"In this wonderful collection, Harrington and Neimeyer have brought together a league of skilled authors whose contributions enlarge our view of bereavement through the prism of contemporary superhero encounters with loss. This is a refreshingly original, clinically astute, playful, and scholarly volume. It is a book for clinicians, educators, and students as well as for the bereaved, those who treat them, and those who love good stories."

*Simon Shimshon Rubin, PhD, professor of clinical psychology and director of the International Center for the Study of Loss, Bereavement and Human Resilience at the University of Haifa, Israel*

"The superhero connection makes this book accessible to a wide audience of people who have enjoyed these characters and who also want to help themselves or others to move through bereavement. Drs. Harrington and Neimeyer have put together what seems impossible: an entertaining way to learn about grief and loss."

*Richard Tedeschi, PhD, distinguished chair at the Boulder Crest Institute for Posttraumatic Growth, USA*

"The authors in *Superhero Grief* cast an intriguing and informative light on the potential transformative power of loss through the lens of the archetype of the superhero. From the impetus of tragedy, these mythical beings find power and purpose, providing lessons on loss for humanity. Thoughtful insight abounds for professionals and grieving people seeking sense-making of their own hero's journey!"

*Donna L. Schuurman, EdD, FT, senior director of advocacy and training and executive director emeritus at The Dougy Center: The National Grief Center for Children and Families, USA*

# Superhero Grief

*Superhero Grief* uses modern superhero narratives to teach the principles of grief theories and concepts and provide practical ideas for promoting healing.

Chapters offer clinical strategies, approaches, and interventions, including strategies based in expressive arts and complementary therapies. Leading researchers, clinicians, and professionals address major topics in death, dying, and bereavement, using superhero narratives to explore loss in the context of bereavement and to promote a contextual view of issues and relationship types that can improve coping skills.

This volume provides support and psychoeducation to students, clinicians, educators, researchers, and the bereaved while contributing significantly to the literature on the intersection of death, grief, and trauma.

**Jill A. Harrington**, DSW, LCSW, is in private practice in the greater Washington, DC, area, where she works as an adjunct professor, grief educator, trainer, writer, and consultant.

**Robert A. Neimeyer**, PhD, directs the Portland Institute for Loss and Transition; actively practices as a trainer, consultant, and coach; and has published extensively on grieving as a meaning-making process.

## The Series in Death, Dying, and Bereavement

Volumes published in the Series in Death, Dying and Bereavement are representative of the multidisciplinary nature of the intersecting fields of death studies, suicidology, end-of-life care, and grief counseling. The series meets the needs of clinicians, researchers, paraprofessionals, pastoral counselors, and educators by providing cutting edge research, theory, and best practices on the most important topics in these fields – for today and for tomorrow.

Series Editors: Robert A. Neimeyer, PhD, Portland Institute for Loss and Transition, Oregon, USA and Darcy L. Harris, PhD, Western University Canada, Ontario, Canada

**Chronic Sorrow**
A Living Loss, 2nd Edition
*Susan Roos*

**Continuing Bonds in Bereavement**
New Directions for Research and Practice
*Edited by Dennis Klass and Edith Steffen*

**Prescriptive Memories in Grief and Loss**
The Art of Dreamscaping
*Edited by Nancy Gershman and Barbara E. Thompson*

**Loss, Grief, and Attachment in Life Transitions**
A Clinician's Guide to Secure Base Counseling
*Jakob van Wielink, Leo Wilhelm, and Denise van Geelen-Merks*

**Non-Death Loss and Grief**
Context and Clinical Implications
*Edited by Darcy L. Harris*

**Superhero Grief**
The Transformative Power of Loss
*Edited by Jill A. Harrington and Robert A. Neimeyer*

For more information about this series, please visit https://www.routledge.com/Series-in-Death-Dying-and-Bereavement/book-series/SE0620.

# Superhero Grief

## The Transformative Power of Loss

**Edited by**

**Jill A. Harrington**

**Robert A. Neimeyer**

Routledge
Taylor & Francis Group
NEW YORK AND LONDON

First published 2021
by Routledge
52 Vanderbilt Avenue, New York, NY 10017

and by Routledge
2 Park Square, Milton Park, Abingdon, Oxon, OX14 4RN

*Routledge is an imprint of the Taylor & Francis Group, an informa business*



*Library of Congress Cataloging-in-Publication Data*
A catalog record for this title has been requested

ISBN: 978-0-367-14558-3 (hbk)
ISBN: 978-0-367-14559-0 (pbk)
ISBN: 978-0-429-05666-6 (ebk)

Typeset in Times
by SPi Global, India

*In devoted memory of the two complex, flawed, and loving*
*true New York characters who created me, gave me my origin story,*
*influenced my story arc, taught me how to embrace*
*vulnerability as well as call upon*
*the power of strength in the face of adversity.*

*Elyse Nanni Harrington*
*(1944–2016)*
*and*
*James Dennis Harrington*
*(1941–2015)*
JAH

*In honor of my own personal Wonder Woman, Agnieszka,*
*who in the midst of global threat and endless separation has secured our bond*
*with the Lasso of Truth and claimed her heritage as the*
*Amazon she was always meant to be.* RAN

We would like to acknowledge the artistry, advocacy, and the impact of actor, Chadwick Boseman, who died at 43 years old shortly after this book began the publication process. Chadwick embodied the superhero Black Panther – personifying the beauty, the character, and the strength of the Black Panther on- and off-screen. His loss to the world and the visual arts is deeply shared by all that were transformed by the power of his humanity – bringing forth the hope of the Black Panther to embolden us to realize that "more connects us than separates us" (Fiege & Coogler, 2018, 02:06:08) and that "we must find a way to look after one another as if we were one single tribe" (Fiege & Coogler, 2018, 02:06:20).

## Reference

Feige, K. (Producer), & Coogler, R. (Director). *Black Panther* [Motion Picture], (2018), United States: Marvel Studios.

# Contents

# Series Editor's Foreword

**Superhero Grief: The Transformative Power of Loss**

The mythology that surrounds death and grief has existed in various forms throughout recorded human history. In almost every ancient civilization, various aspects of death have been represented by a deity or form that was readily recognizable and understood. Consider the god Osiris from Ancient Egypt, who accompanied souls into the underworld; Yama, the god of death in Hindu teachings; the figure of the grim reaper, who first appeared in European art in the early 14th century; and of course, Thanatos, the god of death in Greek mythology. Death, and the vulnerability that it represents, is a universal theme throughout human existence. It is thought that the personification of death in ancient civilizations addressed a need to try to relate to this experience in a meaningful way; interestingly, that need is still salient to us today.

The superhero genre is a current-day mythology that is imbued with themes of sacrifice, death, grief, and transformation. Far more than mere entertainment for the masses, the battles of our superheroes have become the modern-day equivalent of storytelling, passing down the cultural myths and beliefs of modern Western culture. Our superheroes are current-day archetypal figures that represent the human struggle with death, loss, and vulnerability. As the many esteemed authors in this book explore, in each of the superhero's back stories, death presents itself as both tragedy and transformation. We see each of our heroes transformed from being a victim and outcast as a result of earlier, and often devastatingly painful, circumstances into the incredibly strong and dedicated protector of the vulnerable that we know and recognize readily. What is most interesting about this genre is that the real "superpower" of many of these heroes is, in fact, their vulnerability and grief. Without their experiences of death, loss, and grief, they would not have the strength nor the conviction to rise to the call of duty to protect and defend the world from harm.

In its most literal sense, the superhero genre harkens back to our hopes and wishes for a just society, where good and bad are readily delineated, and good eventually triumphs. But this is a simplistic reduction of their stories. It is readily apparent that physical strength and special powers do not erase pain and suffering. Superman is a refugee on earth who is often alienated and misunderstood. With all his superpowers, he cannot resurrect his parents. Batman is still an orphan, who time and again sits alone in his cave. Spider-Man can't bring back his uncle, nor can Wonder Woman bring back her beloved aunt. Through the narratives of our cherished superheroes of today, we see their humanity and vulnerability readily on display alongside their strength and dedication to protect those who are vulnerable and punish those who prey upon that vulnerability.

These back stories are just as important to each of our superheroes as their superpowers. We could say that their experiences of loss and grief created the impetus for the discovery of their powers, providing a sense of meaning and purpose to their lives that benefited humankind. Their struggles with fate and the seemingly random experiences of significant loss mirror our own. Life is not fair. Loss is a universal experience. Grief is painful. However, another part of their experience also reminds us that growth is possible, even after crippling losses. We are capable of far more than we ever thought possible, and we can live our lives with meaning and purpose in honor of those we have loved and lost.

As we turn our attention to the following chapters of this book, we also become aware that many of those who brought our superheroes into existence had suffered from terribly oppressive and violent events themselves. The creation of superheroes brings forth these writers' deepest wishes for a society that fosters the good of its citizens and protects them from harmful, evil forces. If only there had been a superhero figure to intervene during the Holocaust, the Stalinist regime, or other atrocities in human history. Knowing this historical perspective provides us with a greater appreciation of our need for these heroes to remind us of the incredible strength and resilience of the human spirit.

**Darcy Harris,**
**Series Coeditor**

# Preface

From World War II to the present day, superhero fiction has provided a reflective lens for society to process tragedy, inspire hope, and tackle serious sociopolitical issues. With a fierce resurgence in comic books, television, and films in the aftermath of 9-11, the superhero has arisen as one of the most enduring, popular, and influential narratives of modern storytelling. At the origin of almost every superhero story is an experience of profound trauma – most notably the violent death of a parent or loved one and the emergence from the vulnerability of traumatic loss through a transformative process – one that often involves facing the overwhelming force of heartbreak, loss, devastation, and walking through the forging fire of grief. It is not that the superhero is impervious to loss and grief; it is through their process that we can learn lessons of profound pain, survival, transformation, and growth.

Modern psychology has made increasing use of superhero archetypes for those facing enduring life challenges due to their widespread popularity and cross-generational appeal. The use of superheroes in psychology has focused on many forms of trauma, anxiety, and life stressors; however, in no systematic clinical and academic way has the superhero been viewed through the lens of loss, dying, grief, and bereavement. This volume seeks to provide that viewpoint. From life-limiting illness, end-of-life care, bereavement camps to individual and family counseling with adults and children, the use of superhero narratives and archetypes is widely used therapeutically to help individuals and families cope with loss and grief.

In addition to therapeutic care, superhero narratives also provide us with the opportunity for thanatology education. Given the rich storytelling in context to loss, grief, and bereavement, superhero narratives provide lessons of humanity – they are stories written by humans to reflect the struggles of the human condition, with death sometimes being narrated as the ultimate foe or accepted as part of the journey. And through this oftentimes messy and complex journey, we see how all characters (hero, antihero, villain) develop and emerge in their loss.

This volume seeks to teach students, clinicians, educators, and researchers the fundamental principles of modern grief and bereavement theories, concepts, and practice applications through the use of modern superhero narratives synthesized with academic and clinical literature. This book also strives to educate society-at-large about dying, loss, grief, and bereavement, as well as provide support and psychoeducation to the bereaved. Although grief in relation to superheroes has been addressed in sporadic articles, this book is the first of its kind to address major topics in death, dying, and bereavement, illuminated through superhero narratives by authors who are leading academic researchers, clinicians, professionals, and bereaved individuals. Our primary goals are for readers to learn foundational knowledge and skills in thanatology, theory, and practice of grief counseling and psychotherapy; understand the influence of history and culture in bereavement; as well as learn innovative applications and lessons of growth and transformation from the lived personal experiences of the bereaved. This book also contributes significantly to the literature on sudden, violent death as well as the intersection of grief and trauma and the experience of loss as traumatic. With prominence in popular culture and across the lifespan, this volume will provide an opportunity to utilize the visual arts, specifically superhero fiction, as a thanatology teaching medium.

> *Superhero Grief* is an extraordinary compendium of practical and conceptual information addressing the complexities of coping with loss and grief. This book explores the transformative role of traumatic grief as people struggle to redefine their lives in the aftermath of profound loss. It also provides a powerful message of hope for bereaved individuals using superhero examples, personal stories, and therapeutic strategies that offer new meaning, purpose, and strength. This book embodies the spirit of the haunting prison chant "Deshi Basara" from the movie *The Dark Knight Rises,* which simply means, "Rise Up".
>
> **- H. Carl Dickens PhD, Colonel, U.S. Army (Retired), Former Military Psychologist**

## Origins

The origin story of this textbook starts at the Association for Death Education and Counseling (ADEC) 2009 Annual Conference in Miami, Florida. It was at that time I first met M. Katherine Shear, M.D., one of the world's leading researchers in complicated grief. As a doctoral student, I was honored, yet nervous to meet Dr. Shear; however, she put me at ease as I learned one of the true superpowers of most of the luminary scholars, clinicians, and practitioners at ADEC was her approachability, passion, knowledge, and humanity. In her busy schedule at the conference, she made time to meet with me about my dissertation research and a potential mutual project. As I opened my computer to begin the meeting, on the background of my desktop was a fan art depiction of Batman, in the snow, holding roses, outside the tomb of his parents. It caught her eye, and very innocently, she asked me, "What is that a picture of?" I got silent – the cat had my tongue. Not my typical response. In a reflective moment, I gave thought to the old saying about assumptions. First of all,

I had to assume that just because I lived in my universe, not everyone in the universe knew about superheroes and the story of Batman. Second, should this be a moment of truth? After all, I was a doctoral student, and she was a professor. My prefrontal cortex felt like a boomerang between a high level of cognitive control and my unfiltered creative thoughts. As you may be able to tell, the brain became somewhat bold in swaying toward revealing its creative thoughts. Putting aside the fear of being possibly less than academic, I took a breath and said, "That is the superhero, Batman. You know, the character, Bruce Wayne? In his origin story, his parents were murdered in front of him. So, he's a bereaved homicide survivor. And they say one of the top ten 'psychological issues' he contends with is complicated grief." She had a poker face as I sat in somewhat nervous silence – did I just totally discredit myself academically? Visions of all my doctoral work disappearing flashed before me. Dr. Shear then smiled and genuinely asked, "Really? That is very interesting. I'd like to talk more about it when we have time". And so, the idea and recruitment of the cast of characters for a workshop on *Superhero Grief Explored by a Super Grief Panel: The Origin of Batman* at the ADEC 40th Annual Conference 2018 in Pittsburgh, Pennsylvania, began!

The panel consisted of national and international clinicians, researchers, program directors, and educators, who used the film *Batman Begins* (Roven, Thomas, Franco, & Nolan, 2005) as a case study to explore complicated grief, attachment-informed grief therapy, the role of the surrogate caregiver in family resilience, and meaning-making. As the facilitator of the panel, I introduced the audience to the idea of superhero grief and my journey as both a superhero fan and use in my career in social work.

As a kid born in Queens, New York, in the 1970s and subsequently raised on Long Island, I grew up in the epicenter of the creation and era of superheroes – especially in comic books and on television. Art, creativity, and the origin of many superhero creators emerged from the New York City area. My father graduated from DeWitt Clinton High School in the Bronx, where almost two decades previous, superhero creators Stan Lee, Bob Kane, and Bill Finger also graduated. To grow up on Long Island and the New York City area during this time, your source of entertainment was not the Internet, but comic books, movies (in theaters), and television. As a kid, we had a two-dial television with three channels to choose, plus PBS and the ambiguous U channel. Television was something you got to watch very infrequently compared to today, typically during the week after school, with popular TV series, such as *Batman* (Horwitz, 1966–1968) and *Wonder Woman* (Lansbury, Fitzsimmons, & Rodgers, 1975–1979) airing after the last daytime soap opera and before the beginning of the evening news. Also, there were the much-anticipated weekly Saturday morning cartoon lineups, featuring some favorites such as the *Super Friends* (Marshall & Takamato, 1973–1985) and *Underdog* (Biggers, 1964–1973).

Like many other kids, superheroes provided me archetypes of strength and hope. I can remember getting lost walking back from Barboni's Deli to my grandparent's house in Corona, Queens. Scared, I took a breath and envisioned using my Spidey-senses to lead me back to their house on 50th Avenue – a stone's throw away from the Flushing Meadows Corona Park 1939 and 1964 World's Fair remnants. At eight years old, while visiting my grandmother at her home in Rockaway Beach with my father, we walked down 120th Street and spent a much-awaited day at the beach. Being raised from a toddler to swim in both the Long Island Sound and the Atlantic Ocean, I was somewhat necessarily fearless. The next thing I knew, while wading in the ocean, I got caught in the undertow, which, if you are familiar with the riptides at Rockaway Beach, can be deadly. To this day, I still remember pretending I was Wonder Woman and using all the strength I had to push myself up from under the water, saving myself from a tragic ending. However, I think the greatest impression a superhero had in my life was not through a superhero TV show, comic, or film, but by one of their creators.

In the early 1980s, my older and only sibling, Virginia, almost died from complications of double pneumonia, a collapsed lung, and mononucleosis. She had been hospitalized for over a month at Schneider Children's Hospital Long Island Jewish Medical Center. It was during this very scary and painful time that a woman named Doris, who worked with my mother in office administration for a private practice physician, gave hand-drawn pictures to my mother from her brother. She said he was a cartoon artist. As the story goes, Doris told my mother that while her brother was in town, visiting from California, she told him about my sister's critical medical condition and how scared I was for her. I will never forget the day my mom gave us those hand-drawn comic cells. They were from Batman, Robin, and Catwoman with a personal note from her brother, Bob Kane, co-creator of Batman. It was in this total act of kindness that I became a true fan of the Batman, the influence of superheroes, and the true superabilities of humans. To this day, my sister still has the cell of Catwoman hanging in her home on Long Island with a handwritten note from Bob Kane, wishing her a "Healthy and Speedy Recovery". I have hanging in my home, "Best Wishes" from Batman and Robin. They are central to our home as much as the love of superhero stories are central to our lives with our families. The theme, however, that was most central to the character of our lives, was the superpower of kindness exhibited by these two true heroes, neither of which had to reveal their secret identities, but did so to help cheer up two kids under difficult circumstances.

It is with this backdrop that the art of superhero narratives in film, comics, television, and the visual arts has had a great influence in my personal life and also career in social work – more specifically, end-of-life, loss, grief, and bereavement. In understanding the tales of superheroes, as a thanatologist, at the root of these stories, is our continual quest to try to comprehend our own existence, our own losses (individually and collectively), how we survive and make meaning in the face of the profound pain of the loss of our loved ones. Grief, ultimately, is the pain of our love. Just like there is strong, sometimes seemingly unbearable natural pain we bear to bring us into this world, there is also a natural seemingly unbearable, often excruciating pain with bearing the physical loss of our loved ones from this world. You only need see this by watching Scarlet Witch grab her chest as she bears the force of a broken heart (see "Acute Stress Cardiomyopathy") at the moment her twin brother, Quicksilver, is killed (Feige & Wheldon, 2015). In my work, I have seen and used art as a conduit for education and care – in adult and child oncology, hospice, post–9-11 bereaved families, surviving bereaved military/veteran families, and with those traumatically bereaved.

Ensuing the *Superhero Grief* Panel, I was approached by Robert A. Neimeyer to create and develop this volume, in partnership, with the hope that it would contribute in a creative way to thanatology education and care for the bereaved; to harness the love of these visual arts and their narratives for greater knowledge and care of others.

## Organization of the Book

The organization of this book in Part I gives a *Historical Context* in which superheroes were created. Part II utilizes superhero narratives to teach *Modern Grief Theory.* Part III provides case studies of superheroes to teach about *Different Types of Grief.* Part IV looks at *Grief and Culture.* Part V educates readers about *Grief and Family Systems,* specifically on issues related to relationship factors to the deceased. Part VI looks at *Challenges in Bereavement,* while Part VII provides the personal stories of the bereaved, their identification with chosen superheroes, and the five factors of posttraumatic growth. Part VIII gives the reader a glimpse at superheroes in the context of grief and bereavement, *Social Justice, Advocacy, and Leadership*. And finally, Part IX, highlights *Strategies of Care* as well as the *Expressive Arts* and in Part X, we conclude in helping readers to use their own Cerebro ("Cerebro", n.d.) – to open their minds to *Find Super Heroes* in end-of-life care, grief, loss, and bereavement *All Around Them.*

## How to Use This Book

With many esteemed authors in the field of thanatology and personal stories of the lived experiences from the bereaved, we offer a few suggestions for potential audiences in particular: clinicians, educators, researchers, and the bereaved.

For the *bereaved,* we invite you to read through these chapters – to find what may be beneficial for you in coping with loss, trauma, and grief, as well as opening up the possibility of helping you navigate the often painful, unknown, and uncertain terrain of loss. For *clinicians*, broadly applicable to psychologists, counselors, therapists, social workers, and other mental health professionals who provide grief support and grief therapy, one suggestion may be to utilize the film chapters or characters in counseling with the bereaved. There are suggested clinical strategies, approaches, and interventions of care, from a multicultural perspective, including the expressive arts and complementary therapies. *For educators*, whether it be high school, undergraduate, or graduate psychology, healthcare, social science, social work, or any other applicable class, these chapters can be used to teach your students the foundational theories, concepts, and interventions, as well as health and social justice issues surrounding loss, grief, and bereavement. One suggestion may be to ask students to write a paper on the concept of *Continuing Bonds Theory* and how Star-Lord, Superman, and/or Black Panther, depict this theory in the films. Finally, *for Researchers*, this volume helps to elucidate continued work for the scientific agenda in the field of thanatology, most notably, the impact and use of superhero narratives through the visual arts in the care of the dying and bereaved.

# Acknowledgments

In closing, I want to first and foremost acknowledge my family, without whom this volume would never have come to fruition – "I love you 3,000" (Feige, Russo, & Russo, 2019, 00:41:16). I want to thank my loving fiancé-partner, combat military-veteran, and Captain America, David Fulton Carey, for having my six. Also, my scattered, creative, beautiful, and bright Harley-Quinn of a daughter, Madeline Elyse. And most of all, my Drax the Destroyer – my big mush, don't mess with me, unfiltered son, Alexander Daniel. As a mother of a child with autism, there are many of us who try desperately to connect with our children. I am grateful for the art of superheroes, and our shared love of this art, which helped and continues to help me communicate and connect with my son about lessons of good and evil, vulnerability and strength, pain and despair, but most of all hope. It is in these lessons of life that I have continued to speak the language of the superhero to someone with the most special of neuro-diverse abilities. I am super grateful to my family for hours, days, months, years of film/TV watching, dialogue, suggestions, meals brought to me while in the isolation of writing/editing, and the patience exhibited with my many "asks" to read through my work and my often hot-mess, tearing my hair-out creative and editorial frustrations. I would also like to acknowledge my nephew and godson, Robert Collier, for his shared loved of the Batman and superheroes as well as my sister and the Braster Family (Virginia, Kevin, Daniel, Abigail, and Rebecca). It is with the support of a superhero family that you can harness the strongest of all your abilities – hope through love.

It goes without saying that I also want to express my utmost gratitude to my coeditor, Robert "Bob" A. Neimeyer, who provided paramount support in the development and creation of this work. His passion, hard work, knowledge, scholarship, and dedication to the bereaved and to thanatology is unparalleled. He is also to be commended for his legacy in this field as a tremendous supporter of those emerging in this work. Without his creative boldness, I would have never found the voice for mine.

It is without question that I also want to express our gratitude to the many authors who are passionate thanatology colleagues and members of ADEC. They are truly our "Hall of Heroes" for the work they do and their dedication to the dying and bereaved. They are researchers, theorists, practitioners, and educators in end-of-life, dying, grief, and bereavement, to whom we are super grateful for taking a courageous, creative leap in contributing to this book. I would like to personally thank Christopher Hall for cofacilitating and supporting the *Superhero Grief* Panel in 2018 at ADEC, as well as M. Katherine Shear, Robert A. Neimeyer, Irwin Sandler, Phyllis Kosminsky, and Jon Reid. Without their genius, ingenuity, and generosity, this project would not have been born to creation. Bob and I would also like to thank Anna Moore, at Routledge, for her continued dedication and support of this text as well as Senior Editor Darcy L. Harris.

Along with those I have already mentioned, I would like to acknowledge my other very significant and supportive mentors in the field, Edward K. Rynearson, Jack R. Jordan, James A. Martin, and Howard R. Winokuer, without whose support, I would not be the passionate, informed, and dedicated thanatologist I am today. I also would like to thank my colleagues, Kim Ruocco, Lisa Holland Downs, Sharon Strouse, Patti Anewalt, Rayna Vaught Godfrey, Betsy Beard, and Charalambos "Babis" Andreadis, who continually model for me the value of compassionate care and peer support.

I would also like to thank the places and music that made this creative process possible. Thank you to the tranquil and transcendently beautiful community of Lake Naomi, Pennsylvania, where I spent much time in a creative space – developing, writing, and editing this book. Also, a big shout-out and thank you to the genius, operatic music of Hans Zimmer, and to the soundtrack of *Deadpool 2* (2018). To my regret, there was not enough space dedicated to a chapter on the therapeutic use and influence of music.

Finally, I want to acknowledge the "unsung heroes" of this book – the bereaved. It is with the utmost sincere gratitude to all those who shared their lived experiences and personal stories of love, loss, and posttraumatic growth. Your willingness to be vulnerable, share your bending and breaking through the pain of grief, and the transformative power of your loss underscores the true heroic nature of your efforts to help others who are bereaved. Also, we want to thank the innumerable clients in our clinical practices, who are truly the courageous. Those who share their vulnerability, their stories, their pain … who teach us that pain is not weakness leaving the body, but as my colleague Kim Ruocco teaches, that true strength is pain leaving the body and mind. You have taught us how to be better therapists.

I learned how to live by working with oncology patients and their families; I learned how to be a more loving and appreciative parent by working with bereaved parents; I learned the fragility of life by working with those bereaved by sudden deaths; I learned the depths of pride, honor, and resiliency in working with bereaved military/veteran families; I learned compassion and the passion to strive be the best at my work in field of bereavement and thanatology because of the bereaved and those who care for them. They are my superheroes. We hope this book helps have a similar effect on all those who learn about the transformative power of loss through superhero grief.

Jill A. Harrington
"Always a kid from New York"
August 2020

## References

Acute stress cardiomyopathy. (n.d.). Retrieved from: https://www.hopkinsmedicine.org/asc/faqs.html

Biggers, W.W. (Producer). (1964–1973) *Underdog* [Television series]. New York, NY: DFS Program Exchange (former) NBC Universal Television Distribution.

**Cerebro**. (n.d.). Retrieved from: https://www.marvel.com/items/cerebro

Feige, K. (Producer), & Whedon, J. (Director). (2015). *Avengers: Age of Ultron* [Motion Picture]. United States: Marvel Studios

Feige, K. (Producer), & Russo, A., & Russo, J. (Directors). (2019). *Avengers: Endgame* [Motion Picture]. United States: Marvel Studios.

Horwitz, H. (Producer). (1966–1968) *Batman* [Television series]. Hollywood, CA: Twentieth Century Fox Television, Warner Bros. Domestic Television Distribution.

Lansbury, B., Fitzsimmons, C.B., & Rodgers, M. (Producers). (1975–1979) *Wonder Woman* [Television series]. Burbank, CA: Warner Bros. Domestic Television Distribution.

Marshall, L., & Takamato, I. (Producers). (1973–1985) *Super Friends* [Television series]. Los Angeles, CA: Hanna-Barbera Productions.

Roven, C., Thomas, E., & Franco, L. (Producers), & Nolan, C. (Director). (2005). *Batman begins* [Motion picture]. United States: Warner Bros. Pictures.

Various Artists. (2018). *On Deadpool 2 (Original Motion Picture Soundtrack)* [AAC]. New York, NY: Columbia Records.

# Contributors

**Marshall Allen,** MPH, BA in Black Studies and Political Science; Certificate in Black Studies, Multiculturalism, and American Constitutional Democracy; Graduate, University of Missouri, Columbia, Missouri.

**Tashel C. Bordere,** PhD, CT, Assistant Professor, Human Development & Family Science State Extension Specialist, Youth Development, University of Missouri, Columbia, Missouri.

**Cori Bussolari,** PsyD, Associate Professor, Licensed Psychologist, Marriage and Family Therapy Program, Counseling Psychology Department, University of San Francisco, California.

**David F. Carey,** MS, BS, LTC, U.S. Army (Retired), Combat-Veteran (OIF/OEF); National Security Contractor, U.S. Department of Defense, Springfield, Virginia.

**Toya Clebourn-Jacobs,** DSW, LMSW (*Surviving Spouse, Honoring Jamie Ranell Jacobs*), Public Assistance Emergency Management, Spring, Texas.

**Justin Colon,** Baccalaureate student, John Jay College of Criminal Justice, New York, New York.

**Stephen J. Cozza,** MD, DFAACAP, DFAPA, COL, U.S. Army (Retired), Professor of Psychiatry and Pediatrics, Senior Scientist, Center for the Study of Traumatic Stress, School of Medicine, Uniformed Services University of the Health Sciences, Bethesda, Maryland.

**Cheryl Hogsten Dodson**, DNP, MBA, RN, CCM, Assistant Professor of Nursing, Department of Nursing, Methodist University, Fayetteville, North Carolina.

**Kenneth J. Doka,** PhD, MDiv, Professor Emeritus, the Graduate School of the College of New Rochelle, New York; Senior Consultant to the Hospice Foundation of America; Author of over 40 books.

**Lisa Holland Downs,** RN, MSN, FNP-BC, Medical Science Liaison, GENENTECH *A Member of the Roche Group,* Rockledge, Pennsylvania.

**Beverly Feigelman,** MSW, LCSW, Private Practice Psychotherapist, Jamaica Estates, Queens, New York.

**William Feigelman,** PhD, Professor Emeritus of Sociology, Nassau Community College, Garden City, New York.

**Fred C. Fowler,** MD, MBA, Partner, Carolina Digestive Health Associates, Charlotte, North Carolina.

**Malia Fry** (*Surviving Spouse, Honoring GySgt John D. Fry, USMC*), Baccalaureate student, University of Mary Hardin-Baylor, Belton, Texas.

**Donna Gaffney,** DNSc, FAAN, psychotherapist (specializing in loss, grief and trauma among children and families), educational consultant, and founder of DAGaffney Consulting LLC, in Morristown, New Jersey.

**Louis A. Gamino,** PhD, ABPP, FT, Professor (Affiliated) of Psychiatry & Behavioral Science at Texas A&M Health Science Center College of Medicine and Baylor Scott & White Health in Temple, Texas; ADEC Clinical Practice Award (2008).

**Kathleen R. Gilbert,** PhD, FT, Professor Emerita of Applied Health Science, Indiana University School of Public Health, Bloomington, Indiana.

**Rayna Vaught Godfrey,** PhD, Licensed Psychologist, Private Practice (focus on grief, loss and sibling bereavement), Wesna, LLC, Jacksonville, Florida.

**Erica Goldblatt Hyatt,** DSW, LCSW, MBE, Assistant Director of the DSW Program, Assistant Teaching Professor, School of Social Work, Rutgers, the State University of New Jersey, New Brunswick, New Jersey.

**Belinda M. Gonzalez-Leon,** EdD, MBA (*Surviving Spouse, Honoring Alfredo Leon*), Premier Educational Consulting, Miami, Florida

**Jacob Halbert,** MS, PsyD, Institute for the Psychological Sciences, Divine Mercy University, Sterling, Virginia.

**Christopher Hall,** MA, GradDipAdol&ChPsych, BED, CertIVTAE, Chief Executive Officer, Australian Centre for Grief & Bereavement, Mulgrave, Australia.

**Jill A. Harrington,** DSW, LCSW, Private Practice, Harrington Consulting & Counseling Services, Occoquan, Virginia; Adjunct Assistant Professor, The Chicago School of Professional Psychology, Washington DC; Part-time Lecturer, Rutgers University School of Social Work, New Brunswick, New Jersey.

**Ashlynne Haycock,** BS (*Surviving Adult Child, Honoring SFC Jeffrey Haycock, USA & SrA Nichole Haycock, USAF* Veteran), Deputy Director, Policy, Tragedy Assistance Program for Survivors, Arlington, Virginia.

**Weston Haycock,** BA (*Surviving Adult Child, Honoring SFC Jeffrey Haycock, USA & SrA Nichole Haycock, USAF* Veteran), U.S. Senate Staff Assistant, Washington, DC.

**Andy H.Y. Ho**, PhD, EdD, MFT, FT, Associate Professor of Psychology, School of Social Sciences & Joint Honorary Associate Professor, Lee Kong Chian School of Medicine; Deputy Director of Research, Palliative Care Centre for Excellence in Research and Education; Founding Director, Action Research for Community Health, Nanyang Technological University Singapore.

**Gloria Horsley,** PhD, RN (*Bereaved Parent, Honoring Scott Horsley*), Founder and President, Open to Hope Foundation, Palo Alto, California.

**William G. Hoy,** DMin, FT, Clinical Professor of Medical Humanities, Baylor University, Waco, Texas; Former Clinical Counseling Director, Pathways Volunteer Hospice, Long Beach, California.

**John R. Jordan**, PhD, Licensed Psychologist, Retired from Private Practice, Pawtucket, Rhode Island; Developer and Lead Trainer of American Foundation for Suicide Prevention *Suicide Bereavement Clinician Training Program*; Former Clinical Consultant for Grief Support Services of the Samaritans, Boston, Massachusetts.

**Julie B. Kaplow,** PhD, ABPP, Director, Trauma and Grief Center, Hackett Center for Mental Health, Houston, Texas.

**Rachel A. Kentor**, PhD, Assistant Professor, Department of Pediatrics, Baylor College of Medicine Psychology Service, Texas Children's Hospital, Houston, Texas.

**Phyllis Kosminsky,** PhD, LCSW, FT, Private Practice, Westchester, New York; Psychotherapist, The Center for Hope/Family Centers, Darien, Connecticut; Adjunct Faculty, Fordham University School of Social Services, New York.

**Pamela A. Malone,** Ph.D., LCSW-S, FT, Assistant Professor-in-Practice, University of Texas at Arlington School of Social Work, Arlington, Texas; Clinical Supervisor; Private Practice, Blue Lapis Consulting, PLLC, Austin, Texas.

**Christiane Manzella,** PhD, Senior Psychologist, Seleni Institute, New York, New York; Professor, New York University, New York, New York.

**James A. Martin,** PhD, COL, U.S. Army (Retired), Professor of Social Work and Social Research, Bryn Mawr College, Bryn Mawr, Pennsylvania.

**Terry L. Martin,** PhD, former Associate Professor, Hood College, Frederick, Maryland; Private Practice (specializing in dying and grief-related issues); Hospice and Nursing Home Consultant.

**Melinda M. Moore,** PhD, Licensed Psychologist, Assistant Professor, Department of Psychology, Eastern Kentucky University, Richmond, Kentucky.

**Rebecca S. Morse,** PhD, Associate Professor, Director of Research Training, Institute for Psychological Sciences, Divine Mercy University, Sterling, Virginia.

**Joyal Mulheron,** MS, Founder & Executive Director, Evermore, Washington, DC.

**Rebekah Near**, LCAT, CAGS, Licensed Creative Arts Therapist, Grief Counselor, Nashville, Tennessee.

**Robert A. Neimeyer,** PhD, Professor Emeritus, University of Memphis, Memphis, Tennessee; Director, the Portland Institute for Loss and Transition, Portland, Oregon; Private Practice and Coaching; Editor of *Death Studies*; Author of over 500 journal articles and book chapters as well as 30 books.

**Brendan Prout,** MDiv, CTC, CGC, CISR (*Surviving Adult Child, Honoring RADM James G. Prout III)*, Worship Pastor, Quest Church, San Diego, California.

**Jon K. Reid,** PhD, Professor, Southeastern Oklahoma State University, Durant, Oklahoma.

**Kim A. Ruocco**, MSW, Vice President, Suicide Postvention & Prevention, Tragedy Assistance Program for Survivors, Arlington, Virginia.

**Edward Rynearson,** MD, Medical Director, Virginia Mason Medical Center, Grief Services, Seattle, Washington; ADEC Research Recognition Award (2015).

**Mark de St. Aubin**, LCSW, FT, Director of Community Education, Serenity Funeral Home, Draper, Utah.

**Irwin Sandler,** PhD, Regents Professor Emeritus and Research Professor with the REACH Institute and the Department of Psychology, Arizona State University, Tempe, Arizona.

**Selin Santos,** PsyD, Licensed Clinical Psychologist, Department of Hematology and Medical Oncology, Cleveland Clinic, Weston, Florida.

**M. Katherine Shear**, MD, Marion E. Kentworthy Professor of Psychiatry, Columbia University School of Social Work, Columbia University College of Physicians and Surgeons, Director, Center for Complicated Grief, New York, New York.

**Heather Stang,** MA, C-IAYT, Yoga Therapist, The Mindfulness & Grief Institute, Hagerstown, Maryland.

**Sharon Strouse,** MA, ATR-BC, LCPAT, Associate Director, The Portland Institute for Loss and Transition; Private Practice, Art Therapist; Co-founder, The Kristin Rita Strouse Foundation, Baltimore, Maryland.

**Laura Takacs,** LICSW, MPH, Clinical Director, Virginia Mason Medical Center, Grief Services, Seattle, Washington.

**Barbara E. Thompson,** OTD, LCSW, Professor, Russell Sage College, Troy, New York.

**Sarah Vollmann,** MPS, ATR-BC, LICSW, Private Practice (specializing in bereavement) and Lead Counselor at Buckingham Browne & Nichols School in Cambridge, Massachusetts.

**Howard R. Winokuer**, PhD, FT, Grief Educator, Speaker, Consultant and Editor; ADEC Clinical Practice Award (2017); Private Practice, Founder, The Winokuer Center for Counseling and Healing, Charlotte, North Carolina.

# Introduction

## Finding Thanos in "Thanatology" and the Transformative Power of the Visual Arts

*Jill A. Harrington*

Thanatology – what is it? The study of Thanos? The fictional mad titan, so obsessed with the Goddess Death that he massacres millions throughout superhero worlds by genocidal campaigns to bring a balanced correction to the universe (Feige, Russo, & Russo, 2019b)? Although fictional superheroes try to defeat Thanos, even in the end, ultimately, they cannot; in order for Thanos to be snapped out of the universe's timeline, one Avenger had to face the finality of death. In superhero universes, where timelines are continually resurrected in an effort to control our own death-denial, there are time points in which final deaths of characters exist; and in *Avengers: Endgame* (Feige, Russo, et al., 2019b), the death of Iron Man (aka Tony Stark) is one of those final moments. While removing Thanos from the timeline, Tony never truly kills what is "inevitable" (Feige, Russo, et al., 2019b, 00:18:42) – death, as a part of life. Holding true to Thor's observation that "nothing lasts forever … the only thing that is permanent in life is impermanence" (Feige, Russo, et al., 2019b, 1:03:50–1:03:55).

The field of Thanatology addresses this permanent-impermanence and encompasses the study of death as a part of life. The origin of Thanatology begins with the ancient storytelling of Greek mythology (Fonseca & Testoni, 2012). *Thanatos* (death) was the son of *Nyx* (night) and *Chronos* (time), as well as the twin brother of *Hypnos* (sleep). Greeks of this ancient time began to use the word *Thanatos* as the common word for death (Fonseca & Testoni, 2012). *Thanos* is a modern diminutive form of the ancient Greek name, the personification of death, and an immortal God ("Thanatology", n.d.). It is no wonder that in our constant quest about the perplexity of death, throughout the centuries, our modern storytelling of superheroes has characters such as *Thanos,* who represents the ultimate form of annihilation – our own.

From Socrates' talks on the immortality of the soul to Seneca's letters with ubiquitous themes of death, the subject of death and how we survive the impermanence of our loved ones has always been a subject of great significance to humans (Fonseca & Testoni, 2012). Themes of good and evil, all representing life and death, have continually been woven through our storytelling – a preliterate way for us to understand the meaning of our human existence.

Thanatology is a multidisciplinary field of scientific study, emerging in the early turn of the twentieth century, when Metchnikoff, a Russian zoologist, best known for his work in immunology, proposed two new areas of scientific investigation ("Thanatology", n.d.). Using the Greek *Gerontos* (elders) and *Thanatos* (death) and adding *-ology* (the study of) to begin new fields of study, gerontology gained broad acceptance (Fonseca & Testoni, 2012); however, Thanatology, just like the character *Thanos*, was not well received. A lot had to do with the shift in humankind's relationship with death.

In premodern times, death was incorporated as a part of life, shared with family and community. Life was a constant struggle with threats everywhere. Death was accepted, therefore, as a consequence, science was not synonymous with immortality. Deaths occurred at home and were shared by the community; the dead were buried in central locations in towns and cities. For example, Calvary Cemetery in Queens, New York, is one of the largest internment sites in the United States, viewable from the Long Island Expressway and with its centrality, a constant reminder of death-awareness in our everyday lives.

A death-denying society began to emerge around the end of the 19th century with the onset of the Industrial Revolution, when people relocated from rural to urban areas, and dying relocated from family homes to hospitals. Then in the 20th century, scientific advances were viewed as a "weapon in the battle of death" (Fonseca & Testoni, 2012, p. 160), and explanations of the world shifted from theological to scientific. Professionals replaced family members in the care of our dying loved ones (Fonseca & Testoni, 2012). Funerals in the home shifted to professional funeral homes, and our deceased were also being shifted from being interned in central parts of town to more remote locations.

The field of Thanatology did not gain broad acceptance until around the 1950s. Otherwise known as death education, Thanatology is defined as the scientific study of death and the losses brought as a result ("Thanatology", n.d.). Thanatologists include researchers, educators, and practitioners who investigate all aspects of death. Death education became more widely accepted as pioneers in the field, such as Erich Lindemann, Herman Feifel, Elisabeth Kübler-Ross, and Cicely Saunders paved the way for death awareness, compassionate care at the end-of-life, and the concept of grief (Fonseca & Testoni, 2012). In the 1960s, the first college courses on death education began, and since that time, major contributions have emerged in the field.

Since the turn of the 21st century, two new concepts have arisen in the field of Thanatology, which are significant to this book – *Transformative Grief* and *Posttraumatic Growth.* According to Berzoff (2011), Freud was the first theorist to contemplate how loss and grief change the mourner, for better or for worse. Transformative grief postulates that grief offers us an opportunity for new self-narratives, that through "the art of bending and breaking" (Wood, 2016, title), the profound pain of grief can be one of our greatest teachers; that "pain and beauty can coexist" (Wood, 2016, para 7). "Through our grief, we can learn to live with a deeper awareness and appreciation for healthy connection, meaningful growth, and intentional purpose" (Stern, n.d., para 2).

With the inability to escape loss, we are "inevitability" confronted by change, bringing forth our strategies to deal with the inevitable. Transformative grief proposes that we are not limited by our losses, but at the points at which we break, it requires us to find the deepest of our strengths to heal. It suggests that grief is a universal opportunity to choose an educational partnership with loss – to allow one to evolve, grow, and ultimately transform. What Tedeschi and Calhoun (2004) define as the concept of posttraumatic growth, "an experience of positive change that occurs as a result of the struggle with highly challenging life circumstances" (p.1).

So, how can we learn about the transformative power of loss through the modern-day storytelling of superheroes? The first is to understand that Thanos represents what is inevitable – death, even to the mortal creators of these characters. Our superhero stories continue the age-old inquiry about our existence and our extinction – individually and collectively. The trauma of most superhero origins is rooted in death, either of their loved ones, their worlds, or themselves. When we talk about trauma, there are many forms that can bring forth a multitude of varying losses – death and nondeath related. However, at the core of transformative experiences for many pop culture superheroes is the traumatic death-loss of a loved one and their search for sense and meaning in a new assumptive world (Gillies & Neimeyer, 2006). Like us, because their stories are really about human struggles, they grapple with pain, profound loss, and grief. This is the journey of the hero – stripped down to their base, complex, flawed, and full of pain. But how do they arise? Does pain succumb to anger, loathing them in bitterness and vengeance? Or is grief, somehow, the core of their love, the newfound strength that gives them the ability to transform their pain into meaningful positive changes?

The transformative power of loss can be gleaned throughout modern superhero storytelling. For example, *Captain Marvel* shows us this most eloquently. For it is not the power of the Tesseract that is housed in the Space Stone that ultimately transforms Carol Danvers into Captain Marvel, it is her ardent connection to her memories that she leans on as the source of her power. Some of these memories remind her of the enduring love and dedication of her friends, such as Dr. Wendy Larson, otherwise known in Kree, as "Marvelle", – drawing force from their friendship. Most powerfully, Danvers leans on the memories of her strength in the face of adversity – remembering how when fallen, her stubborn courage to draw the strength to continually rise (Feige, Boden, & Fleck, 2019a). In her grief, she leans on her human abilities – the memories of love and her own strengths to give her the fortitude to unleash the most powerful of her human and superhero abilities. Captain Marvel teaches us that loss knocks us down, often not by our own choice. But we can choose to stay down or begin to try to rise. And through that rise be transformed, by which path we ultimately can participate as our own guide. That in grief, which can feel so uncontrollable, we have some control – we play a part in our journey.

This book aims to provide a significant learning experience for students, educators, and mental health professionals as well as the bereaved who are interested in the field of Thanatology and the intersection of superheroes through visual arts storytelling. Visual arts are a powerful medium, not only to entertain but also as an educational tool. Comics, television, and film can be a formidable force for teaching psychology, social work, counseling, as well as the health and social sciences. It is our goal that the education provided in this book will be a source of foundational knowledge, creative application, and support for all those seeking to learn through superhero grief about dying, death, bereavement, and the transformative power of loss.

## References

Berzoff, J. (2011). The transformative nature of grief and bereavement. *Clinical Social Work Journal*, 39(3), 262–269.

Feige, K. (Producer), & Boden, A., & Fleck, R. (Directors). (2019a). *Captain Marvel* [Motion Picture]. United States: Marvel Studios.

Feige, K. (Producer), & Russo, A., & Russo, J. (Directors). (2019b). *Avengers: Endgame* [Motion Picture]. United States: Marvel Studios.

Fonseca, L.M., & Testoni, I. (2012). The emergence of Thanatology and current practice in death education. *OMEGA – Journal of Death and Dying*, 64(2), 157–169.

Gillies, J., & Neimeyer, R.A. (2006). Loss, grief, and the search for significance: Toward a model of meaning reconstruction in bereavement. *Journal of Constructivist Psychology*, 19 (1), 31–65. DOI: 10.1080/10720530500311182

Stern, J. (n.d.). *Transformative grief.* Retrieved from: https://transformativegrief.com

Tedeschi, R.G., & Calhoun, L.G. (2004). Posttraumatic growth: Conceptual foundations and empirical evidence. *Psychological Inquiry*, 15(1), 1–18.

Thanatology. (n.d.). In *Wikipedia.* Retrieved from: https://en.wikipedia.org/wiki/Thanatology

Wood, J. (2016). Transformative grief, Part I: The art of bending and breaking [Blog Post]. Retrieved from: https://www.goodtherapy.org/blog/transformative-grief-part-1-art-of-bending-and-breaking-0224164

# Part I

# Historical Backgrounds: Grief, Loss, and the Creation of Superheroes

# 1 The Rippling Effects of the Holocaust

## The Jewish Influence on the Development of Superheroes

*Howard R. Winokuer and Fred C. Fowler*

Superheroes have been a significant part of the U.S. and world culture for the past 90 years. The Marvel and DC comic universes have touched the lives of millions of children and adults, filling their minds with amazing characters who brought truth and justice to an unjust world. Characters such as Superman, Batman, Spider-Man, and Captain America have captivated readers with their magnificent feats of heroism, providing hope during a period in our history where little hope existed.

What are the origins of superheroes? It seems logical to believe the influences came from U.S. history; however, strong evidence indicates the influencing origins are firmly rooted in the 1930s and 1940s Jewish experiences in Eastern Europe and the subsequent worldwide effects of anti-Semitism (Brod, 2012). It is interesting to note that many writers who created these original characters were Jewish. The characters have a strong connection to the Jewish mode of thought in that "the bad guys that superheroes fight against are, in the final analysis, those people who have oppressed the Jewish people for centuries" (Brod, 2012, p. xx).

It is important to make a distinction between Judaism and Jewishness. Judaism is a religion, whereas Jewishness is associated with a culture, which can also involve the practicing of the Jewish religion. So, an interesting question to ponder is: are the characters Jewish? If they are, it's not in the traditional sense. It's not as if Superman or Iron Man go to synagogue on a weekly basis. And it is important to note that the Jewish writers who created these characters were not advocating for violence as a way to combat anti-Semitism, but rather that "owning their capacity to do violence must not be misconstrued as doing violence" (Breitman, 2012, p. xxii). One could conjecture that it was the artistic response to an attempted genocide of a people – the creation of metahumans with superpowers in a time when Jewish people were oppressed and subjected to a sense of powerlessness.

According to Brod (2012), these writers were not men who fit the traditional definition of what it meant to be manly, but rather were seen as men who were shy, introverted, and unable to live up to the expectations of how a macho man was supposed to act. They fit the stereotype of a typical Jewish man. It seems particularly interesting that people who were perceived as "less then real men created Superman" (Brod, 2012, p. xviii). This may have been a way that these writers created characters that fought for justice in a world where they had no power to do so themselves. It has been hypothesized (Brod, 2012) that the Jewish people lost much of their heritage during the Holocaust and that the creation of superheroes were the writers' attempt to reclaim this heritage.

## 1.1 Artist Origins

In the 1930s two young boys, Jerry Siegel and Joseph Shuster, children of Jewish parents who had fled Eastern Europe, met and created a partnership that eventually created Superman ("Jerry Siegel, Joe Shuster and Superman", n.d.). Their first Superman character was a bald telepathic villain, and the comic book was not successful. They then morphed the character into the bespectacled Clark Kent who was patterned after the famous actors Clark Gable and Kent Taylor. The Jewish component of this character was a hidden identity and the desire to "fit" into society.

Stan Lee, an Army WWII veteran, was a Jewish writer who created many Marvel characters, such as Spider-Man, Thor, the X-Men, Iron Man, the Flash, Dr. Strange, and the Fantastic Four. Born Stanley Martin Lieber, the son of Jewish parents who immigrated to the United States from Romania, Stan became an assistant in 1939 at *Timely Comics*. As was common practice at the time, Jewish-sounding surnames were Westernized to be assimilated into the American and Canadian cultures. Stan changed his name to be accepted within the larger general population, stating, "for journalistic reasons" (Thomas, 2018, para. 12). Also, he was embarrassed and didn't want anyone to associate him with comic books, as he thought one day he would write a great American novel (Thomas, 2006). There was stigma associated with writing comics, as much as being Jewish. Comics were not considered art, or great storytelling, and films based on comics still receive scrutiny for this today.

Another superhero creator was Bob Kane. Born Robert Kahn, Bob was also the son of Jewish parents who had immigrated to the United States from Eastern Europe. Bob similarly changed his name to disguise his Jewish heritage. In collaboration with Bill Finger, Bob created Batman (and Robin), the "Dark Night", one of the most well-known and iconic superheroes in the world (Boxer, 1998). Bruce Wayne, aka "Batman", transforms from a helpless, traumatized child who witnessed the murder of his parents into one of the world's most brilliant detectives and crime-fighting superheroes.

William (Will) Erwin Eisner was born in Brooklyn, New York, and was the grandson of Hungarian immigrants. His family was poor and moved frequently. The family soon found themselves in the Bronx, where he attended DeWitt Clinton High School (as did Stan Lee). There, he met Bob Kane and began creating comics at Kane's behest, who encouraged Will to submit his drawings to *Wow Magazine*. While serving in the U.S. Army during World War II, Will created *Joe Dope,* whose escapades helped soldiers fight the terrible war against the Nazis.

In addition to these writers, other comic book illustrators were also of the Jewish background. What was the commonality of these writers? All grew up in Jewish homes, all were children or grandchildren of people who had immigrated from Eastern Europe, fleeing the Nazi regime and the rippling effects of continued anti-Semitism post-World War II.

## 1.2 The Jewish Influence on the Dawn of the Comic Book Industry

So how did the comic book industry and superheroes get started? In his article addressing the Jewish influence on the creation of superheroes, Kogan (2019) states,

> The American comic-book industry started as an idea largely of Jewish artists in the 1930s and 1940s in New York, trying to give voice to their sense of American identity as Jews at a time where a lot of them couldn't even be explicitly Jewish in public … some of them changed their names to be less Jewish sounding, and they poured that Jewish identity into the characters they drew and the stories they told.
>
> (p. 1)

Magneto, the greatest-known antihero from the X-Men series, may be the best representation of a direct link between sequential art, comic books, and the Holocaust. The X-Men franchise chronicles the exploits of a group of mutant humans, each of whom possesses a unique power typically manifesting itself in childhood/adolescence. The X-Men, led by Francis Xavier, seek peaceful integration with society as a whole and fight for justice. Another group, the Brotherhood of Mutants, seeks the opposite. Led by Magneto, the members of the Brotherhood view themselves as *Übermensch*, who, based on their superior abilities, should dominate society and execute their own form of perceived justice. The Brotherhood embraces the paranoia that humankind wishes to destroy them out of fear and jealousy. Consequently, Magneto and his followers work for the destruction of humans and any X-Men who oppose them.

Stan Lee and Jack Kirby, both Jewish, created the X-Men, and Marvel Comics published the first issue in 1963 (Lee & Kirby, 1963). Consistent with practices of the industry in the 1960s, Marvel avoided overt references to religion. No indication of Magneto's experience of the Holocaust appeared until *Uncanny X-Men #150* was published in August 1981. Speaking to Cyclops, Magneto comments on the death of Cyclops's love interest, Jean Grey, saying, "I know something of grief. Search throughout my homeland; you will find none who bear my name. Mine was a large family and it was slaughtered – without mercy, without remorse" (Claremont & Cockrum, 1981, p. 1). This could refer to any number of events, but Magneto reveals himself later. He verbalizes regret and remorse at injuring a young woman. "I remember my own childhood – the gas chambers at Auschwitz, the guards joking as they herded my family to their death" (Claremont & Cockrum, 1982, p. 1). "As our lives were nothing to them, so human lives became nothing to me" (Claremont & Romita, 1985, p. 1).

The story only refers to Magneto, or Max Eisenhardt as he was known then, as a survivor of Auschwitz. No mention of his religion appears. As issue 150 concludes, the reader is left with the impression that Magneto has experienced an epiphany, repenting from the attitudes and actions of his adult life. This transition, however, did not occur under the direction of Lee and Kirby who were no longer directly involved with the franchise. Chris Claremont, also Jewish, became the writer of the X-Men stories in 1975. Until he came along, the X-Men series had languished and sold poorly. Claremont revitalized the series by focusing on character development. Magneto's history was born. Despite numerous references to Auschwitz, Claremont never identified Max or Magneto as Jewish. "I wanted to keep everybody wondering exactly where we going to land with this, partly because on one level, the Holocaust is a uniquely Jewish experience, but on another level, it was also, in European terms, a more universal experience as well. The Holocaust was specific to Judaism, but it also embraced a significant number of other minorities" (Riesman, 2019, p. 1).

Bryan Singer's 2000 film, *X Men*, firmly established Magneto's Auschwitz connection. In the opening sequence, Max is separated from his parents at the death camp as his mother is herded to the gas chamber and the crematorium. In his grief and anguish, we see Magneto's powers emerge as he twists and pulls the iron gates of the camp. His Jewish identity is finally established in a four-part series published by Marvel in 2009 entitled *Magneto: Testament.* The story opens with Max enrolled in school in Berlin. He is bullied by his classmates and school authorities for being Jewish. The story chronicles the major events of the Holocaust as Max and his family are caught up in them. They flee to Warsaw with its large Jewish population, but on September 1, 1939, Germany invades Poland. Max's family is killed, and he is sent to Auschwitz where he becomes a Sonderkommando – a prisoner who assists his captors by herding other prisoners to the gas chambers. Thus, he experiences the horrors of the camp knowing that he and his comrades allowed it to happen. This shapes his psyche to make him a man of action who is not afraid to make preemptive strikes against an enemy to protect himself. The artwork of the series shows the young Max as wide-eyed at all he sees going on around him. By the end in 1945, his eyes have narrowed to unfeeling slits.

When considering Holocaust survivors, people such as Elie Wiesel and Simon Wiesenthal comfort and reassure us. They were, respectively, an indefatigable humanitarian and a relentless agent of justice. Magneto, on the other hand, disturbs us. He is a vigilante willing to kill the innocent in order to ensure that anyone who might threaten him dies. He makes his own rules. Justice is whatever he decides it should be. We feel compassion for his traumatic childhood and his losses but shrink from his attitude toward humanity. We are torn between sympathy and repulsion. As the oppressed, who becomes the oppressor.

## 1.3 Conclusions

In conclusion, we have discussed that many superheroes were created by Jewish writers, so therefore it is perhaps not surprising that comics about the Second World War and/or the Holocaust have proliferated (Pettitt, 2019). In the *Uncanny: X-Men* series, "the Holocaust forms a particularly important backdrop to the story which several characters, including Magneto and Kitty Pryde, are revealed as having direct connections to the atrocity; the Nazi genocide therefore forms part of the context of many of the subsequent narrative arcs" (Pettitt, 2019, p. 156). More recently, DC Comics, in the 60th anniversary of the Superman series, published a tripart commemorative series. In this series, Superman and Lois Lane travel back in time to Nazi-occupied Europe, where they discover the truth of the concentration camps. Unfortunately, despite their attempts, they are unable to save the lives of the Jewish people in the camps (Pettitt, 2019).

The superhero must be viewed against the background and characteristics of these writers, i.e., so many of these writers and their families were refugees and were impacted by the world events of the time and rippling effects of the Holocaust. For these Jewish writers, whose characteristics were the opposite, the superheroes they created were often their alter ego. The struggles and losses the writers faced in their own lives were – in a different manner – reflected in the story themes developed for the superhero. This may have been a way that these writers created characters that fought for justice and a world where they had no power to do so themselves. Brod (2012) hypothesized that the Jewish people lost much of their heritage during the Holocaust and that the creation of superheroes were the writers' attempt to reclaim this heritage.

## References

Boxer, S. (1998). Bob Kane, 83, the cartoonist who created Batman is dead. *The New York Times*. Archived from the original on September 29, 2015.

Breitman, B. (2012). Psychological dimensions of Jewish men and violence. In H. Brod, *Superman is Jewish?: How comic book superheroes came to serve truth, justice and the Jewish-American Way* (pp. xxvii). New York: Simon and Shuster.

Brod, H. (2012). *Superman is Jewish?: How comic book superheroes came to serve truth, justice and the Jewish-American way* (p. xxii). New York: Simon and Shuster.

Claremont, C., & Cockrum, D. (1981). *Uncanny X-Men #150*. Marvel Comics Group.

Claremont, C., & Cockrum, D. (1982). *Uncanny X-Men #161*. Marvel Comics Group.

Claremont, C., & Romita, J. (1985). *Uncanny X-Men #199*. Marvel Comics Group.

Jerry Siegel, Joe Shuster and Superman. (n.d.). Retrieved from: http://www.thecomicbooks.com/old/super.html

Kogan, Z. (2019). *Superheroes, Jews and Israel: The origin story*. Retrieved from: https://www.jewishboston.com/superheroes-jews-and-israel-the-origin-story/

Lee, S., & Kirby, J. (1963). *X-Men #1*. Marvel Comics Group.

Pettitt, J. (2019). Remembering the Holocaust in American superhero comics. *Journal of Graphic Novels and Comics* 10(1), 155–166.

Riesman, A. (2019). How Magneto became Jewish. *Sequential Art*, p. 1. Retrieved from: https://www.vulture.com/2019/06/dark-phoenix-how-the-x-men-magneto-became-jewish.html

Thomas, R. (2006). *Stan Lee's amazing marvel universe*. New York: Sterling Publishing.

Thomas, R. (2018). How Stanley Lieber wrote his first comic book story and became "Stan Lee". *Time*. Retrieved from https://time.com/5452565/stan-lee-name-change-history/

# 2 And Then Came Superman

## Parallels with the Man of Steel and His Creators

*Jill A. Harrington and Howard R. Winokuer*

Since garnishing the cover of the June issue of *Action Comics #1* in 1938, dressed in his signature red cape lifting a car over his head, the Man of Steel has been a global iconic image of truth and justice for over eight decades (Sommerlad, 2018). With strength emanating from a radiant core of antioppression, Superman has been one of the most beloved, powerful, and influential superheroes, not because he was one of the first, but because of what he stands for – a symbol of hope. His origin story begins with traumatic loss, much like the origin stories of his creators. For many years, it was speculated that the two geeky teenage boys created Superman as a way to attract girls at their Ohio high school. However, over the years, a deeper story has emerged, revealing parallels between the lives of the creators – Jerry Siegel and Joe Shuster – and their creation – Superman. This chapter will briefly explore some of the shared similarities of Superman and his creators with a special focus on the influence of loss, grief, and oppression.

### 2.1 Man of Steel, Forged by Loss

What is most obvious about the bespectacled character Clark Kent is that he is unpopular, acts weak, and is awkward, especially around women such as Lois Lane. Superman, in his alter-ego, gives him confidence, power, and popularity. How could this not be the main impetus for the creation of a superhero by two geeky adolescent boys who met in high school in the 1930s and shared a love for science fiction, comics, and pulp publishing? For many decades, this was thought to be the most influential factor in Siegel and Shuster's creation of Superman; however, 70 years later, Brad Metzler, author of *Book of Lies* reveals that "America did not get Superman from our greatest legends, but because a boy lost his father. Superman came not out of our strength but out of our vulnerability" (Colton, 2008, para 12).

Metzler's work helped to reveal origins to the creation of Superman that were more profound. Although first published in 1938 by DC Comics, writer Siegel and artist Shuster conceived the idea of Superman in 1932, shortly after the sudden, tragic death of Siegel's father. On June 2, 1932, Mitchell Siegel, a Jewish immigrant from Lithuania, was working in a secondhand clothing store in Cleveland, when according to the police report, three men attempted a robbery, and in the upheaval, Siegel, 60, collapsed on the floor and died (Colton, 2008). There remains debate over whether Siegel was shot by the burglars; however, the account that Mitchell Siegel died of a heart attack during the robbery remains in the coroner's report (Colton, 2008).

Metzler contends that the profound and sudden loss of Siegel's father was the greatest influence in the creation of Superman (Colton, 2008), transforming his grief with his friend into a loss narrative. In the earliest surviving artwork, Superman comes to the rescue of a man being held up by a masked robber. Gerard Jones, comic-book historian, reflects about the death of Mitchell Siegel, "it had to have an effect.... Superman's invulnerability to bullets, loss of family, destruction of his homeland – all seem to overlap with Jerry's personal experience. There's a connection there: the loss of a dad as a source for Superman" (Colton, 2008, para 15).

Soon after Mitchell Siegel's death, in 1933, still developing their character, Siegel wrote a book titled *Dan Dunn,* about a bulletproof action hero with super-strong, supernatural powers, which he then used to write a crime story, and Shuster drew into comic format. They entitled it *The Superman* (Daniels & Kidd, 1998). This version of Superman would go on to be the archetype of the world's first beloved comic book hero. Central to the origin story of Superman is the loss of his biological parents, Jor-El and Lara. Throughout all of the story arcs, the most recurrent theme is Superman's deep sense of the loss of his father and his continued bond with Jor-El.

## 2.2 Jewish Origins

***Immigrants and Loss of Homeland.*** The loss of Superman's parents is predicated on the destruction of his homeland, Krypton, which forges a central theme to the identity of Clark Kent – that of an immigrant. In the midst of the impending violent destruction of their planet, their people, and their way of life, Jor-El and Lara are faced with the heart-wrenching decision to separate from their infant son, placing baby Kal-El in a one-person spacecraft destined for Earth, to ensure his survival as they faced death (Roven, Nolan, Thomas, Snyder, & Snyder, 2013). This, too, mirrors the agony and plight of many Jewish European immigrants fleeing Nazi Germany and the Holocaust – making agonizing decisions that would rupture them from their families, their homeland(s), and their way of life to survive. Some families made sacrifices, much like Jor-El and Lara, to stay behind because there were only enough resources for a few to go. Many faced death and possibly, like Krypton, the extinction of their people, while those who fled and survived were marred by a massive traumatic historical catastrophe – impacted by the rippling effects of profound traumatic loss for their generations and those thereafter. They fled to many countries, seeking harbors of safety.

Siegel and Schuster were both the sons of recent Jewish immigrants who fled from anti-Semitism in their native countries of Lithuania and Russia

(Sommerlad, 2018). Both families found a perceived sense of safety in Glenville, a Jewish neighborhood on the east side of Cleveland. It was there, at Glenville High School, that Jerry Siegel met the bespectacled Joe Shuster. Sharing a love of science fiction and comic books, their camaraderie was also forged by their shared Jewish backgrounds, culture, and history (Sommerlad, 2018).

***Discrimination, Anti-Semitism in America, and Hidden Identity.*** America, unfortunately, was not the safest of harbors for those Jewish families seeking refuge from hatred and discrimination. Between the 1880s and 1920s, American Jews were also being persecuted as two million Jewish people sought refuge in the United States (Klapper, n.d.). This surge of immigration fueled a backlash, particularly from those who did not like newcomers of any kind, especially those who were anti-Semitic. Jewish families sought to build their own safe harbors in forming their own communities, such as Glenville, where families could look out for one another, share Jewish cultural activities, organizations, and religion and raise their families. However, threats were all around and always present. Schuster and Siegel were growing up at a time when violent crime was rampant in America, and the newspapers were filled with stories of mobsters, murders, and mayhem. This mass migration of Jewish people into the United States unleashed a wave of anti-Semitism from the Anglo-American elite (Morris, 2017), as well as from American Nazis, and pro-Hitler German-American Bund arose (Vollum & Adkinson, 2003). As a result, they created a world where a super man may much be needed to fix the problems (Jones, 2004).

In this time of profound anti-Semitism throughout the world, including America, like many Jewish people of that time, Siegel and Shuster used pseudonyms (such as Joe Carter) to hide their Jewish identities and assimilate themselves into the Anglo-Christian community. They did this because many faced employment discrimination as well as fear from publishers and Hollywood studios that the general public would not patronize Jewish art or films. Jewish creators of films were "invisible in the movies Jews made … names were changed to uphold a screen myth of ethnic anonymity, and Julius Garfinkle became John Garfield" (Champlin, 1988, para. 17).

Kal-El, Superman's Kryptonian name, in which the suffix "El" is Hebrew (Sommerlad, 2018), is changed by his adoptive parents, Martha and Jonathan Kent, to help him assimilate as an immigrant-alien in the predominating midwestern Anglo-Christian culture as Clark Kent. This hidden identity is much like that of his creators, who hid behind Anglo-Christian names while donning super artistic gifts. Thematically, the story of Superman is a conduit for the experience of many Jewish people endeavoring to integrate into the predominantly American Anglo-Christian culture, shrouding their identity and heritage behind the suit of a new name. However, beneath these concealed identities, they stand true to the ones that are socially obscured. And in this yearning to assimilate in the challenge of exclusion, while enduring so many intergenerational losses, underneath the "S" is a symbol of hope to create an America where Jewish people were strong, resourceful, and resilient

(Champlin, 1988; Sommerlad, 2018), much like Superman and the experiences of his creators.

***Oppression from Nazi Germany and Jewish Mythology.*** Superman was created during the rise of the Third Reich, and in the following year, 1939, World War II began. Siegel and Shuster were very aware of the persecution of the Jewish people in Nazi Germany, Russia, Italy, and other parts of Europe, coupled with sometimes less obvious but still insidious forms of anti-Semitism in the United States. When asked why they created Superman in the 1930s Siegel expressed, "hearing and reading of the oppression and slaughter of helpless, oppressed Jews in Nazi Germany … I had the great urge to help the downtrodden masses, somehow. How could I help them when I could barely help myself? Superman was the answer" (Sommerlad, 2018, para 7). Interestingly, while World War II was being fought, Siegel and Shuster did not depict Superman fighting and defeating the Axis powers. They knew with his superpowers he could defeat them in fictional history; however, with real Americans fighting and dying in the war, they felt it might disparage their efforts. So, in order to keep Superman out of the war, but demonstrate his patriotism, Siegel and Shuster had Clark Kent's (aka Superman) X-ray vision malfunction during his preinduction physical, causing him to be declared 4-F, which means he was medically unfit for military service. To continue to demonstrate his patriotism, Superman combatted Fifth Columnists activities (e.g., Nazi sympathizers) in the United States, instead of fighting overseas (Mintz & Roberts, 2010).

What role, then, did Jewish mythology play in the development of Superman? Siegel and Shuster, both of Jewish religion and culture, were strongly influenced by the fleeing migration of their immigrant parents from a dangerous homeland. As a partially assimilated immigrant, the strongest connection to a Hebrew influenced superhero is how Superman parallels the stories of Golem and, most importantly, Moses.

In Jewish folklore, a golem, is an enlivened anthropomorphic being that is created by mud or clay. The most renowned Golem tale involves Judah Loew ben Bezalel, the late 16th-century rabbi, who created a golem and brought it to life through rituals of Hebrew incantations to defend the ghettos from anti-Semitic persecution in Prague (Bilefsky, 2009). Superman's strength and creation of a savior for the Jewish people supports a parallel with a golem; however, the strongest connection is tied to the story of Moses, who was also a savior of his people, fleeing the persecution by Egyptians of the Jewish people, who also faced trauma, loss, displacement, and migration, with faith and Moses as a symbol of hope.

Kal-El (suffix in Hebrew meaning "God"), like Moses, is sent alone, in a spaceship (basket) through the universe (river) because it is known that he is fated to be the savior of millions of people (oppressed Hebrews) (Sommerlad, 2018). It was this great oppression by the Egyptians where the story of Moses was born; wherein with his great strength and courage, Moses led his people out of Egypt, saving them through a great Exodus to the safe harbor of a promised land – the land of Canaan. Throughout his story, Superman mourns for Krypton, the same way Moses mourns for his lost family. This is also synonymous with the survivor's guilt many of those who escaped concentration camps felt while their families and friends perished (Sommerlad, 2018).

Because of this symbolism, Superman and many other comic superheroes were banned throughout Nazi Germany and all its occupied territories (Corey, 2008). They understood the significance of their meaning and the power that hope could bring to the oppressed.

## 2.3 Therapeutic Means by Narrative Reconstruction

Therapeutic writing can take many forms – it can be journaling, creative writing, storytelling, etc. In writing about loss and grief, the use of narrative reconstruction can help the individual shape and make meaning around the loss experience (Neimeyer, Klass, & Dennis, 2014).

The origin and story of Superman have many parallels to the lives of his creators, Jerry Siegel and Joe Shuster, two geeky teens, drawn together in high school by their love of comics, fantasy, science fiction, pulp publishing, and their shared heritage. Writing for the school newspaper, bespectacled, introverted, and awkward with girls, these are all synonymous with their lives and their superhero. But, underlying their Man of Steel was a story forged by loss and grief – not just of their individual losses, but of the collective losses of a people. Superman is a therapeutic grief narrative and a story of integrating profound loss with strength and hope through the greatest of all adversity.

## References

Bilefsky, D. (2009). Hard times give new life to Prague's golem. *The New York Times*. Retrieved from: https://www.nytimes.com/2009/05/11/world/europe/11golem.html

Champlin, C. (1988). The founding fathers of Hollywood: An empire of their own: How the Jews invented Hollywood. *Los Angeles Times*. Retrieved from: https://www.latimes.com/archives/la-xpm-1988-09-25-bk-4083-story.html

Colton, D. (2008). Superman's story: Did a fatal robbery forge the man of steel? *USA Today*. Retrieved from: https://usatoday30.usatoday.com/life/books/news/2008-08-25-superman-creators_N.htm

Corey, R. (2008). *Media and the Making of Modern Germany: Mass Communications, Society, and Politics from the Empire to the Third Reich*. New York: Oxford University Press.

Daniels, L., & Kidd, C. (1998). *Superman: The Complete History: The Life and Times of the Man of Steel*. London: Titan.

Jones, G. (2004). *Men of Tomorrow: Geeks, Gangsters, and the Birth of the Comic Book*. New York: Perseus.

Klapper, M.R. (n.d.). *20th century Jewish immigration*. Retrieved from: https://teachinghistory.org/history-content/beyond-the-textbook/25059

Mintz, S., & Roberts, R. (2010). *Hollywood's America: Twentieth-century America through film* (4th ed.). Oxford, UK: Wiley Publishing.

Morris, T. (2017). Tracing the history of Jewish immigrants and their impact on New York City. *Fordham News*. Retrieved from: https://news.fordham.edu/inside-fordham/faculty-reads/tracing-history-jewish-immigrants-impact-new-york-city/

Neimeyer, R.A., Klass, D., & Dennis, M.R. (2014, July–December). A social constructionist account of grief: Loss and the narration of meaning. *Death Studies*, 38(6–10), 485–498.

Roven, C., Nolan, C., Thomas, E., & Snyder, D. (Producers), & Snyder, Z. (Director). (2013). *Man of steel* [Motion Picture]. Los Angeles, CA: Warner Bros. Pictures.

Sommerlad, J. (2018). Superman at 80: The Jewish origins of the man of steel and the "curse" that haunts the actors who play him. *Independent*. Retrieved from: https://www.independent.co.uk/arts-entertainment/films/features/superman-jewish-origins-film-adaptations-curse-jerry-siegel-christopher-reeve-henry-cavill-a8344461.html

Vollum, S., & Adkinson, C.D. (2003). The portrayal of crime and justice in the comic book superhero mythos. *Journal of Criminal Justice and Popular Culture*, 10(2), 96–108.

# Part II

# Understanding Superhero Grief Through Postmodern Grief Theory

# 3 Transformations in the Field of Grief and Bereavement

## From Clark Kent to Beyond Kübler-Ross

*Christiane Manzella*

Human beings are storytellers. Our stories reflect how we live, love, die, grieve, make war, and peace. The superhero stories considered here are embedded in Western culture and are 20th- and 21st-century inventions. Yet, superheroes are not unique to Western cultures or to the 20th and 21st centuries. For example, the Mahabharata, the epic story from India, has embedded within it the Bhagavad Gita, the story of the god Krishna teaching Arjuna, a mortal Prince, about how to fight a war, brother against brother, while also teaching Arjuna about life, love, and death (Eswaren, 2007). Essentially, Krishna is teaching Arjuna to be a superhero. McClelland (1979) might posit that the Superhero stories developed because the Western culture values power and war. It is clear that the DC and Marvel comic superhero stories reflect a world that is threatened by and at war with evil – a major theme in the superhero narratives. However, a more subtle and perhaps not always so apparent theme in the superhero stories is that of love and loss. These superhero stories clearly reflect the ways love and grief are deeply intertwined.

The superheroes who star in this chapter are Wonder Woman as depicted in the film, *Wonder Woman* (Roven, Snyder, Snyder, Suckle, & Jenkins, 2017b), and Superman, as represented in two films, *Batman v Superman: Dawn of Justice* (Roven, Snyder, & Snyder, 2016) and *Justice League* (Roven, Snyder, Berg, Johns, & Snyder, 2017a). Why these two superheroes? Because while the most dominant story is that each fought to overcome evil, underlying their stories of love, loss, and legacy is that each loved and fought evil *while being significantly bereaved.*

### 3.1 Wonder Woman's Story

In *Wonder Woman* (Roven et al., 2017b), Diana Prince is the daughter of Queen Hippolyta and Zeus, making her a half-god with superpowers. She only finds out years later in the epic battle with Ares (son of Zeus and god of war) that she, herself, is a god and, therefore, the god killer. As a girl, Diana secretly trained with her aunt, General Antiope. Everything changes when an American pilot spying for the British, Steve Trevor, somehow flies through the protective sphere around the island. Diana rescues him, and they all learn that war is engulfing the world. Soon after, the island is invaded by German soldiers, and the ensuing battle ends with the death of many Amazonians, including Diana's beloved aunt, General Antiope, who dies saving Diana's life. Diana takes the sword and lasso of Hestia and leaves the island with Steve Trevor to fight the evil Ares. As battles rage, Diana falls in love with Steve, but Steve dies in combat, sacrificing himself to save humanity. Ares tries to convince her to join him to destroy humanity, but she says no, humans are worth loving. In *Justice League* (Roven et al., 2017a), strong memories of love – of humans and Steve – and her deep hope of triumphing over evil propel Diana back to her role and identity as Wonder Woman.

## 3.2 Superman's Story

Superman, born the infant Kal-El, was from the planet Krypton. Like all on Krypton, Kal-El faced certain death because of the imminent destruction of his birth-planet. His parents sent him to Earth, as an infant, on a small spaceship just before Krypton was destroyed, thus rescuing him. The spaceship crash-landed and was found by his Earth parents, Martha and Jonathan Kent, who adopted him and named him Clark. They protected him, cared for him, and loved him. And he loved them. They helped him learn how to use his superpowers and how to fight evil. In *Batman v Superman: Dawn of Justice* (Roven et al., 2016) and *Justice League* (Roven et al., 2017a), Lois Lane knows that Clark Kent and Superman are the same person. In *Batman v Superman: Dawn of Justice* (Roven et al., 2016), Superman dies saving his Earth mother, Martha. In *Justice League* (Roven et al., 2017a), Superman is brought back to life.

## 3.3 Postmodern Grief's Story: Overview

Modern understandings of grief have moved from stage-based models proposed by Lindemann (1994) and Kübler-Ross (1969). Kübler-Ross's model of coping (denial, anger, bargaining, depression, and acceptance) was developed through her conversations with the dying and was widely applied in describing grief as well as in counseling the bereaved. Now, as new understandings about the grief process are being developed and communicated in the literature, we have a more nuanced view that more accurately reflects the wide range of grief responses (e.g., Klass, 2015; Neimeyer, 2004).

There is recognition that those who are bereaved can adapt and cope with grief (Worden, 2018); that grief integrates in oscillations between loss orientation and restoration orientation in waves, moving from acute grief to an integrated grief (Neimeyer, 2004; Stroebe & Schut, 2010); and that grief is not depression (Zisook & Shear, 2009). Also, grief can be healthy and adaptive for grievers to maintain an ongoing bond with the deceased (Klass, 2015), rather than simply "cutting the tie" with the deceased.

We also recognize that grief is clearly related to the ways we love and form attachments (Bowlby, 1980; Shear, 2015). There is a growing awareness of the neurobiological underpinnings that shape love and the grief process (i.e., Kosminsky & Jordan, 2016; Schore, 2019). We form attachments from birth to death, which really can be understood as love (Bowlby, 1980). When a relationship ends, through death or some other way, grief *is* the normative process (Neimeyer, 2004; Worden, 2018).

From his research and clinical work, Worden (2018) developed the *Task Model* of grieving that empowers the bereaved; the bereaved can cope and adapt to loss. The first task for the bereaved is to recognize that the death is real. At first, there is shock and bewilderment and disbelief. The challenge at this time is to recognize, face, and internalize the reality that the death is real. Worden (2018) describes the second task as working through the pain of the grief. This can include physical pain, such as insomnia, appetite changes, and emotional pain, such as sadness, yearning, and anger. This time can be challenging because many times those who are bereaved are reluctant to describe or experience these feelings due to many in our death-denying society who reject "emotional displays" around the pain of grief. The third task is to adjust to an environment in which the deceased is missing. This time often involves learning new skills and making internal adjustments. The fourth task is to emotionally relocate the deceased and move forward with life while maintaining a continuing bond with the deceased – maintaining this ongoing bond if it is adaptive and healthy. The fourth task can be the most challenging task in the grieving process. A bereaved person usually goes back and forth from task to task because these tasks are not linear (Worden, 2018).

Stroebe and Schut (2010) developed the Dual Process Model of Grief. They described grief as a process that oscillates between a loss-oriented response and a restoration-oriented response to grief. The loss-oriented response usually dominates early in the grief process and involves primarily emotional responses, especially sadness, yearning, and anger. The restoration-oriented focus reflects the bereaved person's attempts to do and learn new things, assimilating the loss while learning to live life without the deceased. Emotional and cognitive distress oscillates between loss and restoration. Grief gradually becomes less intense and painful (Stroebe & Schut, 2010) and assimilates and integrates into a new normal (Neimeyer, 2004).

## 3.4 Is Grief Depression? Worden's Tasks and the Dual Process Model of Grief

In the movie, *Justice League* (Roven et al., 2017a), Diana Prince is found carrying out restorations at the Louvre. She seems to be in an almost dream-like state, slowly restoring the face of a marble sculpture. Was she depressed? It is important to distinguish grief from depression (Zisook & Shear, 2009). Freud (1917/1957) wrote, "In mourning it is the world which has become poor and empty; in melancholia, it is the ego itself" (p. 246), similar to the contemporary concept of depression. What seems clear is that Diana was not depressed.

Following Steve Trevor's death, Diana turned away from and shut down her identity as Wonder Woman. She was functioning at a high level and yet had not faced the reality of Steve's death (Worden's Task I) or faced or worked through her own emotional pain about his death as well as her own deep pain and disillusionment about not having been able to save the world (Worden's Task II). She only returned to her identity as Wonder Woman again because she was roused to engage with life and fight evil (Worden's Task III and Task IV). We also see that Diana oscillated between the loss orientation and the restoration orientation (Stroebe & Schut, 2010), returning to her role as Wonder Woman and again actively embracing her identity as Wonder Woman, dedicated to fighting evil and saving humanity and Earth.

## 3.5 Neurobiological Underpinnings

Clark Kent (Kal-El) and Diana Prince were clearly loved by their parents. This suggests we can assume that the relationship between Clark (Kal-El) and his Kryptonian mother and Diana and her mother started as an affectively connected dyadic relationship during the first months of their lives. Thus, as babies, Kal-El, Diana, (and the other superheroes) were loved, and each baby's right brain and each mother's right brain became activated and synchronized, forming the basis and capacity for mutual dyadic love through their lives (Schore & Marks-Tarlow, 2019). And, when each was bereaved, the neural pathways that developed in the limbic portion of the brain (completed at about three months old), the same neural pathways that are associated with love and separation distress, were activated (Porges, 2011; Schore, 2019; Schore & Marks-Tarlow, 2019). Love shaped the choices Superman and Wonder Woman made as each took huge risks to save and protect all those they loved and, importantly, people they didn't even know, out of love. And, the pinnacle of Superman's legacy of service and love is that rather than allow his mother to die, he died to save her (Roven et al., 2016).

Another aspect of interpersonal neurobiology and grief that can be explored through the superhero stories is the polyvagal system. The polyvagal system includes the 10th cranial nerve, the vagus nerve (the wanderer), the longest nerve in the body. The polyvagal system has three components: the ventral vagal complex that regulates social engagement, which reflects a relaxed and safe state, "rest and digest"; the sympathetic nervous system, "fight or flight"; and the dorsal vagal complex, which is the unmyelinated primitive pathway that regulates the shut down or "drop dead" response, the survival response of last resort (Porges, 2011). The polyvagal system is like a personal surveillance system asking: "Is this situation safe?" and is a major part of the affect regulation system that stems from the early forming, autonomic, nonconscious neurobiological processes in the limbic portion of the brain that is at the heart of emotional coregulation (Porges, 2011; Schore, 2019).

In *Justice League* (Roven et al., 2017a), the evil Steppenwolf obtains resources to destroy the world. The other superheroes are desperate and need Superman, so they decide to try to bring Superman back to life. They place Clark's body in the amniotic fluid in the Mother Ship. In a burst of energy, Clark comes back to life. He is completely confused and can only see with his x-ray vision. Victor (a cyborg and superhero) tries to stop his machine arm from firing, but it seems that Victor's sympathetic nervous system is not in his control and activated: Fight! His arm shoots out a huge destructive burst. Even though Wonder Woman tries to stop Superman from acting as she cries out, "Kal-El! The last son of Krypton, remember who you are!" (Roven et al., 2017b, 1:15:31), Superman retaliates. There is a huge amount of wreckage. While his superpowers were intact, Superman's neural system was not fully engaged, and his capacity for accurate neuroception, helping him know he was safe, was profoundly impaired. Like many who are bereaved or traumatized, neuroception of danger impaired his sense of safety (Porges, 2011) and interfered with his capacity to oscillate between loss and restoration orientation; to effectively function (Stroebe & Schut, 2010).

Just like a clinician working with a bereaved person would do, Wonder Woman recognized what Clark needed and tried to help him come into a ventral vagal state so he could accurately discern that he was safe (Schore, 2019). She appealed to his babyhood self and deepest identity, Kal-El, but this didn't work because his capacity for coregulation was profoundly disrupted, most likely because of having been brought back to life after having been dead. Perhaps his ventral vagal nerve had to remyelinate to again function efficiently. The most effective soothing happened when Lois Lane was brought to Clark, still wearing the engagement ring he had planned to give her before he died and that Martha sadly gave to her after Clark's funeral. It seems that Lois was still actively engaged in Task II, working through the pain of his death (Worden, 2018) or was perhaps stuck in the loss orientation (Stroebe & Schut, 2010). They embrace and he carries her high into the sky. Through coregulation, his neural functioning returned (and she was soothed, too). He was again able to function efficiently as Superman and as Clark Kent. Just as Lois held Clark, a clinician's role is listening well and holding – therapeutic holding – knowing where the person is (i.e., which task?) while helping coregulate. This can happen through softening the gaze, modulating the voice, and facilitating right brain to right brain resonance, bringing about a sense of love and safety (Kosminsky & Jordan, 2016).

Superhero stories can provide clues to understand life, love, and grief. Are you "blowing through the roof" because of pain, grief, or needing healing, love, and coregulation? Or are you frozen because of grief, unable to feel joy or love or even pain? As you read about grief and watch the superhero story films again or for the first time, see what clues emerge for you!

## References

Bowlby, J. (1980). *Attachment and loss*. New York: Basic Books.

Eswaren, E. (2007). *The Bhagavad Gita*. Tomales, CA: Nilgiri Press.

Freud, S. (1917/1957). Mourning and melancholia. In J. Strachey (Ed. & Trans.), *The standard edition of the complete psychological works of Sigmund Freud* (vol. 14, pp. 243–258). London: Hogarth Press.

Klass, D. (2015). Continuing bonds, society, and human experience: Family dead, hostile dead, and political dead. *Omega*, 70 (1), 99–117.

Kosminsky, P.S., & Jordan, J. (2016). *Attachment-informed grief therapy. The clinician's guide to foundations and applications*. New York: Routledge.

Kübler-Ross, E. (1969). *On death and dying*. New York: Macmillan.

Lindemann E. (1994). Symptomatology and management of acute grief 1944. *The American Journal of Psychiatry*, 151(6 Suppl), 155–160.

McClelland, D. (1979). *Power: The inner experience* (2nd ed.). Irvington, CA: Irvington Publishers.

Neimeyer, R.A. (2004). *APA video series: Systems of psychotherapy: Constructivist therapy*. Washington, DC: American Psychological Association.

Porges, S. (2011). *The Polyvagal theory. Neurophysiological foundations of emotions, attachment, communication, and self-regulation*. New York: W.W. Norton & Company.

Roven, C., Snyder, D., Berg, J. & Johns, G. (Producers), & Snyder, Z. (Director), (2017a). *Justice league* [Motion Picture]. USA: Warner Bros. Pictures.

Roven, C., & Snyder, D. (Producers), & Snyder, Z. (Director). (2016). *Batman v Superman: Dawn of justice* [Motion Picture]. USA: Warner Bros. Pictures.

Roven, C., Snyder, D, Snyder, Z., & Suckle (Producers), & Jenkins, P. (Director), (2017b). *Wonder woman* [Motion Picture]. USA: Warner Bros. Pictures.

Schore, A.N. (2019). *Right brain psychotherapy*. New York: W.W. Norton & Company.

Schore, A.N., & Marks-Tarlow, T. (2019). How love opens creativity, play and the arts through early right brain development (pp. 64–91). In A.N. Schore (Author). *Right brain psychotherapy*. New York: W.W. Norton & Company.

Shear, M.K. (2015). Complicated grief. *New England Journal of Medicine*, 372, 153–160.

Stroebe, M., & Schut, H. (2010). The dual process model of coping with bereavement: A decade on. *Omega*, 61(4), 273–289.

Worden, J.W. (2018). *Grief and counseling and grief therapy: A handbook for the mental health practitioner* (5th ed.). New York: Springer Publishing Company.

Zisook, S., & Shear, K. (2009). Grief and bereavement: What psychiatrists need to know. *World psychiatry: Official journal of the World Psychiatric Association (WPA)*, 8(2), 67–74.

# 4 Loss and the Heroic Quest for Meaning

## A Conversation with Robert A. Neimeyer

*Robert A. Neimeyer and Jill A. Harrington*

[**Portland, Oregon** – hometown of Jessica Cruz, otherwise known as a Green Lantern and part of the Green Lantern Corps. It was here, in Portland, where one night in the woods Jessica and her friends were out for a hike and accidentally discovered two men burying a dead body. The men, alarmed, shot Jessica and her friends – leaving them for dead. However, Jessica survived. Debilitated by survivor's guilt and traumatic grief in the aftermath of violent death loss, Jessica became reclusive, sequestering herself in her apartment. From the parallel universe of Earth-3, her profound grief and anxiety attracted a powerful emerald ring, which fed off fear, in opposition to the Earth-1 green lantern rings, which were attracted to courage. The ring latched onto Jessica and amplified her fear. Now a villain, Jessica, quickly drew the attention of Lex Luthor, who wished to control her and the ring's destructive power. However, she also drew the attention of a certain superhero, a homicide loss survivor himself, who wanted to help support Jessica in transforming her pain and power to a heroic quest for meaning – Batman! With his help, Cruz learned how to harness her grief and pain, integrating her loss with a newfound power and purpose. She joined Batman and found meaning as part of the Justice League. She is known as the superhero, Green Lantern (Johns, 2018). It is here that I find myself in Portland, Oregon, at the doorstep of Dr. Robert Neimeyer, who we would consider in our field, a grief and loss leader – our Batman. Who has spent a tremendous part of his professional career studying and supporting the bereaved on their heroic quest for meaning through profound loss. It is here, like Batman, he begins the origin story of his Justice League of Grief, gathering a worldwide team of talented, dedicated, and compassionate educators to create the Portland Institute of Loss and Transition. As he opens the door, I am greeted with a warm smile, and with his known welcoming and calming voice, he invites me to join him in conversation.]

JH: Dr. Neimeyer, you've long been identified with a "constructivist" or meaning-oriented take on grief and transition. So, from that perspective, can you briefly describe meaning reconstruction and the experience of loss?

RN: Sure, Jill. Constructivism essentially suggests that, for better and worse, we fallible human beings seek to construct the meaning of our lives as we go along, looking for a thread of coherence in the random events that befall us, striving to build relationships that support us, and seeking shorter-term and long-term life directions that give us a sense of ultimate purpose and value, a kind of provisional grounding in the shifting sands of time. Significant loss – that inevitable companion on the journey – stretches and sometimes sunders these fragile strands in our tissue of meaning and often forces us to return to the loom to reweave the fabric of our lives, sometimes reaffirming previous identities, values, and relationships, and sometimes reconstructing them. Typically, this is a deeply emotional and often complicated process, especially when the losses are profound or traumatic, and in suffering them, we lose a sense of predictability, justice, and even a sense of who we are or were in the process. Another way of saying this is that loss challenges the life stories or narratives on which we have relied for orientation, and grieving is the emotional quest to learn the lessons of loss and to reconstruct our life story in a way that is sustainable now.

JH: Hmm. That makes sense. And maybe so we can connect with the theme of this book – Why do you think the superhero narrative exists?

RN: Good question! But I think the answer is really as simple as it is profound. Joseph Campbell spent a lifetime analyzing the "mono-myth" that percolates through essentially every world culture – the "hero's journey", in which Odysseus, Moses, Penelope, Gilgamesh, Siddhartha, or George Washington is banished by crisis or circumstance to a dark and dangerous realm, undergoes all sorts of trials of the body and of spirit, and eventually returns to the familiar world transformed, as a bearer of crucial knowledge, possessor of special power, or wisdom figure who leads others toward the right path that ensures cultural, communal, or personal survival. The superhero narrative, in all its creative variety, really represents our own historical epoch's version of this universal mythic structure – often scaled down to reveal the ironic humanity of the hero. It speaks to our capacity to transcend suffering or to transmute it into something of ultimate value for others and ourselves.

JH: Yes, I can see that. But let's look at that in the specific context of death and loss. Do you think that finding meaning following loss is central to most superhero narratives?

RN: I have to chuckle a little at that question! It's a bit like asking a Buddhist if experience teaches that attachment is a bad idea, or asking a Christian whether forgiveness is important! Of course, I see a quest for meaning as omnipresent in human life, though we rarely consider it as long as we can live with taken-for-granted meanings that remain unchallenged or untested by our experience. And we certainly can hold tight to safe and familiar meanings that diminish our lives and others by ignoring the call to something more risky and noble. But when it is our loved ones who die violently (as in the case of Spider-Man, Batman, Iron Man, or Captain Marvel), or our world that is destroyed or threatened (as in the case of

Wonder Woman, Captain America, Superman, or the Black Panther), we are prompted to engage deeply with the questions, *Who am I, in my most central identity? What now is mine to do? How can the world be set right, and what is my role in doing this?* Every hero from Achilles to Aquaman is confronted by these questions of ultimate identity, purpose, and meaning, and each in one way or another answers the call.

JH: Given that most superheroes have experienced the sudden, violent death of a family member, how do you think violent death affected the superhero's capacity to make meaning of the tragic event?

RN: Typically, it affected it by decimating it. As commonly happens in the wake of tragic loss – including the tragic suicide of my own father before I turned 12 – traumatic loss devastates us and calls into question our "assumptive world" and its corollary assumptions – that we can anticipate what comes next, understand it, and in some measure, control it. Cataclysmic losses give the lie to all of this, and we are commonly cast into a place of darkness, incomprehension, profound aloneness, and self-doubt. How we handle this determines whether we will emerge embittered, hateful, victimized, and disempowered, or galvanized, self-developing, assertive, and powerful. The former can be understood as succumbing to meaninglessness, and the latter can be read as a potent commitment to the pursuit of meaning.

JH: So, you think this trauma also lends itself to the survivor's transformation. Do you think this transformative process also triggered growth after loss for most superheroes?

RN: Certainly, although it might be more accurate to say that the superheroes-to-be lent *themselves* to the *trauma*, experienced it fully in a way that shook them to the roots, and then pressed them to confront their demons and grow into the persons they were meant to be. We see something of the same in our research on difficult, complicating grief and its capacity to tear down what was, to make way for what might now be.

JH: Okay, let's get practical. Fictionally speaking, if you were approached by superheroes who were grieving profound losses, what are some ways you might work with them in a grief therapy session to assist them in searching for significance and meaning in loss?

RN: I love it! This is where the rubber meets the road, where theory meets practice. Not to dodge the question, but I see therapy as "leading from one step behind", meaning that at each moment of the encounter I try to attune myself to what the client is *almost* saying, as I listen between the lines of the story he or she is telling me to discern the implicit questions, emotions, needs, and possibilities that invite fuller voicing, exploration, and engagement in our dialogue. Therapy is less about what the therapist does or plans to say and more about what the therapist hears and helps the client address, not only in words in their sessions but also in brave and bold actions between them. Another way of saying this is that therapy of any real kind is not a rehearsed manualized procedure, so much as an improvisational and often surprising dialogue, one that takes both (or in the case of couples, family, or group therapy, all) parties in directions that neither (or none) of the participants could have anticipated. But fair enough. You channel the superhero or heroes and give me a few sentences from each, and I'll respond. *Ready, set – go!*

JH: Okay, here goes:

"Dr. Neimeyer, my name is Clark Kent, otherwise known as Superman. Both of my biological parents died when I was just an infant. I don't even remember them. Most of what I know about my biological parents, I have learned through memory sticks. Some other orphaned or bereaved children I have met don't have memory sticks in a crystal cave as I do. But they tell me they learn about their parent/s who have died from the memories and stories of others. I know it has been helpful for me to be lucky enough to communicate with the memories of my deceased father, but sometimes that doesn't even seem enough. How can I help other kids and myself to connect with memories, to find a connection with our parents who have died and help that bring us forward to create meaning in our lives?"

RN: First, Clark, let me say that I feel a tingle of admiration for the way you frame this heartfelt question, which bridges from your own vulnerable longing for the parents you never knew to the plight of other grieving children engaged in a similar quest in the course of their own bereavement. In a sense, acknowledging your personal quest to know your parents both validates your humanity, whatever planet you hail from, and lifts up the similar efforts of other children to connect *who* they were and *whose* they were to the more mature people they are becoming. That in itself is a noble gift, and very much in keeping with your character. Second, I appreciate how you recognize that building what psychologists call a "continuing bond" with deceased loved ones doesn't necessarily require us to retreat into a Fortress of Solitude to do so. As you noted, most of the kids you talked about did just the opposite. They rescued recollections of their parents from the memories of others, usually through the normal process of asking for or spontaneously being offered stories about them by other people who knew them. What a gift it can be to sit down with the family photo album with a loving grandparent and hear about what our father was like when he was our age, or to be told and retold how devoted our mother was to us when we were a little baby. It is mainly when these stories are silenced out of a fear that they will trouble us that we feel isolated and alone in our grief, which can then become as frozen as an arctic wasteland. Stories shared, in tears and laughter, thaw this grief and make it more fluid.

I also have to say that I love your language around "memory sticks!" I know you meant the second word as a noun, like a kind of USB drive from the planet Krypton. But playfully, I also imagine that part of reconstructing rather than just relinquishing or letting go of bonds of attachment when a loved one dies is to look to find ways that memory *sticks*, considered as a verb, in the sense that it becomes an indelible resource to us in our bereavement and in our lives going forward. For kids as well as adults, one way to help memories stick is with a whole creative range of art therapy techniques, from encouraging young children to draw pictures and tell stories about their mommy or daddy, through prompting adolescents to compile a playlist of music they associate with their folks or their family on their smartphones, to having emerging adults undertake a legacy project about their parents by researching their lives, interviewing others, and then sharing a brief biography about them on Facebook or in other social media. Might you consider extending your narrative skills as a journalist, Clark, by attending a Portland Institute training session in expressive arts approaches to grief,[1] and maybe organize a grief camp getaway to the Fortress of Solitude? You might even consider renaming it the *Fortress of Solidarity* for that special occasion!

JH: Ha, ha, ha! I love the image of Clark Kent as an expressive arts therapist! That should get Lois Lane's attention! Okay, here's another:

"Hi, Dr. Neimeyer, my name is Pepper Potts, and my husband, Tony Stark, otherwise known as Iron Man, died saving half the universe and ridding it of the tyranny of Thanos. Tony was the love of my life, not at all because he was a superhero. Well, I mean Iron Man was part of who he was, but I loved him because he was *Tony* – complex, complicated, and brilliant, sometimes battling his own self-interest for the good of humanity. Tony and I grew slowly in love with one another, and selfishly, I did not really want him to be a hero. But I knew that he could never really be Tony if he didn't do everything he could to save those lost in the universe by the devastation Thanos wrought. So, I encouraged him to join the rest of the Avengers and jump through time to save countless lives and make the universe whole again. I even fought by his side, as Rescue and was there when he sacrificed himself to hold the Infinity Stones and snapped his fingers to bring back all those eradicated by Thanos five years before. I sat by as he was dying, and let him know that I would be okay along with our daughter, Morgan, who joked that she loved her dad "3,000" (Feige, Russo, & Russo, 2019, 00:41:16), as he also did her. I wanted to release him from any guilt he might have felt by dying and leaving us. I wanted to give him permission to let go, to release him from his suffering.

It's been months now since his death, and I can't help thinking that maybe I should have done more. Even though I knew he was dying, maybe I could have done more to save him. I replay those images in my head when I was there with him, and he was dying. Maybe I didn't make the right choice? Maybe I should have tried to rescue him. But, there is a part of me that knows he was dying, and I had to accept that and allow him to be at peace. But, another part of me is confused and conflicted. I feel stuck in this place of confusion and guilt. Did I do enough?"

RN: Pepper, I was among the countless tearful witnesses to that tragic, beautiful exchange between you, and was moved beyond words by the nobility of Tony's sacrifice, and the equal nobility with which you embraced it and him, and reassured him that you and Morgan would be okay. The great Chilean poet, Pablo Neruda, once said: *Se nada nos salva de la muerte, al menos que el amor nos salve de la vida* – If nothing can save us from death, may love at least save us from life. In that telling moment when life met death, each of you, in word and deed, lovingly "saved" the other. But of course, it was not simply Tony who was complicated – we all are. In your case, a strong and selfless superheroic part of you accepted Tony's ultimate sacrifice and granted him permission to travel to a place beyond time. But another part – his partner and the mother of his beloved child – would have done anything to turn back the hands of the clock, perhaps pressing the restart button on that *Endgame* (Feige et al., 2019) to have it all turn out differently. This part feels confusion, conflict, and contrition, not affirmation, acceptance, and altruism. And so, this part needs more than rational reassurance that you did all you could.

As I listen to you, I wonder if your spontaneous use of "part language" suggests a way forward. Just as you have more than one part within you, so too *Tony* is a part of you – a kind of *hologram*, of a psychological sort, who might still have something to tell you or teach you about life and loss, if we could invite him into the room, offer him a comfortable chair, and help that anguished, hurting, and regretful part of you find voice and ask the questions of him that you are asking of me. If we could visualize him, hear his voice bearing on those questions, and perhaps bearing an undying love for you and Morgan, would that be a helpful step? If so, might we make some time for that healing encounter in our next session? In between, I'd like to send you a quote from a wise mentor of mine that I think you might find meaningful.[2] What thoughts or questions might you have about that?

JH: That was beautiful and so powerful. I am at a loss for words. However, if I were speaking as Pepper, I would certainly be making an appointment for the next session!

So just one final question: What are the most important *Lessons of Loss* we can learn about meaning reconstruction and the narratives of superheroes?

RN: Cool. How about these?

1. Human suffering is universal. Do something about it.
2. You will never be prepared for all that may come. Get used to it.
3. Evil arises from self-interest, unmitigated by empathy for others.
4. You are more than you know yourself to be, and less than you imagine.
5. Beneath all of your visible powers are invisible vulnerabilities.
6. Face the terror of your fear. And learn from it.

7. Find the mask that speaks the truth of who you must be. And find someone with whom you can take it off.
8. You cannot go it alone. However strong you are, you need the help of others like and unlike you.
9. Return to the world you left. And learn to love it.
10. Know that your life, like all lives, is an act of creative fiction. Make it a good story.

## Notes

1 Readers interested in learning more about these and other meaning-oriented tools for grief therapy are encouraged to explore the training and certification programs offered by the Portland Institute for Loss and Transition at www.portlandinstitute.org.

2 Speaking in the gendered language of mid-20th-century America, George Kelly, the originator of personal construct psychology, wrote:

In a broad sense, each of us gives his life for something, something noble or something ignoble, though mostly something in between. Some do it decisively in one abrupt and frightening gesture. Some do it slowly and unobtrusively, sacrificing themselves little by little. Some face death outright; others stumble in its general direction. To seek to die well is an object of the full life and those who fail to live well never succeed in finding anything worth dying for. Thus life and death can be made to fit together, each as the validator of the other (p. 259).

[Source: Kelly, G. A. (1965). Suicide: The personal construct point of view. In N. L. Farberow & E. S. Shneidman (Eds.), *The cry for help* (pp. 255–280). New York: McGraw-Hill.

## References

Feige, K. (Producer), & Russo, A. & Russo, J. (Directors). (2019) *Avengers: Endgame* [Motion Picture]. United States: Marvel Studios.

Johns, G. (2018, January 18). *Green lantern (Jessica Cruz).* DCUGuide. https://dcuguide.com/w/Green_Lantern_(Jessica_Cruz)_(New_52).

# 5 Continuing Bonds Across the Universes

## Superheroes and Enduring Connections

*Christopher Hall*

### 5.1 Paradigm Shifts

The progress of scientific discovery is often seen as a continuous, incremental advance, where new discoveries add to the existing body of scientific knowledge. This view of scientific progress was challenged by Kuhn (1962), who argued that science proceeds with a series of revolutions interrupting normal incrementing progress. He called these revolutions "paradigm shifts", and one such shift took place in the field of thanatology two decades ago. Reflected in the 1996 publication of *Continuing Bonds: New Understandings of Grief* (Klass, Silverman, & Nickman, 1996), the authors argued for a shift away from the idea that successful grieving requires "letting go" or "breaking the bond" with the deceased and saw a move toward a recognition of the potentially healthy role of maintaining continued symbolic bonds with the them. This shift in thinking also fundamentally altered how we approach interventions with the bereaved.

Freud's 1917 publication of "Mourning and Melancholia" (1917/1957), which attempted to explain within a scientific framework the process of grief work, has been credited with establishing a 20th-century psychology of grief (Walter, 1994). Freud's concept of "grief work" aimed at detaching energy from memories and thoughts of the deceased, in order to reinvest that energy in available relationships. Interestingly, Freud's theoretical model did not match his personal experience following the death of his daughter, which he described nine years later in a letter to a friend whose son had died. He now understood that love was something "which we do not wish to relinquish" (Freud, 1961, p. 239).

In terms of seeking closure, Freud also wrote in 1923 that "In the instance of the loss of a very significant object, the total mourning process may never be completed" (Freud, 1961, p. 31). Freud's concept of grief work remained a dominant theme in theoretical models for many years. Lindemann (1944), who worked as a psychoanalyst around the time of World War II, described the resolution of grief as being the "disconnection from the deceased, readjustment to life and the formation of new relationships" (p. 43). Lindemann developed the concept of morbid (or unresolved) grief, which was seen in cases where the bereaved person failed to complete the final task, the focus of which was breaking bonds with the deceased.

## 5.2 Continuing Bonds

Klass, Silverman, and Nickman's model of "Continuing Bonds" (1996) gave voice to an emerging consensus in the field – that although death ends a life, it does not end a relationship. Grief is actually about managing a changed relationship to the person who has died, rather than letting go, disconnecting, or finding some kind of "closure". Rather than "saying goodbye", there exists the possibility of the deceased being both present and absent. They argued that after a death, bonds with the deceased do not necessarily have to be severed – we have memories and shared experiences with others that will always remind us of these connections.

Bereaved individuals are assumed to be able to reconnect with life while still creating places of memorialization, retaining personal possessions, and developing routines and rituals that honor the deceased person (Klass, 2006). The bereaved person needs to make adjustments to how they experience and "express" the relationship they have to the person who has died.

Based upon a sociological analysis of grief, Walter's (1994) biographical model of grief highlights the continuing influence of the dead on the living. He claims that the purpose of grief is to enable the bereaved to construct a consistent and personally held biography of the deceased, so they may integrate their memory into their ongoing life. Often this will be done through conversations with family, friends, and neighbors who knew the deceased person when they were alive.

The development of this bond is conscious, dynamic, and changing, the expression of which can be found in a variety of forms. The deceased may be seen as a role model, and the bereaved may turn to the deceased for guidance or to assist them in clarifying values. The relationship with the deceased may be developed by talking to the deceased or by relocating the deceased in heaven, inside themselves, or joined with others whom they predeceased. The bereaved may experience the deceased in their dreams, by visiting the grave, feeling the presence of the deceased, or through participating in rituals or by treasuring linking objects. Many people build the connection out of the fabric of daily life. Frequently this continuing bond is co-created with others. A number of studies have found that approximately half of the bereaved population experience the sense of presence of the deceased (Datson & Marwit, 1997), although the true incidence is thought to be much higher, given a great reluctance among the bereaved to disclose its occurrence to clinicians.

Ongoing research is still examining when continuing bonds are helpful and when they are not. Writers have attempted to distinguish the conditions under which it is adaptive from those where it is maladaptive. Evidence suggests that individuals who experience insecure styles of attachment are more prone to chronic grief trajectories (Bonanno, Wortman, & Nesse, 2004), contributing to maladaptive rather than adaptive forms of continuing bonds with the deceased.

Field (2006) identifies a type of continuing bonds expression that represents failure to integrate the loss due to extreme avoidance in processing the implications of the loss. These conflicting findings are likely explained by Klass's (2006) assertion that the original concept never implied causality, but rather suggested that the impact of continuing or relinquishing bonds is dependent on the nature and integration of the bond, not its simple presence or absence. Continuing bonds must always be considered within a cultural context, and there needs to be assessment of the ways the bond influences adaptation to the loss.

This chapter will now explore two superhero characters – Iron Man and Batman and how the construct of continuing bonds is expressed within their narratives.

## 5.3 Tony Stark/Iron Man

Through its 11 years and 22 films, the Marvel Cinematic Universe (MCU) is an American media franchise centered on a series of superhero films, based on characters that appear in American comic books published by Marvel Comics. The first MCU film was *Iron Man* (Arad, Feige, & Favreau, 2008) and multiple films culminating to *Avengers: Endgame* (Feige, Russo, & Russo, 2019), which has become the highest grossing film of all time, generating nearly 2.8 billion dollars in its theatrical release.

The 2008 origin film introduces "Iron Man" to audiences. The central story arc is one of redemption and concerns the evolution of Tony Stark, the glamorous head of a weapons manufacturing company, into Iron Man. Tony is shaken when he's taken hostage and realizes that his weapons have fallen into the wrong hands. He, along with a fellow captive, build an exo-skeleton that is not only a suit of armor but also a weapon and a means of transport and escape. Tony escapes but his fellow captive sacrifices himself in order to secure Tony's survival. Wracked with guilt, Tony uses this experience to refocus his attentions and all his resources to create an improved version of the exo-skeleton, which will be dubbed Iron Man by the media. At the end of *Iron Man* (Arad et al., 2008), he reveals to the world a now iconic catchphrase, "I am Iron Man" (1:57:10). Unlike other superheroes such as Superman, Stark unveils his secret identity.

From the beginning of the series, what makes Iron Man a superhero "is a flaw – a heart defect" (Sragow, 2010, para. 10). The first movie is about the way he strengthens his heart, literally and metaphorically, with the help of his friends – and his breakthrough miniaturized arc reactor, which prevents metal fragments from entering his heart and killing him.

In *Iron Man 2* (Feige & Favreau, 2010), we see a strained relationship between Tony and his father, Howard. *Captain America: Civil War* (Feige, Russo, & Russo, 2016) reveals that Tony's (unknowingly) final, bitter interaction with his father left Tony feeling guilt over never having been able to tell his father that he loved him. With time travel a possibility in *Avengers: Endgame* (Feige et al., 2019), Tony is given an opportunity to be with his father in the

1970s, immediately before Tony was born. This allows for a conversation between men who were not able to express affection as father and son. They both talk about their concerns of failing their children. Tony worries about losing his daughter and Howard is anxious about becoming a father. Tony's ability to connect with his father in this moment because being a father himself gives him new perspective on why Howard neglected him as a child. On the other hand, Tony's able to forgive both his father for his lack of support and himself for never having the courage to take the first step toward reconciliation. As Tony departs, he hugs and thanks his father and finds some much-needed understanding to fill his biggest emotional void.

In *Avengers: Endgame* (Feige et al., 2019), we learn that Tony now has a daughter and is reluctant to rejoin the Avengers. Tony Stark at the end of the film sacrifices himself for the greater good and gives up seeing his daughter again, which is particularly touching because he knows how difficult it is to grow up with an absent father. But this decision is all the more meaningful because he learned to forgive his father and hopes his daughter may also understand his sacrifice. "He's found meaning in forgiveness, in the importance of being a father, and in the power of sacrifice" (Tan, 2019, para. 8).

These conversations, whether imaginal or perceived as real, can serve as connections to the deceased as well as repair work for the bereaved. Actions, such as Tony's service as head of Stark Technology and leader of the Avengers, as well as his *Endgame* sacrifice, are all examples of continuing bonds.

## 5.4 Bruce Wayne/Batman

In May 1939, DC comics introduced Bruce Wayne, who was human, was vulnerable, and possess no superhuman powers – Batman. As depicted in the 2005 motion picture, *Batman Begins* (Roven, Thomas, Franco, & Nolan, 2005), central to Batman's mythology is the witnessing, as a young boy, his parents murdered outside a theatre. These murders are the defining moment of his human life and that of his alter-ego. In fact, young Bruce is so deeply wounded by seeing his parents killed that he eventually makes the commitment to fight injustice wherever it may present itself. After years of traveling the globe, in which he painstakingly sculpts his mind and body, Bruce Wayne eventually finds his way back to Gotham City. His huge inheritance provided the means to equip a crime fighter's laboratory on a grand scale, and while maintaining secrecy, Wayne begins to design and construct Batman's crime-fighting arsenal. Wayne's genius-level intellect, nearly limitless resources, and savvy crime-fighting skills mold that character that is Batman.

His father, whom he is both proud of and has a warm relationship with, conveys to him the importance of resiliency when he comforts his son after a fall, "Why do we fall Bruce? So, we can learn to pick ourselves up" (Roven et al., 2005, 10:41). As a young adult his mentor and later to become villain, Ducard, asks Bruce, "Do you still feel responsible for your parents' death?"

Bruce Wayne replies, "My anger outweighs my guilt" (Roven et al., 2005, 17:05). Although the source of this anger remains unexplored, we do know that anger may serve to thwart continuing bonds of involvement (Field, Gal-Oz, & Bonanno, 2003). Anger can also impede the processing of more vulnerable emotions such as fear, anxiety, and loss (Foa, Riggs, Massie, & Yarczowers, 1995; Forbes, Haslam, Williams, & Creamer, 2005).

Moments later Ducard says, "You are stronger than your father", to which Bruce replies "You didn't know my father". Ducard responds with, "But I know the rage that drives you. An impossible anger strangling the grief until the memory of your loved one is just poison in your veins. One day you catch yourself wishing the person you loved never existed. So, you would be spared your pain… Your anger gives you great power but if you let it, it will destroy you" (Roven et al., 2005, 00:19:58–00:20:50).

The death of his parents inspired new ambitions and goals (continuing bonds) in the figure of Batman. Alfred provides a linking object to these losses through their shared history and grief. When the young Bruce says to Alfred "I miss them Alfred, I miss them so much", Alfred responds with, "So do I master Bruce, so do I" (Roven et al., 2005, 16:50).

## 5.5 Conclusions

There does not appear to be a simple one-to-one relationship between types of continuing bonds and bereavement outcomes (Ho & Chan, 2018). The nature of these bonds encompasses a wide variety of behaviors. Loss is not the sole defining factor in each hero's life, just as it is not the sole defining factor in a real-life person who is bereaved.

Even though superheroes are fictional, the lessons they teach us are real and can be used as vehicles of meaning for both the bereaved and those who support them. The real appeal of superheroes dealing with loss is to serve as a reminder that though all our favorite heroes are super, they're also human. What we really admire is not the superpowers but the hero, the one who overcomes their doubts and adversities and then acts to make the world a better place, and in doing so finds a way for the person that they love to accompany them on that journey.

## References


Arad, A., Feige, K. (Producers), & Favreau, J (Director). (2008). *Iron man* [Motion picture]. USA: Marvel Studios.

Bonanno G. A., Wortman C. B., & Nesse, R. M. (2004). Prospective patterns of resilience and maladjustment during widowhood. *Psychology and Aging*, 19(2), 260–271.

Datson, S., & Marwit, S. (1997). Personality constructs and perceived presence of deceased loved ones. *Death Studies*, 21(2), 131–146.

Feige, K. (Producer), & Favreau, J. (Director). (2010). *Iron man 2* [Motion picture]. USA: Marvel Studios.

Feige, K. (Producer), Russo, A., & Russo, J. (Directors). (2016). *Captain America: Civil war* [Motion picture]. USA: Marvel Studios.

Feige, K. (Producer), Russo, A., & Russo, J. (Directors). (2019). *Avengers: Endgame* [Motion picture]. USA: Marvel Studios.

Field, N., Gal-Oz, E., Bonanno, G. (2003). Continuing bonds and adjustment at 5 years after the death of a spouse. *Journal of Consulting and Clinical Psychology*, 71(1), 110–117.

Field, N.P., (2006). Unresolved grief and continuing bonds: An attachment perspective. *Death Studies*, 30(8), 739–756.

Foa, E. B., Riggs, D. S., Massie, E. D., & Yarczowers, M. (1995). The impact of fear activation and anger on the efficacy of exposure treatment for posttraumatic stress disorder. *Behavior Therapy*, 26(3), 487–499.

Forbes, D., Haslam, N., Williams, B. J., & Creamer, M. (2005). Testing the latent structure of posttraumatic stress disorder: A taxometric study of combat veterans. *Journal of Traumatic Stress*, 18, 647–656.

Freud, S. (1957). Mourning and melancholia. In J. Strachey (ed. & trans.), *The standard edition of the complete psychological works of Sigmund Freud* (Vol. 14, 152–170). London: Hogarth Press. (Original work published 1917)

Freud, S. (1961). The Ego and the Id. In J. Strachey (ed. & trans.), *The standard edition of the complete psychological works of Sigmund Freud* (Vol. 19, 31) London: Hogarth Press. (Original work published 1923)

Ho, S. M. Y., & Chan, I. S. F. (2018). Externalised and internalised continuing bonds in understanding grief. In D. Klass & E. M. Steffen (Eds.), *Continuing bonds in bereavement: New directions for research and practice* (pp. 129–138). New York: Routledge.

Klass, D. (2006). Continuing conversation about continuing bonds. *Death Studies*, 30(9), 843–858.

Klass, D., Silverman, P. R., & Nickman, S. L. (Eds.), (1996). *Continuing bonds: New understandings of grief.* New York: Taylor and Francis.

Kuhn, T. S. (1962/2012). *The structure of scientific revolutions: 50th Anniversary Edition* (4th ed.). Chicago: University of Chicago Press.

Lindemann, E. (1944). Symptomatology and management of acute grief. *American Journal of Psychiatry*, 101(3), 141–149.

Roven, C., Thomas, E., Franco, L. (Producers), & Nolan, C. (Director). (2005). *Batman begins* [Motion picture]. United States: Warner Bros. Pictures.

Sragow, M. (2010, April 30). Justin Theroux puts a shine on our favorite shellhead in “Iron Man2”. *The Baltimore Sun.* Retrieved from https://www.baltimoresun.com/entertainment/bs-xpm-2010-04-30-bs-ae-film-summer-preview-20100429-story.html.

Tan, L. A. G. (2019, May 7). Closure after “Endgame”: Proof that Tony Stark has a heart. *The Harvard Crimson.* Retrieved from https://www.thecrimson.com/article/2019/5/7/avengers-endgame-commentary.

Walter, T. (1994). *The revival of death.* London: Routledge.

# 6 Understanding Grieving Styles

## Batman on the Couch

*Kenneth J. Doka and Terry L. Martin*

In writing this chapter, we break two cardinal rules of psychological counseling. The first is to never analyze a client that one has neither treated nor met. Second, do not treat fictional characters. Yet, as we examine the assignment of the editors – to illustrate a concept of grief therapy by applying it to a superhero, it is difficult not to focus on Batman as an interesting illustration of the concept we developed on grieving styles (see Martin & Doka, 1999; Doka & Martin, 2010).

Batman is an exceptional superhero in a number of significant ways. First, Batman is a superhero without superpowers. Unlike Superman, he cannot fly and does not possess super-senses such as hearing. Batman is not faster than a speeding bullet. In fact, bullets only bounce off him because of his protective suit. He is not invested with some of the powers of a spider, nor can he live underwater and command sea creatures. And while Batman has developed his cognitive and physical abilities and has created significant assistive technologies, he is fully human – born and bred in a normal, though, highly wealthy and philanthropic, family.

Second, Batman's origin story – both in the original DC cartoon books as well as in Christopher Nolan's *The Dark Knight Trilogy* (2005, 2008, 2012), allows for more extensive character development. We see the seminal influences on his life – especially his father and later butler–guardian, Alfred. We witness his first terrifying encounter with bats as a young boy and understand its symbolic connection to the loss of his parents.

In addition, Batman is far more aware of the moral ambivalence that surrounds his role in Gotham City, his home. He vigorously fights for the law – yet outside the law. There is ambivalence about his role both within the police and city government – even his more colorful criminal nemeses taunt him that he is not that different from them.

Finally, and most important, Batman's origin begins in loss. Asking his parents as a child to leave the theater early for some air, he and his family are confronted by a desperate criminal who, in panic, kills his parents in front of the now-traumatized boy (Roven, Thomas, Franco, & Nolan, 2005). This seminal trauma of parental loss drives his new persona and mission. Batman will now reform the corrupted city of Gotham – confronting the lawless. He, in effect, becomes a model of male grief. But the question for this chapter is: What pattern, or grieving style, does Batman exemplify?

## 6.1 Understanding Grieving Styles

The concept of grieving styles originally began as a paper, "Take It Like a Man", presented to ADEC (The Association for Death Education and Counseling) in 1994. In that paper, we proposed that there was a male grieving pattern, or style, that indicated males responded less in emotional ways and more in cognitive and behavioral ways. We also affirmed that despite the affective bias of contemporary Western counseling, this pattern was no less effective than the more emotive style (Doka & Martin, 1994).

While the paper was well accepted, our ideas continued to evolve. As many women began to identify with the pattern, we started to realize that gender was only one factor that affected grieving patterns. We acknowledged that while gender norms and socialization play an important role in grieving styles, other factors, such as culture, temperament, and developmental experiences, influenced what grieving pattern an individual adopted. We affirmed that gender was a significant though not determinative variable in an individual's grieving style (see Martin & Doka, 1999; Doka & Martin 2010). In these works, we recognized that grieving styles existed along a continuum and also identified four points on that continuum. Underlying our theory was the concept of *emotion regulation* (Gross & Munoz, 1995). Briefly stated, this concept asserts that in each individual, the psychic energy generated by grief will be diverted to different domains such as affective, cognitive, or behavioral.

### *6.1.1 Intuitive Grievers*

The intuitive style is the one generally associated with grief. That is hardly surprising because much of the original research on grief was conducted with widows. In the intuitive style, individuals often describe their experience of grief as one of waves of emotion – sadness, anger, loneliness, yearning, guilt, and relief, to name but a few. The expression of grief reflects those inner emotions. Intuitive grievers report such reactions as crying, shouting, and withdrawing. In short, they emotionally act out grief. An example of this can be seen in the film *Batman v Superman: Dawn of Justice* (Roven, Snyder, & Snyder, 2016), when Martha Kent and Lois Lane share tearful and tender moments during the funeral held in Kansas for Clark Kent, who, as Superman, was just killed in a battle with Doomsday.

Because their primary reaction is emotional, it is unsurprising that adaptation involves processing these emotions. Adaptive strategies work well that allow the ventilation of emotions and feelings. Thus, most traditional approaches to dealing with loss can be effective with intuitive grievers such as individual therapy and traditional support group modalities. Intuitive grievers who do not need formal support often find it helpful to share and explore their emotions with others – family, friends, or clergy.

### *6.1.2 Instrumental Grievers*

Instrumental grievers populate the other end of the continuum. Here their grief is experienced in more cognitive and behavioral ways. They will think about the person, ruminate about the loss. Emotion is a secondary response here. While intuitive grievers emote in vivid colors, instrumental grievers experience such feelings as pastels.

This will be evident in their expression of grief – again, more likely to be behavioral or cognitive. They will often reminisce or review decisions and events around the loss. They will often grieve through doing. For example, one man found it therapeutic to sculpt the perfect memorial stone for his still-born child. In the film *Justice League* (Roven, Snyder, Berg, Johns, & Snyder, 2017), we see Wonder Woman as an instrumental griever as she makes it her mission to find and pull together members of the league in a way to honor and carry on the legacy of Superman.

Instrumental grievers may need validation that their way of grieving is appropriate – assurance that the absence of tears or profound and open emotional reactions is neither a character flaw nor symbolizes a lack of connection and affection. Cognitive and active therapies will often work with instrumental grievers, as will psychoeducational approaches. Ritual, too, can offer a powerful mechanism for instrumental grievers to "do" their grief. With male instrumental grievers, counselors can also use approaches compatible with the male role such as storytelling. Counselors and therapists also need to recognize that instrumental grievers may use humor as a way to cope with emotions and also may find it helpful to "dose" their emotions – moving into and out of emotional expression, especially when the emotions seem too intense.

While traditional support groups may not meet the needs of instrumental grievers, other modalities may work well. For example, cognitive approaches such as discussion and reading groups as well as educational programs like How to Handle the Holidays, can appeal to instrumental grievers. Also, problem-solving groups such as living alone or raising children as a single parent also can attract.

### *6.1.3 Blended Grievers*

Blended grievers are in the middle of the continuum. As such, blended grievers share experiences, expressions, and adaptation strategies of both intuitive and instrumental grievers. We see this in the character Alfred throughout *The Dark Knight Trilogy*. Alfred carries on with the practical tasks of taking care of the Waynes' estate and orphan child Bruce, while also sharing in affective expressions of grief throughout the film series narrative journey. Examples of this can be observed during the after-funeral scene in *Batman Begins* (Roven et al.,

2005), when young Bruce cries and tells Alfred how much he misses his parents, and Alfred shares that he misses them as well. Later, in *The Dark Knight Rises* (Thomas, Nolan, Roven, & Nolan, 2012), Alfred makes an impassioned plea with adult Bruce about the consequences of his hatred and with heartfelt sorrow leaves Bruce, as he shares that he cannot standby and bury another member of the Wayne family.

Blended grievers will often have varied experiences and use strategies depending on the relationship to the deceased, the situation experienced, and the time since the loss. They may be open to a range of different therapeutic modalities.

An argument may be raised as to whether a goal of therapy should be to facilitate movement to the center of the continuum – to encourage a more blended style. Our answer would not encourage such moves. We would hold that each style has its own advantages and disadvantages. Therapy should help an individual utilize the strengths and weaknesses in their approach. Crisis, after all, is a poor time to teach new skills.

### *6.1.4 Dissonant Grievers*

Dissonant grievers exist outside of the continuum. Here there is a discontinuity between the way an individual experiences grief and the way that person expresses grief. For example, someone might experience grief at a highly affective level, yet he or she, for one reason or another, represses those emotions.

## 6.2 Case Study

### *6.2.1 Batman as a Dissonant Griever*

As portrayed in films of *The Dark Night Trilogy,* Bruce Wayne, also known as Batman, clearly is a dissonant griever. He has a very strong and continued emotional responses to his parents' deaths. He has strong emotions – though rarely expressed. He exhibits a strong sense of guilt – feeling perceived responsibility for his parents' murders. In his mind, it was his desire to leave the theater that caused the confrontation with the desperate thief, which resulted in his parents' violent deaths. His major way of handling that guilt is an intense rage not only at the outlaw who accosted his family but also at the entire criminal element in Gotham.

Yet rather than deal with these emotions, Bruce chooses to act out his guilt in rage through the persona of Batman. His anger compels him to act as a vigilante outside the law. One can even see both delight and a streak of vindictive revenge as Batman confronts criminals. Even his allies within Gotham's police and administration struggle, as he does, with moral ambivalence at Batman's vigilante crusade. In fact, Bruce has begun to realize that the way he is coping with his loss – his violent Batman alter ego – has inhibited his ability to sustain romantic relationships and affected his relationship with a major source of support – his former guardian and family butler, Alfred.

### 6.2.2 Batman in Therapy

When Bruce Wayne began therapy, the presenting issue was Bruce's desire to improve his relationships with women. Bruce sought intimacy, but the nature of his extracurricular alter ego of Batman required a level of secrecy that inhibited any close relationships. Wayne described the assumption of his alter ego, Batman, as a legacy to his deceased parents as well as his way both to avenge their loss and cope with his grief.

As Bruce and his therapist began to address grieving styles, Bruce initially identified as an instrumental griever. Keeping the city safe was, he rationalized, his way of creating a legacy to his parents – an active way to cope with his loss, highly compatible with the instrumental pattern. The therapist gently challenged Bruce's perception of his style. It was clear to the therapist that underlying Bruce's inner experience of grief were deep emotions – especially guilt that his desire to leave the theatre resulted in his parents' sudden deaths. Instrumental grievers do not experience grief with such vivid emotions.

The strongest emotions that Bruce was experiencing were both anger and guilt. He deeply regretted leaving the theatre early – feeling that if he and his parents had left after the performance ended, the streets would not have been empty, and his family would not have been accosted. Bruce's therapist began to explore that guilt with Bruce – reminding him that he was a child at the time to take on such a burden.

As they began the exploration, they began to discuss Bruce's developmental experiences. Bruce recounted that he had a close relationship with his father, one built on his deep respect for his father. His father would always remind Bruce that the Waynes had been given much, and therefore much was expected of them. The Waynes should be tough and strong; excessive emotional displays were discouraged. Bruce recounted that once when he was frightened by bats emerging from a cave, his father took him to the cave to face his fears.

This proved a turning point in therapy. Bruce realized that his assumption of his Batman role was an attempt to reassure his father that he had confronted his fears – both of bats and the criminals that had shattered their lives. He then began to see the ways that his guilt converted into an anger that put him at continued risk, challenged the law, and sometimes led to acts of violence that were both destructive of property and even led to the deaths of those Bruce defined as criminals. In expressing these emotions in the supportive environment that the therapist had created, Bruce realized he no longer needed his father's approval of his assumed hyper-masculine role.

In the course of the intervention, two therapeutic rituals had great significance to Bruce, as they allowed him to act on his emotions in a more socially acceptable way. First, there was a ritual of reconciliation, where Bruce left flowers at the spot where his parents were killed, apologizing to them for placing them – however inadvertently – in danger. Second, as therapy moved toward termination, Bruce conducted a ritual of transition, viewed by Alfred and the therapist – burying Batman with all due honors.[1]

## 6.3 Conclusions

Since therapy terminated, Bruce Wayne continues to do well. He is active in both Wayne Enterprises as well as the Wayne Foundation. In fact, the Wayne Foundation has begun two new, important national initiatives. The first is that they have begun a significant effort to assist young orphans. Second, the Wayne Foundation is funding research, support groups, grief camps, and other initiatives designed to support children coping with parental bereavement – a special emphasis is on those whose parents died through violence. In therapy, Wayne decided these programs would be a far better legacy to his parents and a more helpful resolution to his own emotional struggles.

Since therapy, Bruce's relationship with Alfred has improved. Moreover, working through his guilt and rage and acknowledging his underlying intuitive style has generally improved his ability to relate to others. Once a loner, he now has many friends. And, perhaps most important, he is now engaged.

There is one more major change in Bruce's life. Bruce Wayne has moved from Gotham City – relocating both Wayne Industries and the Wayne Foundation. Gotham's crime rate has continued to rise. Metropolis seems much safer.

## Note

1 Such rituals are fully described in Martin and Doka (1999) and Doka and Martin (2010), along with rituals of affirmation and continuity.

## References

Doka, K., & Martin, T. (1994). *Men don't cry: Rethinking males and grief. Annual Meeting of ADEC*, April, Portland, OR.

Doka, K., & Martin, T. (2010). *Grieving beyond gender: Understanding the ways men and women mourn*. New York: Routledge.

Gross, J., & Munoz, R. (1995). Emotional regulation and mental health. *Clinical Psychology: Science and Practice*, 2, 151–164.

Martin, T., & Doka, K. (1999). *Men don't cry, women do: Transcending gender stereotypes of grief*. New York: Taylor & Francis.

Roven, C., Snyder, D., Berg, J., & Johns, G. (Producers), & Snyder, Z. (Director), (2017). *Justice league*. USA: Warner Bros. Pictures

Roven, C., & Snyder, D. (Producers), & Snyder, Z. (Director). (2016). *Batman v superman: Dawn of justice*. USA: Warner Bros. Pictures

Roven, C., Thomas, E., & Franco, L. (Producers), & Nolan, C. (Director). (2005). *Batman begins* [Motion picture]. United States: Warner Bros. Pictures.

Thomas, E., Nolan, C., & Roven, C. (Producers), & Nolan, C. (Director), (2012). *The dark knight rises*. USA: Warner Bros. Pictures.

# 7 Bruce Wayne, Batman, and Attachment-Informed Grief Work

*Phyllis Kosminsky*

In *Song of Myself,* Walt Whitman writes: "Very well then, I contradict myself; I am large, I contain multitudes" (Whitman, 2005, p. 123). None of us is just one thing; we all contain multitudes. We are weak and strong, generous and withholding, kind and cruel. Perhaps this is why Batman (aka Bruce Wayne) is among the most well researched and most widely considered superheroes: he's just like us, except for being a billionaire, crime-fighting vigilante who wears a bat costume. When we first meet him in *Batman Begins* (Roven, Thomas, Franco, & Nolan, 2005), Bruce is an innocent and relatively carefree child. We see him run from a playmate and accidentally fall into a deep hole, where he is swarmed by bats – a nightmarish experience from which his father tenderly rescues him. This nightmare pales in comparison to the fateful night when Bruce's parents are murdered in front of him during a botched robbery outside a theatre in Gotham. Bruce vows to avenge his parents' deaths, and this vow inspires his transformation from a child to a man to Batman. Of course, it is not, in fact, a transformation but an assumed identity. Underneath his batlike attire, Bruce is still the same person and, in many ways, the same child that he has always been.

## 7.1 Attachment-Informed Grief Work

How does Bruce's early trauma factor into his expectations about life, people, and relationships? How does it affect his ability to trust, to be vulnerable? All of these are elements of what we can broadly refer to as attachment orientation (Bowlby, 1982). Attachment, and more specifically, the security or insecurity of a person's orientation to attachment, has been identified as a significant factor in mental and physical health and emotional functioning. And in hundreds of studies of adult grief and its variations, attachment security has been identified as a significant factor in how people cope with loss (Kosminsky & Jordan, 2016).

One of the things we learn from working with bereaved people is that just as every relationship is different, so is every loss. Simply put: to understand the way that someone is responding to a loss, we have to understand what it is that they have lost.

## 7.2 What Did Young Bruce Lose?

A recurring theme and central life lesson for young Bruce is that *adversity is what teaches us how to survive*. After rescuing his son from the bat-filled well, Dr. Wayne carries him into the house and poses a question that serves to reframe his son's experience. "Why do we fall?" he asks, and then answers with: "So that we can learn to pick ourselves up" (Roven et al., 2005, 0:10:41). Putting him to bed, Thomas Wayne asks Bruce if he knows why the bats attacked him. Still tearful, Bruce shakes his head, and Thomas tells him: "You know why they attacked you, don't you? They were afraid of you. All creatures feel fear". "Even the scary ones?" Bruce asks. "Especially the scary ones!" his father reassures him, and at last, we see a small smile come to Bruce's face (Roven et al., 2005, 0:11:06).

However, some adverse events are more than a person, especially a child, can survive unscathed. Young Bruce and his parents are out for the evening and have just exited the Gotham City theater when they are confronted by an armed robber who shoots first Bruce's father, and then his mother. As Thomas Wayne dies in his son's arms, Bruce is struck by a crushing wave of terror, guilt, and grief. These feelings will follow him into adulthood, and the strategies he employs to avoid them will restrict his emotional growth, limit his ability to form meaningful relationships, and deprive him of the chance to regain the sense of belonging and safety that was taken from him in childhood.

After a period of retreat, during which he learns the skills that will become essential to his crime-fighting campaign, Bruce Wayne returns to Gotham. In *The Dark Knight* (Thomas, Nolan, Roven, & Nolan, 2008), Bruce Wayne has fully assumed his dual identity: he is the man and the Batman. Both of these identities are masked: Bruce Wayne, the playboy, is a character as different as Bruce can construct from the lonely, isolated man inside; he is also an effective cover for Bruce's crime-fighting alter ego. There is some overlap between Bruce and Batman: both of these characters live without the comfort of human connection. And that's how it has to be, because intimacy equals vulnerability, something that neither Bruce nor Batman can afford. As he tells us in *Batman Begins*, "I don't have the luxury of friends" (Roven et al., 2005, 1:38:38). Later, when Bruce arrives at his home to find a roomful of people celebrating his birthday, he angrily instructs Alfred, "You need to send these people away right now!" (Roven et al., 2005, 1:40:15). He does not want people around, and the greater their proximity, the greater his determination to get away from them.

## 7.3 Understanding the Impact of Early Parental Loss on Attachment Orientation

These and other comments made by Bruce, both in and out of his Batman attire, suggest an avoidant orientation to attachment, a departure from the secure attachment to his caregivers that he enjoyed as a child. In light of what has been reported by researchers and clinicians on the impact of early traumatic loss, this is not surprising. “Some people adapt to loss . . . by withdrawing from others, attempting to use avoidance to reduce the pain and fear of further loss” (Mancini, Robinaugh, Shear, & Bonanno, 2009).

It is impossible to say what the trajectory of Bruce’s attachment development might would have taken been had he not suffered the sudden loss of his parents. The answer to the question of “what has been lost”, in reference to Bruce Wayne, is simple: all has been lost. Bruce Wayne’s adaptation to the ache of lost security is to suppress and deny his need for others. He has become the very personification of someone who avoids attachment.

Avoidance with respect to attachment has been described as having two underlying factors: one has to do with the individual’s view of other people, and the other with their assessment of the risk associated with forming attachments. “Fearful avoidant attachment” describes someone who avoids forming relationships because, having been hurt in the past, they are afraid of being hurt again. “Dismissive avoidant attachment” refers to a tendency to undervalue other people and to minimize the potential benefit of forming interpersonal relationships (Hazan & Shaver, 1987). From his comments about friendship and his rejection of other people, it would appear that Bruce Wayne is dismissive, but over the course of *Batman Begins* (Roven et al., 2005) and in *The Dark Knight* (Thomas et al., 2008), it becomes clear that there is more to his avoidance than his belief in the general pointlessness of relationships with others. His independence is both a defense from his feelings of need and a form of camouflage. In his Batman suit, Bruce Wayne is physically disguised; in his refusal to allow any penetration of his emotional shell, he maintains an effective disguise of his interior life and the longing for family that has never left him.

## 7.4 The *Lego Batman* Movie (2017): Remolding the Archetypal Hero

As outside observers with access to his internal world, we are privy to a truth about Batman/Bruce Wayne that the people closest to him suspect, and sometimes try to assert: that despite his insistence on isolation and independence, there is a part of him that has not been able to excise his longing for connection. The canon of Batman films is filled with evidence of Batman’s struggle to reconcile his desire for intimacy with his fearful need to avoid it. We see evidence of this struggle in scenes with Alfred, in poignant interactions with various love interests, even in moments of solitary reflection when memories of his earlier life remind him of what he had and lost.

However, in what is perhaps a fitting medium for the message, the nature of Batman’s emotional complexity is communicated most directly in the 2017 film *The Lego Batman Movie* (Lin, Lord, Miller, Lee, & McKay, 2017). Part parody, part homage, with its cartoon depiction of the Dark Knight, *The Lego*

*Batman Movie* offers us a transparently literal portrayal of Batman's struggles with intimacy and their roots in his early trauma. When your actors are made out of plastic, subtlety is not really the point. With limited ability to communicate subtext, characters proclaim their self-discoveries and emotional breakthroughs with bullet point simplicity.

Here is Batman at the beginning of the film. Alfred has walked into the room and surprised his young master, who has been looking at a family portrait: (cue sad music in the background)

BRUCE: (inner dialogue) Hey mom, hey dad. I saved the city again today. I wish you could have seen me. I think you would have been really proud.
ALFRED: Were you looking at the old family pictures again?
B: Oh yeah, those, no, I wasn't. (Lin et al., 2017, 0:18:56)

Later, in an amusing twist on storylines involving the frustrated attempts of the women in Bruce's life to get him to commit, Batman responds dismissively to the Joker's claim that he is Batman's "greatest enemy".

B: You think you're my greatest enemy?
J: Yes, you're obsessed with me!
B: No, I'm not!
J: Are you saying that there is nothing, nothing special about our relationship?
B: Whoa. Let me tell you something, Jaybird. Batman doesn't do "ships".
J: What?
B: As in "relation*ships*". There is no *us*. Batman and Joker are not *a thing*. I don't need you. I don't need anyone. You mean nothing to me. No one does. (Lin et al., 2017, 0:11:33)

The Joker is so enraged by Batman's dismissal that he embarks upon what he intends to be the final, epic destruction of Gotham and everyone in it. To get Batman out of the way, the Joker manages to send him to the Phantom Zone, the domain to which the most dangerous criminals in the Lego multiverse are conveyed. Faced with Phyllis, the gatekeeper of the Phantom Zone, Batman insists that he is in fact not a villain but a hero. Unconvinced, Phyllis shows Batman a montage of scenes in which his self-absorption has hurt those around him, including Alfred, Robin, and Mayor Barbara.

Throughout his history, Batman has been portrayed as a "dark" hero – tortured by his past and unrelenting in his pursuit of vengeance. But in the Phantom Zone, he is forced to see that it is not only the bad guys who have been hurt by his solitary campaign against evil. In refusing the help of others and pushing away anyone who has sought to know him, Batman has left a trail of wounded would-be friends, family, and partners. Chastened, Batman pleads with Phyllis to allow him to return to Gotham so that he can help his friends defeat the Joker.

## 7.5 Traumatic Loss: Intrusive Memories, Avoidance, and the Fear Response

Understandably, many traumatic loss survivors are determined to suppress memories of the trauma in the hope that this will enable them to put it behind them. However, the nature of traumatic memory is that rather than gradually being absorbed into an individual's personal narrative, it remains in the fore-front, a vivid and intrusive presence. The continuing intrusion of traumatic memories triggers flashbacks and sustains a heightened sense of fear. This results in intensified efforts at avoidance, including avoidance of people and places that the individual experiences as potential triggers (Mancini et al., 2009).

This is clear in the case of Bruce Wayne, who has taken what must be regarded as an extreme course of action to avoid thinking about the murders of his parents. His single-minded dedication to fighting all crime has given his life a focus and has arguably allowed him to find meaning in his loss (Neimeyer, 2001). But it has also cast him into a bottomless pit of isola-tion. He denies any need for others, dismisses any expression of concern, any offer of friendship or help. He has withdrawn from any meaningful human contact and from all appearances personifies dismissive, avoidant attachment. Knowing what we do about his past, however, we (along with Alfred) are in a position to recognize that Bruce/Batman's avoidance is fear-based: he has been wounded to the core, and he is protecting himself against ever being hurt again. Rather than risk the pain of loss, he will not love or allow himself to be loved.

## 7.6 Clinical Considerations

In Bruce Wayne's story, we see the cost that unresolved trauma has imposed, and this theme could be amplified in work with survivors of traumatic loss. An introduction to this theme could include a dialogue in which the client and clinician use the film or film series as a therapeutic tool to explore Bruce/ Batman's avoidance. For example:

- Bruce is very self-reliant – he doesn't depend on anyone else to help him in his fight against crime. Can you think of another character from a movie or video game who operates this way?
- What is the "face" that Bruce projects to the world? How would you describe the difference between this "face" and what he feels inside?
- If you were Bruce's friend and knew what he had been through, what would you say to him? What if he said he was fine and didn't want to talk?

In addition to individual grief counseling, clients can benefit from participation in a support group. Perhaps if he could become less fearfully avoidant in relating to others, Bruce/Batman might be open to talking with other survivors of violent loss, an experience that would further open him to his own feelings and those of others. The interventions suggested could clear the way for posttraumatic growth and allow Bruce to connect with his feelings, develop meaningful relationships, and sustain a bond with his parents grounded not just in fear but in love.

## 7.7 Posttraumatic Growth

We do not seek out traumatic experience, but sometimes events that threaten to destroy us lead, over time, to a heightened sense of strength and capacity for survival. These events can also provide transformative lessons about what truly matters in life (Tedeschi & Calhoun, 2004).

Upon his return to Gotham, Batman is met by a disgruntled Commissioner Barbara. She walks away from him, saying, "I don't know why you even bothered to come back".

BATMAN: I came back because I was afraid.

BARBARA: What?

BATMAN: The reason I came back was the same reason I left you. I was afraid of feeling the pain you feel when you lose someone close to you. Gotham needs us. So I came back. So what do you say? Will you work with me? I need your help. (Lin et al., 2017, 1:22:36)

The battle with the Joker is still to come, but in this scene, we know that Batman has achieved a more personal victory, finally freeing himself from the force field of his early trauma. Near the end of the movie, Batman tells Robin:

> Sometimes losing people is part of life. But that doesn't mean you stop letting them in. Some very wise people taught me that. This is my family. But it's your family, too.
>
> (Lin et al., 2017, 1:32:31)

Not a man of steel, this superhero. But in this case, being made of plastic turns out to be just what our man needs to become his most human self.

## References

Bowlby, J. (1982). *Attachment* (2nd ed.). New York: Basic Books.

Hazan, C., & Shaver, P.R. (1987). Romantic love conceptualized as an attachment process. *Journal of Personality and Social Psychology*, 52(3), 511–524.

Kosminsky, P. S., & Jordan, J.R. (2016). *Attachment informed grief therapy: The clinician's guide to foundations and applications*. New York: Routledge.

Lin, D., Lord, P., Miller, C., & Lee, R. (Producers), & McKay, C. (Director) (2017). *The Lego Batman movie* [Motion picture]. USA: Warner Bros. Pictures.

Mancini, A.D., Robinaugh, D., Shear, K., & Bonanno, G.A. (2009). Does attachment avoidance help people cope with loss? *Journal of Clinical Psychology* 65(10), 1127–1136.

Neimeyer, R.A. (2001). *Meaning reconstruction & the experience of loss*. Washington, DC: American Psychological Association.

Roven, C., Thomas, E., & Franco, L. (Producers), & Nolan, C. (Director). (2005). *Batman begins* [Motion picture]. United States: Warner Bros. Pictures.

Tedeschi, R.G., & Calhoun, L.G. (2004). Post traumatic growth: Conceptual foundations and empirical evidence. *Psychological Inquiry* 15(1), 1–18.

Thomas, E., Nolan, C., Roven, C. (Producers), & Nolan, C. (Director). (2008). *The dark knight* [Motion picture]. United States: Warner Bros. Pictures.

Whitman, W. (2005). "Song of myself". In: *Leaves of grass* (150th ed.). New York: Penguin Classics.

# Part III

# Types of Grief: Brief Case Studies of Superheroes

# 8 Deadpool and Anticipatory Grief

*Cheryl Hogsten Dodson*

The concept of anticipatory grief was originally identified by Lindeman (1944) and appeared in the literature as one of the products from an investigative inquiry into the symptoms and management of acute grief. According to Rando (2000), the literature surrounding anticipatory grief is incongruent, the concept has been the subject of considerable debate, and its conceptualization has been through many evolutions since its introduction in 1944. More current literature, like Townsend and Morgan (2017), describes anticipatory grief as experiential grief that is the result of an expected or pending loss of something highly valued. The valued entity can be tangible or intangible, and the loss can be real or perceived (Townsend & Morgan, 2017). Despite the numerous entities that can be lost and subsequently grieved, anticipatory grief is often discussed in the context of life-limiting illness, such as terminal cancer, amyotrophic lateral sclerosis (ALS), or Alzheimer's disease. Anticipatory grief associated with death or disease can be experienced by those facing their own mortality as well as individuals awaiting the expected loss of a loved one (Moon, 2016).

Simon (2008) outlined the symptomology of anticipatory grief, noting that individuals may experience several physical symptoms like disturbances in sleep and appetite, headaches, nausea, and decreased energy levels. These individuals may also find themselves overcome by a vast array of emotions like disbelief, worry, anxiety, fear, sorrow, anger, guilt, powerlessness, and hopelessness. Anticipatory grief may also lead to cognitive concerns and alterations, spiritual trepidations or strengthening, emotional detachment, and social isolation (Simon, 2008).

## 8.1 Case Study: Deadpool

As seen in the film *Deadpool* (Kinberg, Reynolds, Donner, & Miller, 2016), anticipatory grief can affect anyone, even a former Special Forces operator turned mercenary then antihero, namely Wade Wilson, better known as Deadpool. Wade met the girl of his dreams, Vanessa. They fell in love and prepared to settle down. Life was perfect until Wade was diagnosed with terminal cancer. His once bright and exciting future was suddenly transformed into a bleak and hopeless one.

Anticipatory grief began almost instantly for Wade at the time of his diagnosis. He started to grieve the imminent loss of his life and the consequent loss of his future, specifically his future with Vanessa. In the hospital scene right after diagnosis, Wade said, "I'm memorizing the details of her face. Like it's the first time I'm seeing it. Or the last" (Kinberg et al., 2016, 27:38). Additionally, Wade quickly exhibited physical symptoms of anticipatory grief. He was seen in his and Vanessa's apartment, sleepless in the middle of the night, staring out of the window, burdened with sadness and despair. Wade also knew his death would subject Vanessa to the pain of loss. As Wade's narration alludes, he knew that the only way he could save Vanessa's life was by saving his own, because "the worst part about cancer isn't what it does to you, but what it does to the people you love" (Kinberg et al., 2016, 36:02). However, the mere impossibility of saving himself left Wade visibly hopeless and riddled with guilt.

As sometimes seen in anticipatory grief, Wade withdrew himself from Vanessa so that he might spare her the pain and burden of his illness, allowing her to remember him the way he was and not the way he was soon to become (Kinberg et al., 2016). Struggling to accept his fate and desperate for an alternate ending to his story, Wade accepted an offer from a mysterious man who claimed he could cure the cancer. There was just one small catch to this cure; it also came with superhero abilities. Most would argue that the acquisition of superhero capabilities is not such a bad deal, especially in light of being freed from the grip of a terminal illness. However, Wade's gamble for a cure was much more than he bargained for (Kinberg et al., 2016).

Although Wade was cured of cancer, the unexpected consequences of his cure increased his real and perceived losses, which continued to overshadow his gains. The torturous treatments that gave rise to his cure and new superhero powers left Wade severely disfigured. As his friend Weasel put it, "Your face is the stuff of nightmares" (Kinberg et al., 2016, 59:18). Being cancer free wasn't enough to save Wade; his self-concept was now destroyed – a powerful intangible loss that many nonfictional patients who are disfigured experience. Wade believed he was so grotesque that Vanessa would never be able to look at him, let alone love him. His grief intensified, as did his social isolation and withdrawal from others. Energized and fueled by anger, Deadpool was born and so was his mission to destroy Ajax – the man who ruined his life (Kinberg et al., 2016). For Wade, his anticipatory grief culminated with killing Ajax and realizing that, even after Vanessa saw his face, her love for him was unwavering and unconditional.

## 8.2 Conclusions

Unlike the grief that takes place after a death, anticipatory grief can be preparatory in nature, imparting a sense of control and allowing the dying individual – or the loved ones of a dying person – to prepare for death (Kübler-Ross, 1969; Zilberfein, 1999). This can be anything from reconciliation with others to designation of subsequent ownership of treasured items to even planning a memorial or funeral. In *Deadpool* (Kinberg et al., 2016), Wade began preparing for his death by taking an inventory of his most prized possessions, detailing their relative value to Vanessa. Also, perhaps with a preparatory purpose, Wade promised to find Vanessa in the next life and planned to play the Wham song *Careless Whisper* (Michael & Ridgeley, 1984, track 8) outside her window when he did – so she'd know it was him (Kinberg et al., 2016).

Although there is general agreement that anticipatory grief can have a protective value that facilitates healthy postloss grieving, there are those who argue the opposite, noting that anticipatory grief can trigger premature detachment, robbing the dying individual and their loved ones of any possibilities that remain for their relationship prior to the actual death (Rando, 2000; Townsend & Morgan, 2017). This premature detachment is illustrated clearly in *Deadpool* as Wade prepares to leave. He tells Vanessa, "… cancer is a shit-show… and under no circumstances will I take you to that show" (Kinberg, et al., 2016, 30:57).

Unlike real life, Wade's terminal cancer didn't end in death. The miracle of being cured from an incurable cancer and becoming a superhero is a departure from the reality of most people in similar circumstances. The majority of people with a diagnosis of terminal cancer will not only die as a result but will also likely experience various manifestations of anticipatory grief. Their symptoms will be highly individualized and depend heavily on the grieving person's past life experiences and coping mechanisms. Despite the defined symptomology of anticipatory grief, there are no set rules to its manifestation or expression. "Each loss is different in its own way" and so is the grief experienced before and after the loss (Doka, 2016, p. 23).

Individuals should be encouraged to embrace the unique nature of their pending loss and subsequent grief. Regardless of how anticipatory grief is manifested, it is not the responsibly of caregivers and clinicians to tell people how they should respond to loss. As long as an individual is not at risk for self-harm or harming others, caregivers and clinicians' main focus should be a supportive one ensuring autonomy of the grieving individual.

It is essential for caregivers and clinicians to be nonjudgmental and accepting of both the grieving individual and the individual's grief. Such an attitude facilitates the development of trust between the grieving person and the caregiver or clinician. This mutual trust is fundamental to a supportive and therapeutic relationship (Townsend & Morgan, 2017).

Whether formal or informal, support for grieving individuals is critical. Support can range from psychotherapy to peer support to even empathetic family and friends. It can be provided individually or in groups. Disease-specific support may also be helpful for those with a terminal or life-limiting illness. The provision and type of support should be tailored to the grieving individual.

Education should be provided to normalize and validate the feelings and experiences of individuals experiencing anticipatory grief. In the case of those facing the death of a loved one or the loss of their own life, education about dying and death may also be necessary. Educating individuals about loss, grief, dying, and death not only normalizes and validates their feelings, but can also reduce anxieties, fears, and feelings of guilt.

Bottom line, caregivers and clinicians must be accepting, creative, and thoughtful when caring for and supporting individuals faced with loss, especially losses associated with dying and death. Remember, individuals' responses to loss are as unique as their fingerprints. Individuals experiencing anticipatory grief need support and must be allowed to grieve on their own terms, so long as safety is not a concern.

## References

Doka, K.J. (2016). *Grief is a journey*. New York, NY: Atria Paperback.

Kinberg, S., Reynolds, R., & Donner, L.S. (Producers), & Miller, T. (Director). (2016). *Deadpool* [Motion picture]. United States: Twentieth Century Fox.

Kübler-Ross, E. (1969). *On death and dying* (50th anniversary ed.). New York, NY: Scribner.

Lindeman, E. (1944). The symptomatology and management of acute grief. *American Journal of Psychiatry*, 151(6) (Suppl.), 141–148.

Michael, G., & Ridgeley, A. (1984). Careless whisper. On *Make it big* [CD]. London, England: Epic.

Moon, P.J. (2016). Anticipatory grief: A mere concept? *American Journal of Hospice and Palliative Medicine*, 33(5), 417–420.

Rando, T.A. (2000). Anticipatory mourning: A review and critique of the literature. In T.A. Rando (Ed.), *Clinical dimensions of anticipatory mourning: Theory and practice in working with the dying, their loved ones, and their caregivers* (pp. 17–50). Champaign, IL: Research Press.

Simon, J.L. (2008). Anticipatory grief: Recognition and coping. *Journal of Palliative Medicine*, 11(9), 1280–1281.

Townsend, M.C., & Morgan, K.I. (2017). *Essentials of psychiatric mental health nursing: Concepts of care in evidence-based practice* (7th ed.). Philadelphia, PA: F.A. Davis Company.

Zilberfein, F. (1999). Coping with death: Anticipatory grief and bereavement. *Generations*, 23(1), 69–74.

# 9 Superman and Secondary Losses

*Belinda M. Gonzalez-Leon*

The death of a loved one, a primary loss, brings with it the loss of practices, customs, and everyday routines, and therefore these secondary losses are losses in addition to the death. "Losses that occur as a result of, or coincident with the primary losses" (Mahon, 1999, p. 297) are considered secondary losses. Poole et al. (2016) state that a loss is any end or separation of attachment that is "usually accompanied by a set of secondary losses" (p. 195). Secondary losses bring grief and mourning as well as sadness, anger, guilt, confusion, physical pain, weeping, and lack of sleep (Coolican, Corr, Moretti, & Simon, 2011).

Those affected by a death may feel that everything is changing or that much is disappearing from their life. Although primary loss is major, secondary losses are no less important. Secondary losses are unique to each person, but they cover a wide range of damage, including the losses of income, security, roles, home, identity, caregiving, business, purpose, friends, community, self-confidence, relationships, memories, beliefs, belongings, milestones, faith, celebrations, hope, and goals. It could be as simple a loss as not having the person who fixes your hair, repairs the appliances, folds the clothes, or walks the dog. Secondary losses can be micro actions that are associated with our loved one who has died and that can trigger grief.

Coolican et al. (2011) also cite secondary losses as losing the ability to perform certain actions. This could be the inability to work, which incurs financial strain that may already be burdened by a loss of income from a loved one's death. Secondary losses can be dreams and future plans that will no longer be realized because of the primary loss. New routines have to be adopted, and memories will continue to be clouded by memories of death (Mahon, 1999). Secondary losses are immediate or can be experienced even years later. Kübler-Ross and Kessler (2005) note that secondary losses tend to reveal themselves over time, which leaves the bereaved to endure in what feels like painful perpetuity. The complexity and multitude of secondary losses adds to the difficulty of mourning the primary loss.

Perhaps the greatest secondary loss is the loss of who you were – your identity. You may lose interest in a particular pursuit or perhaps lose autonomy because of new reliance on others. You were a particular person, but after a primary loss, you become a different person not just because of the responsibilities you take on but also because the direction of your life has changed and is emotionally impacted by the loss. "Now that you are inconsolable, it feels like the new you is forever changed, crushed, broken, and irreparable … what is left is a new you, a different you, one who will never be the same again or see the world as you once did" (Kübler-Ross & Kessler, 2005, p. 76).

Although Kübler-Ross and Kessler (2005) acknowledge the loss of identity after the death of a close other, they do not deny the existence of a new identity that does emerge after enduring primary and secondary loss. Resiliency is defined as "the strength and speed of our response to adversity" (Grant & Sandberg, 2017, p. 13). It is with time and with each secondary loss that we adapt to or overcome that resiliency is built up. By dealing with the everyday secondary losses we encounter, we are able to take the next step and move on to the next day because we find purpose or because we have no choice but to do so. You may have no choice but to go to work or be the only one who can take care of your children. "Grief reactions in bereaved persons typically lead to … those efforts that individuals make … to cope with their losses and their grief … to adapt to a new world in which they find themselves" (Coolican et al., 2011, p. 221). If anything, secondary losses force us to adapt, resolve, and develop a new identity out of survival.

## 9.1 Case Study: Superman

Mahon (1999) describes secondary loss grief as a prolonged pain because these losses continue to compound over time. Therefore, it is important to find a way forward, to cope with and manage these losses. The character Clark Kent in the film *Man of Steel* (Roven, Nolan, Thomas, Snyder, & Snyder, 2013) arrived on Earth as an orphan when he was too young to realize and understand the primary death loss of his parents. However, despite being raised by loving Earth parents, he encountered difficulties growing up because as an alien he possessed special powers and strength. Poole et al. (2016) included grief over the loss of one's prior life or the loss of control due to so much uncertainty in the future as secondary losses. These were losses that Clark Kent experienced without truly understanding, and this is the same for the majority of the bereaved.

As Clark Kent grew older, each time he experienced a power, it reminded him that he was different (compounded with typical teenage angst) and that he was on Earth because of his parents' deaths. And that in his parents dying, he also lost his planet, culture, race – everything. However, it is with each and every loss that he endures that he must undergo a separate grief for each and every incident (Rando, 1988). As children grow and reach various levels of development, it is possible to experience grief at each stage because with maturity comes a new level of recognition and realization of death (Mahon, 1999). Special moments as the first day of school, learning to ride a bicycle, and high school graduation all serve as reminders of the individuals not present to share in the moment or to be the guide and support needed for the milestone. We see Clark Kent struggle through these experiences because with each comes the acceptance of the great devastation that leads to his survival (Roven et al., 2013). Mahon (1999) states that joyful moments are, unfortunately, oftentimes overshadowed by both the primary and secondary losses as the bereaved navigate the landscape of loss and learn how to identify, cope with, and integrate these losses.

Both of Clark Kent's adoptive parents were vital in helping him cope and develop his identity (Roven et al., 2013). His mother is portrayed as the always supportive and understanding parent who knows how to calm his fears and help him center himself. Clark's father is the structure and discipline that he needs to keep him on the straight and narrow path, which eventually leads to his development as a "superhero" of great morals and values. His parents instill in him the belief that his survival of tragedy was for a purpose and that his parents' deaths had meaning, which is found by most survivors of loss. "One of the central goals in mourning is an effort to find ways to understand the meaning(s) of the losses one has experienced" (Coolican et al., 2011, p. 221). This family base and subsequent journey is what allows Clark to heal and cope.

What we also see in Clark Kent is what Bozeman (1999) explains in that our first experience with death greatly influences following experiences because memories and feelings regarding that first death affect how we feel future losses. For Clark Kent, the death of his adoptive second father on earth is what wrecks his stability and moral compass. He strains to decide between following his adoptive father's request to hide his powers versus his biological father's encouragement to use his special abilities in order to fulfill his destiny (Roven et al., 2013). These secondary or even tertiary losses weigh heavily on him and affect his closest family and friends as we watch them struggle along with him.

It is interesting that as Superman, Clark Kent is given the opportunity to "speak" with his biological father by use of a digital memory bank. It is a bittersweet experience that allows Superman to receive guidance and then decisively take action because he finally has his father's teachings to direct him. It is reflective of what Coolican et al. (2011) refer to how grieving persons will try to restructure their relationship with the deceased "so as to maintain a continuing bond or special connection" (p. 221). This is a scene that many of us would like to play out but will never be able to. At times I find myself speaking to my deceased husband about ordinary occurrences such as a new store that opened in our neighborhood ("Hey! Did you see what just opened on that empty corner? You wouldn't believe how much the town has changed".) or more important matters such as a concern about our children. Many times, I can feel what his guidance would be, and I can see the seriousness on his face.

In the end, Superman is able to cope with several of his secondary loss issues and finds meaning as well as purpose in his losses. Superman shows his audience that it is the very journey of his grief that permits him to become the hero with a strong and unwavering fidelity to serve and protect humankind despite being an adopted son of Earth. He allows us to become witnesses to how secondary losses can eventually become secondary gains along the path of grief.

## 9.2 Conclusions

A month before my forty-sixth birthday, my husband of twenty years died leaving me with two daughters that had barely turned five and seven years of age. My husband was my older daughter's confidant, my younger daughter's teddy bear, the one who would put gas in the car weekly, cooked almost every night, drove the girls to school in the morning, watched every single episode of our favorite TV series with me on the sofa, would kill all the bugs in the house, walked the dog daily, would deal with the landscapers, and the person I consulted with for everything. My secondary losses were significant in regard to the daily operations of life.

There is an old Spanish song that states, "la costumbre es mas fuerte que el amor" (Gabriel, 1984, track 10), which translates to English as, "the custom is stronger than love" but better explained as "a habit is greater than love". Secondary losses are customs and habits that are ripped from our lives through the death of a loved one and at times can be more painful than the absence of the person. As a mother with young children, my struggle to maintain the responsibilities of a household exacerbated my feelings of grief in losing my spouse. Through my personal experience, I finally understood the lyrics of the song because of my secondary losses.

My saving grace was my steadfast stubbornness in keeping my daughters' world unchanged as much as possible. I maintained the same wake-up time, bedtime, and mealtime. They continued at the same school with the same friends. We continued to celebrate birthdays and visit amusement parks. With great pain and at great lengths, I kept the status quo to minimize their secondary losses so their primary loss adaption could be better. I actively mitigated secondary losses to make the overall grief less than it already was. As I struggled to keep their world sane, I found that the tenacity of routine also gave me comfort and healing. As Clark Kent's journey led him to a new understanding and appreciation of his role as Superman, I too have walked a long path in becoming a new person. My world is not the same as it was five years ago, but it is not a sorrowful and depressing life – rather one filled with the everyday joys of family and friends. For it is only by recognizing and confronting each and every moment of grief, that we can heal and move forward to experience what life can offer and become our own superhero.

## References

Bozeman, J.C. (1999). A journey through grief: An analysis of an adult child's grief in the loss of a mother. *Illness, Crisis, & Loss*, 7, 91–99.

Coolican, M.B., Corr, C.A., Moretti, L.S., & Simon, R. (2011). Donor families, distinctive secondary losses, and "second death" experiences. *Progress in Transplantation*, 21(3), 220–227.

Gabriel, J. (1984). Costumbres [Record]. On *Canta A Juan Gabriel Volumen 6*. México: Ariola Eurodisco.

Grant, A., & Sandberg, S., (2017). *Option B: Facing adversity, building resilience, and finding joy*. New York: Alfred A. Knopf.

Kübler-Ross, E., and Kessler, D. (2005). *On grief and grieving: Find the meaning of grief through the five stages of loss*. New York: Scribner.

Mahon, M.M. (1999). Secondary losses in bereaved children when both parents have died: A case study. *Omega*, 39(4), 297–314.

Poole, J.P., Ward, J., DeLuca, E., Shildrick, M., Abbey, S., Mauthner, O., & Ross, H. (2016). Grief and loss for patients before and after heart transplant. *Heart & Lung: The Journal of Cardiopulmonary and Acute Care*, 45(3), 193–198.

Rando, T. (1988). *How to go on living when someone you love dies*. New York: Bantam Books.

Roven, C., Nolan, C., Thomas, E. Snyder, D. (Producers), & Snyder, Z. (Director). (2013). *Man of steel* [Motion Picture]. United States: Warner Bros. Pictures.

# 10 Magneto and Ambiguous Loss

*Cori Bussolari*

Magneto is one of the most complicated and fascinating characters in the X-Men universe, as his story exemplifies his experience with a multitude of ambiguous losses. These include both the death of his biological family, friends, and community during the Holocaust, as well as his subsequent loss of trust toward others, loss of his belief that humanity is worth caring about, and loss of his identity.

Coined by Pauline Boss in the 1970s while interviewing the wives of pilots deemed missing in action in Vietnam and Cambodia, an ambiguous loss is an unresolved loss that "complicates grief, confuses relationships, and prevents closure" (Boss, 2010, p. 137). There are two types described in the literature (Boss, 1999, 2007). The first is the physical absence with psychological presence ("Leaving without good-bye") (Boss, 2007, p. 105). The loved one is missing physically, but kept psychologically present. Examples include kidnapping, immigration, deportation, adoption, or situations where there is no body to bury. The second type refers to a psychological absence with physical presence ("Goodbye without leaving") (Boss, 2007, p. 105) such as in Alzheimer's disease, addiction, relational and identity changes, a significant preoccupation that takes our loved one away (Boss, 1999, 2007) or knowing that one might develop a terminal disease (Sobel & Cowan, 2003).

A primary component of ambiguous loss is ambivalence, or a "conflict between positive and negative feelings toward a person or set of ideas. The resolution of ambivalence essentially hinges on helping a person to recognize his or her conflicting feelings" (Boss, 1999, pp. 61–62). Ambiguous loss is considered highly traumatic because it is "painful, immobilizing, and incomprehensible so that coping is blocked" (Boss, 2010, p. 139). The experience can last for years without any resolution and may also heighten the risk for developing prolonged grief symptoms, depression, and posttraumatic stress (Lenferink, Eisma, de Keijser, & Boelen, 2017).

Given the chaotic nature of ambiguous loss, there is no pattern or structure regarding grief. In response to this dilemma, positive coping guidelines were developed (Boss, 2010) to help illuminate particular health-supporting and resilient behaviors rather than the grief process. These include finding meaning, tempering mastery, identity reconstruction, normalizing ambivalence, revising attachment, and discovering hope. Using these guidelines, I will present a case study of Magneto in order to understand this multifaceted man in relation to his trauma and loss.

## 10.1 Case Study: Magneto

Max Eisenhardt was a teenage, Jewish boy living with his family during late 1930s Germany. They were subjected to Nazi-inspired hatred and violence culminating in death camp interment and the horrific murder of his family. Although Max survived the genocide, we see how his painful losses and his singular focus on survival created the formidable, albeit traumatized, antihero, Magneto (Donner, Singer, Kinberg, Goodman, & Vaughn, 2011; Kinberg, Parker, Donner, Hallowell, & Kinberg, 2019).

> ***Finding Meaning*** *("There's so much more to you than you know, not just pain and anger. There's good in you too, and you can harness all that. You have a power that no one can match, not even me".)*
>
> (Donner et al., 2011, 1:21:28)

In order to find meaning, we are tasked to adapt to our new life and make sense of unfathomable circumstances. Magneto's sense of predictability and stability had been dramatically challenged, eroding his trust in humans, and he found purpose through survival. Magneto was part of the Sonderkommando,[1] where his primary goal was to help an old friend, even at the cost of doing perceivably horrible things like stealing gold fillings to pay for favors.

Years later, due to his fanatical desire to make sure that a mutant genocide would not happen, he participated in several violent acts. Magneto justified his actions because he believed he was making sacrifices for the greater good. Only within his friendship with Professor X, was he able to repurpose his focus away from fear and vengeance, as observed when he helped save the world and his chosen family, after initially trying to destroy it (Kinberg, Singer, Parker, Donner, & Singer, 2016).

> ***Tempering mastery*** *("I've been at the mercy of men just following orders. Never again".)*
>
> **(Donner et al.,** 2011, **1:55:38)**

Max's deep feelings of powerlessness and the subsequent awakening of Magneto arose after being at the mercy of the Nazis and fear of a mutant genocide. In response to Professor X's comment, "We can help them", Magneto asked, "Can we? That's how it starts and ends with being rounded up, experimented on, and eliminated" (Donner et al., 2011, 0:49:41). Magneto struggled with seeing multiple perspectives, particularly more balanced beliefs, such as the idea that although there were terrible humans, there were also people worth helping. While he perceived his intentions as worthy, he was often unable to use his powers in a measured and thoughtful manner. Magneto identified strongly with his torturers and justified killing all humans, similar to the Nazis, noting, "Let's just say, I'm Frankenstein's monster …" (Donner et al., 2011, 0:25:01).

> ***Reconstructing identity and Revising Attachments*** *("I know you think you've lost everything, but you haven't … you have more family than you know. You never had the chance to save your family before, but you do now ...".)*
>
> (Kinberg et al., 2016, 1:59:05)

Magneto displayed ongoing identity confusion, particularly around whether he was the caring person that his father and Professor X hoped he would be or a rageful, godlike savior. This was also seen when he tried to live a "normal" life as a working-class man with a wife and child, who were murdered by humans. A distraught Magneto looked at the sky, after he killed the men who killed his family, and yelled, "Is this what you want from me? Is this what I am…?" (Kinberg et al., 2016, 0:36:45). Yet, his connections with his chosen X-Men family trumped all of his anger. Magneto realized that he did not need to hold on to rigid roles and could develop a more fluid identity. He could fight for what was right as Magneto, but also be part of something supportive and loving, as Erik. Magneto revised his ambivalent attachments to the X-Men, by both staying connected to them, but not completely being part of them, something like a "both/and, not either/or" (Boss, 2010, p. 144), leading to what appeared as an identity integration.

> ***Discovering Hope*** *("Just because someone stumbles and loses their path, doesn't mean they're lost forever".)*
>
> (Singer et al., 2014, 1:20:36)

An important aspect of grieving is to eventually reconstruct meaning so that we can access hope. In turn, hope helps cultivate meaning and gives us purpose. Magneto's clear purpose throughout his life was demonstrated in the form of survival and retribution, thus, he resisted Professor X's overt belief in the best of humanity. Magneto deemed humans as inherently evil and that the only way to survive was to act swiftly and violently, that is, hurt others before they can annihilate you. Professor X nurtured feelings of hope Magneto was often unable to access. Although Magneto felt powerless to save the people he cared about for most of his life, he was shown ways he could still help his loved ones. When the two old friends once again sat down for a game of chess at the end of *Dark Phoenix* (Kinberg et al., 2019), one could see that there was hope for his future and friendships.

## 10.2 Conclusions

The very nature of ambiguous loss can leave someone struggling to create meaning and feel safe in an unpredictable and fear-inducing world. These losses are often the most traumatizing and stressful due to the lack of closure or rituals for support. Within this context, "closure is a myth" (Boss, 2010, p. 141), and thus, it is helpful to look at areas of resilience rather than a specific grief process. Magneto truly personifies the many forms that our grief can take. For Erik, his anger, fear, and need for retribution continued to grow, creating Magneto. While there is never an excuse for his violent acts, we can't help but additionally notice those areas of resilience that only Professor X could see, such as his deep love of his chosen family and desire to create a safe world where others do not need to live in fear. These are the areas needing nurturance, and, even more than his awe-inspiring powers, these are his greatest strengths.

## Note

1 German Nazi concentration camp prisoner units forced to dispose of gas chamber victims.

## References

Boss, P. (1999). *Ambiguous loss: Learning to live with unresolved grief.* Cambridge, MA: Harvard University Press.

Boss, P. (2007). Ambiguous loss theory: Challenges for scholars and practitioners. *Family Relations: An Interdisciplinary Journal of Applied Family Studies*, 56(2), 105–111.

Boss, P. (2010). The trauma and complicated grief of ambiguous loss. *Pastoral Psychology*, 59 (2), 137–145.

Donner, L.S., Singer, B., Kinberg, S., & Goodman, G. (Producers), & Vaughn, M. (Director). (2011). *X-Men: First class.* United States: Twentieth Century Fox.

Kinberg, S., Parker, H., Donner, L.S., & Hallowell, T. (Producers), & Kinberg, S. (Director). (2019). *Dark phoenix.* United States: Twentieth Century Fox.

Kinberg, S., Singer, B., Parker, H., & Donner, L.S. (Producers), & Singer, B (Director). (2016). *X-Men: Apocalypse.* United States: Twentieth Century Fox.

Lenferink, L.I.M., Eisma, M.C., de Keijser, J., & Boelen, P.A. (2017). Grief rumination mediates the association between self-compassion and psychopathology in relatives of missing persons. *European Journal of Psychotraumatology*, 8 (Suppl 6).

Singer, B., Donner, L.S., Kinberg, S., & Parker, H. (Producers), & Singer, B. (Director). (2014). *X-Men: Days of future past.* United States: Twentieth Century Fox.

Sobel, S., & Cowan, C.B. (2003). Ambiguous loss and disenfranchised grief: The impact of DNA predictive testing on the family as a system. *Family Process*, 42(1), 47–57.

# 11 Batman and Masked Grief

*Jon K. Reid*

Bereavement typically begins with acute grief, a period immediately after a loss, in which the bereaved person experiences feelings, thoughts, or behaviors that are painful and uncomfortable. To varying degrees these reactions typically become more tolerable over time using one's naturally occurring social support systems and personal coping strategies. But, what about those persons whose grief reactions do not subside or become integrated over a reasonable period of time? As early as 1944, Lindeman wrote about the type of grief that does not follow a natural or typical trajectory. He used terms such as pathological grief, morbid grief reactions, delayed grief, and chronic grief (Lindemann, 1944). Worden (2018) utilized similar terms, specifically: chronic grief reactions, delayed grief reactions, exaggerated grief reactions, and masked grief reactions.

After a sudden and/or violent death, also known as traumatic loss, survivors are often inundated and overwhelmed with numerous thoughts, feelings, and sensations that go beyond normal reactions. These can intrude into periods of wakefulness as well as during sleep for years to come, often with no predictable end in sight. Several responses to traumatic loss have been identified, particularly when grief does not follow a typical trajectory that involves expressing grief, adjusting to the world without the loved ones, and finding meaning in life.

Worden (2018) includes several factors that can predict complicated mourning, such as the presence of multiple losses, early parental loss, death by murder, and the "absence of a social support network" (Worden, 2018, p. 136) of people who know the bereaved and will offer support. Family and friends often distance themselves from individuals who have experienced violent and traumatic loss.

Worden (2018) describes masked grief reactions as experiencing symptoms or behaviors that can be maladaptive, impairing, or causing difficulty but not identified by the griever as related to their loss. In comparison to other types of grief, in which "the patient knows that the symptoms began around the time of the death and are the result of the experience of the loss, those with masked grief do not associate their symptoms with a death" (Worden, 2018, pp. 148–149). Using the work of Parkes (1972, 2006) in building a definition of masked grief,

Worden (2018) describes the bereaved as developing nonaffective symptoms. Citing Deutsch (1937), Worden (2018) goes on to explain that "the death of a beloved person must produce some kind of reactive expression of feeling" and that in the absence of an expression of overt feelings, "this unmanifested grief will be expressed completely in some other way" (p. 147). Rather than being clearly expressed as reactions to grief, "masked grief turns up as either a physical symptom or it is masked by some type of aberrant or maladaptive behavior" (p. 148).

Additionally, Worden (2018) offers several clues to help diagnose those with masked grief or unresolved grief reactions, such as: making "radical changes to their lifestyle following a death" (p. 151); avoiding "friends, family members, and/or activities associated with the deceased" (p. 151); and engaging in "self-destructive impulses and actions" (p. 152). People usually experience this kind of complicated grief reaction because at the time of the loss, the grief was absent, was masked, and/or its expression was inhibited.

## 11.1 Case Study: Batman

The story of Bruce Wayne, from the film *Batman Begins* (Roven, Thomas, Franco, & Nolan, 2005), takes place in the fictional Gotham City, where Bruce was born into a family of extreme wealth. At an early age, while playing in the garden with his friend Rachel, Bruce fell into an abandoned well and was swarmed by bats. Though rescued by his father, this frightening experience led to night terrors. His continued fear resulted in the family leaving the theater one night and being mugged in an alley. His parents were murdered right in front of him (Kershner, 2008, p. 28).

Young Bruce blamed himself for placing his family in danger – high self-blame being a risk factor for complications in bereavement. Days later, the boy knelt at his bedside and swore by his parents' spirits that he would "avenge their deaths by spending the rest of [his] life warring on all criminals" (Langley, 2012, p. 36). With no remaining family Bruce was raised by the family caretaker, Alfred Pennyworth. His wish for specific revenge on the man who killed his parents was thwarted some years later, and Wayne spent subsequent years traveling the world and training in martial arts to fulfill his self-imposed promise to make Gotham City safer.

Bruce Wayne's grief reaction would not be considered typical, although he seemingly tried to adapt to his parents' deaths. He was not able to form stable relationships, he continually robbed himself of sleep, and he put himself in life-threatening situations that left him with numerous injuries and scars. Pain did not dissuade him from continuing his battle against evil, but it is doubtful that he ever realized that his grief was masked. Although one could argue that Wayne found meaning by fighting crime and protecting innocent victims, his style of life placed him at constant risk of death or mortal injury, certainly not consistent with the discovery of meaning in life as advocated by Viktor Frankl (1946). This is what makes Bruce Wayne's response to grief as complicated as an assessment of complicated grief. However, there is little doubt in the psychological realm the recognition of his masked grief reactions.

Bruce's approach to coping fits well into the paradigm identified by Dr. William Worden as one style of abnormal grief reactions – specifically masked grief. In addition to the multiple losses, early parental loss, and lack of family/social support, there is the obvious use of a mask in his attire as Batman, with which Bruce Wayne transforms himself into a superhero, an avenger who disrupts criminal behavior and punishes criminals. When asked why he wears a mask, his response is that, "it's not to hide who I am, but to create what I am" (Batman #624, 2004, as cited in Langley, 2012, p. 62). Even so, behind his mask, Bruce Wayne hides his life as a superhero while figuratively masking his unresolved grief.

Though Batman's actions have saved the lives of many, he has nonetheless paid a price in his personal life. Bruce acknowledges in *Batman Begins* (Roven et al., 2005) that he finds it difficult to form new relationships and has the insight that he seems to push people away. He is unable to convince his most trusted friend, Rachel Dawes, that he is anything more than just a rich playboy or a revenge seeker. Though Bruce often appears in public with beautiful ladies, "it seems that his life … is lonely and unfulfilling" (Kershnar, 2008, p. 29).

## 11.2 Conclusions

In the life of Bruce Wayne, the losses continued to add up. In addition to the murders of his parents, the love of his life, Rachel, was murdered, and his home, Wayne Manor, was burned down (Roven et al., 2005). His pledge to make Gotham City safer did not assuage the guilt and pain he felt over his parents' deaths, leading to numerous risky behaviors and the delay of usual developmental tasks as he moved into adulthood. His story, however, like many superhero stories as well as real-life stories of survival, offers hope to those who have faced tragedy. Others find his discovery of meaning following tragedy to be inspiring (Rosenberg, 2013). And his story eventually "ends" with happiness in the form of achieving a family of his own creation, far away from Gotham City in movie sequels, offering hope to many who have worn the mask of grief.

## References

Deutsch, H. (1937). Absence of grief. *Psychoanalytic Quarterly*, 6, 12–22.

Frankl, V.E. (1946). *Man's search for meaning*. Boston, MA: Beacon Press.

Kershnar, S. (2008). Batman's virtuous hatred. In M.D. White & R. Arp (Eds.), *Batman and philosophy: The dark knight of the soul*. (pp. 28–37). Hoboken, NJ: John Wiley & Sons.

Langley, T. (2012). *Batman and psychology: A dark and stormy knight*. Hoboken, NJ: John Wiley & Sons.

Lindeman, E. (1944). The symptomatology and management of acute grief. *American Journal of Psychiatry*, 151(6), 141–148.

Parkes, C.M. (1972). *Bereavement: Studies of grief in adult life*. New York, NY: International Universities Press.

Parkes, C.M. (2006). *Love and loss: The roots of grief and its complications*. New York, NY: Routledge.

Rosenberg, R.S. (2013). Our fascination with superheroes. In R. S. Rosenberg (Ed.), *Our superheroes, ourselves* (pp. 3–18). New York, NY: Oxford University Press.

Roven, C., Thomas, E., & Franco, L. (Producers), & Nolan, C. (Director). (2005). *Batman begins* [Motion picture]. United States: Warner Bros. Pictures.

Worden, J.W. (2018). *Grief counseling and grief therapy: A handbook for the mental health practitioner* (5th ed.). New York: Springer.

# 12 Wonder Woman and Delayed Grief

*Pamela A. Malone*

Delayed grief is also known as inhibited, postponed, or suppressed grief in that it is expressed or felt later as an avoidance of aspects of the loss, its accompanying pain, and the full realization of its implications (Jeffreys, 2011; Worden, 2018). It can appear as a disengagement from experiencing emotional grief responses or reactions. Delaying grief postpones the grief reaction for weeks, months, and even years. People vary in their ability to tolerate pain and may postpone or delay their grief reaction to a time when they have built up some reserves or resilience, or when they have sufficient support and emotional safety. The person will appear to lack grief, inhibit grief, or delay grief. A number of possible causes or existing factors may be associated with a person's inability to process, feel, or display grief.

Grief can be interrupted by other more pressing concerns or responsibilities, leaving little time or bandwidth for personal grief. A woman whose husband has died leaving her a single parent may spend her emotional energy and time on managing her children's grief and other needs. She may become task-focused in dealing with both raising children and maintaining the household. This is especially true if she lacks practical support at the time of her loss. Her avoidance of grief may impart an idea of "life goes on" as a way to protect herself and the family from strong emotions that could impede daily functioning (Rubin, Malkinson, & Witztum, 2012). This delay of grief allows the individual to do what must be done to survive; however, in this sole restoration focus mode, they delay or inhibit the process of attending to their loss.

Grief may be delayed due to the conflicted emotions of the griever who is unwilling or unable to confront its depth and impact. The relationship with the deceased may be fraught with negative experiences and terrible memories. Consider a woman who has been the victim of childhood sexual abuse (CSA) by an uncle who is now deceased. This involves an isolation of emotions that include the terror and the grief, which may initially be inextricably woven together. "As well, because of the pain, humiliation, and sheer sense of betrayal that CSA involves, the urge to suppress these volatile feelings is strong" (Fleming & Belanger, 2001, p. 324). She may need to protect herself from the negative aspects before she can make emotional space to remember and think about the positive aspects of the relationship. Recalling the positive aspects of the relationship will take time, and delaying grief until then is understandable.

Grief can also be postponed or delayed because the person does not feel safe enough or entitled to release these feelings. This is especially true if the loss is not recognized or acknowledged. It can also occur when there is stigma associated with the cause of death as in an overdose or suicide death. Consider a father whose 16-year-old son died by suicide. This father, who had already struggled with alcoholism, buried himself in work and drink for many years, in essence delaying and postponing the inevitable pain of grief. He suppressed his grief with alcohol only to have it surge in full force during sobriety.

In situations that involve a crisis such as a natural or human-made disaster or war, there is often no time to grieve. Many of these grievers redirect their energy to focus on survival and protection of self and others. Grief is put on hold or delayed until there is time and space for it.

## 12.1 Case Study: Wonder Woman

Themes of loss, grief, and bereavement are rampant in movies in which Wonder Woman (Diana Prince) stars, and delayed grief is prominent. As seen in the film *Wonder Woman* (Roven, Snyder, Snyder, Suckle, & Jenkins, 2017b), the Amazonian princess is raised on Paradise Island, a sheltered island created by Zeus to keep the Amazons safe. She is the only child on the island surrounded by strong, powerful, and agile woman warriors. As a young girl she begins to emulate them and as an adolescent begins to secretly train as a warrior with her aunt, Antiope, the general of the Amazon warriors. Her training becomes more earnest with her mother's begrudging approval for her aunt to train her even harder. As a young woman, Diana meets Captain Steve Trevor, an American pilot, whose plane crash lands in the sea surrounding Paradise Island. Diana saves him from drowning, and they immediately fall in love. She is horrified as Steve tells her about the war raging in the world outside the island. Diana sees the first Amazon killed by bullets during an arduous battle with soldiers who appeared from the world outside the island and subsequently bears witness to the deaths of many Amazonian warriors. Antiope, Diana's aunt, is shot by one of the soldiers and dies in Diana's arms, allowing her no time to grieve because the battle continues.

Diana's mother, Queen Hippolyta, informs her that if she chooses to leave the island she can never return. Diana shows great sadness leaving both her mother and the safety of Paradise Island. She evidences even more sadness while watching wounded soldiers disembark from the ship and when the village people are gassed by the Germans. She bears witness to the ravages of war as men lay dying, horses are beaten to move supplies, and women and children starve in the area known as No Man's Land. As the war to end all wars rages on, Diana fights alongside Captain Steve Trevor and his men and watches with great concern as Steve goes up in his plane. When she realizes

Steve's intention in flying a plane full of bombs she screams "Steve, no…." as the plane explodes over enemy lines (Roven et al., 2017b, 2:01:11). At the end of the film, Diana looks at photos of deceased soldiers posted in the village square, sees one of Captain Steve Trevor, and smiles through her tears as she looks up at the sky where she last saw him. This leaves a stoically bereaved Diana to mourn her first and only love.

In *Batman v. Superman: Dawn of Justice* (Roven, Snyder, & Snyder, 2016), Bruce Wayne discovers Diana is a demi-god and decides she is needed to fight in the alien invasion of Earth. He emails a picture of her with Steve Trevor as a way of coaxing her into action. He tells her, "We have to stand together"; she responds, "One hundred years ago I walked away from mankind. From a century of horrors. Men made a world where standing together is impossible" (Roven et al., 2016, 2:19:21). The world did not hear from her since Steve Trevor's death, as she delayed her grief for 100 years.

In the *Justice League* (Roven, Snyder, Berg, Johns, & Snyder, 2017a) film Diana sees Bruce Wayne working on a troop carrier airplane and states, "I once knew someone who would've loved to fly it" (Roven et al., 2017a, 32:05). Later when they are arguing about Superman's death, she tells Bruce Wayne, "At some point you have to move on"; he responds, "Steve Trevor tell you that?" (Roven et al., 2017b, 1:04:49). Bruce Wayne continues to push her by saying, "I'd never heard of you until Luther lured you out by stealing a picture of your dead boyfriend. You shut yourself down for a century so let's not talk about moving on" (Roven et al., 2017b, 1:05:21). In planning how to save the world, Diana tells Bruce Wayne, "It's my job and I haven't been doing it. I've been reacting. Not leading. They're all Steve Trevor" (Roven et al., 2017b, 1:22:38). In discussing loss and the difficulty in trusting others, she tells Victor Stone, "I lost someone I loved once. I shut myself off from everyone". And in a realization of the implications her delayed grief had on her life, she acknowledges to Victor, "But I had to learn to open back up again. The truth is I'm still working on it too" (Roven et al., 2017b, 41:47–42:02).

## 12.2 Conclusions

Wonder Woman is an excellent portrayal of delayed grief. She is initially overwhelmed by the immediate needs of mankind during a time of war and focuses on survival and saving the world. She does not allow herself to express her grief publicly (Worden & Winokuer, 2011) thereby inhibiting or suppressing her grief. Her grief is buried as she sequesters herself for 100 years, which continues to be delayed when she reenters a world that still needs her to fight and save others. However, through her relationship with Bruce Wayne and members of the league, she begins to realize that delaying her grief has led to a life of isolation, inhibiting the potential good she could have on the world. It is here we see her begin to welcome the opportunity to work on her profound feelings of loss. This demonstrates that even with the deepest and most prolonged grief, there is hope for healing.

## References

Fleming, S.J. & Belanger, S.K. (2001). Trauma, grief, and surviving childhood sexual abuse. In R.A. Neimeyer (Ed.), *Meaning reconstruction & the experience of loss* (pp. 311–329). Washington, DC: American Psychological Association.

Jeffreys, J.S. (2011). *Helping grieving people – when tears are not enough: A handbook for care providers*. New York, NY: Routledge.

Roven, C., Snyder, D., Berg, J., & Johns, G. (Producers), & Snyder, Z. (Director). (2017a). *Justice league* (Motion Picture). United States: Warner Bros. Pictures.

Roven, C., & Snyder, D. (Producers), & Snyder, Z. (Director). (2016). *Batman v. superman: Dawn of justice* (Motion Picture). United States: Warner Bros. Pictures.

Roven, C., Snyder, D., Snyder, Z., & Suckle, R. (Producers), & Jenkins, P. (Director). (2017b). *Wonder woman* (Motion Picture). United States: Warner Bros. Pictures.

Rubin, S.S., Malkinson, R., & Witztum, E. (2012). *Working with the bereaved: Multiple lenses on loss and mourning*. New York, NY: Routledge.

Worden, J.W. (2018). *Grief counseling and grief therapy: A handbook for the mental health practitioner*. New York, NY: Springer Publishing Company.

Worden, J.W., & Winokuer, H.R. (2011). A task-based approach for counseling the bereaved. In R.A. Neimeyer, D.L. Harris, H.R. Winokuer, & G.F. Thornton (Eds.), *Grief and bereavement in contemporary society: Bridging research and practice* (pp. 57–67). New York, NY: Routledge.

# 13 The Flash and Disenfranchised Grief

*William Feigelman, Beverly Feigelman and Justin Colon*

Disenfranchised grief is a term originally coined by Dr. Kenneth Doka and was the subject of a book (Doka, 1989), which was subsequently revised (Doka, 2002). Defined simply, it refers to a lack of social support and validation from social intimates to a perceived loss or death. People's lack of compassion to the death suggests that the mourner is grieving unnecessarily (Doka, 2002). Examples include stillbirth death-loss, loss of a pet, or surrendering a child for adoption. Neimeyer and Jordan (2002) discuss disenfranchised grief as essentially an empathic failure between society and the mourner in which they fail to have their experience understood by those around them and instead often feel offended, wounded, or abandoned by a lack of an empathic response to loss. Many bereavement analysts might claim that the theory of disenfranchised grief is sufficiently broad to account for the unique grief difficulties of the suicide and drug-overdose death bereaved, in much the same way that Guy (2004) explains how overdose death bereaved parents are left with a feeling that it may not be legitimate for them to grieve for their deceased children.

Yet, we would also contend that drug overdose, suicide deaths, and stigmatized deaths (i.e., homicide-suicide, familicide, sexual-related deaths) may bring with them a sense of intense shame and humiliation. Worden (2009) claims, in a chapter devoted to special types of losses, that AIDS-related deaths can be ones that bring with them unspeakable social losses, where because of the associated stigma, some survivors fear they will be rejected and judged harshly if the cause of their loved one's death becomes known. So, they may lie and attribute the death to cancer or something other than AIDS (Worden, 2009). Behaviors such as these are repeatedly reported by suicide, substance-overdose, or addiction-related death survivors at support group meetings and at sharing sessions during bereavement-healing conferences. Many suicide and substance-overdose death bereaved parents routinely misrepresent the cause of a family member's death to other close family members, coworkers, and friends, fearing that the person's reputation will be greatly diminished by the revelation of his or her death cause.

In one dramatic example (taken from a support group meeting observation), the father of a 20-year-old son remained reluctant and unwilling to disclose his own father's death (by suicide) to his son, fearing that the boy would no longer respect his deceased grandfather after learning that the grandfather had taken his life. The intense shame that these bereaved people experience points to a perceived need to preserve the good reputation of their deceased relatives. Not only do the bereaved feel that others won't acknowledge and legitimatize their grief but they also fear that the memory of the deceased loved one will be permanently tarnished, and they fear that they, too, will be ridiculed, avoided, and even judged blameworthy by the revelation of the death cause. It is a protective action by the bereaved, in preservation of the dignity for their loved one and their family. We believe that this process can go beyond the concept of disenfranchisement, which is simply a lack of social validation of a loss, to active processes of social stigmatization.

## 13.1 Case Study: The Flash

The Superhero The Flash, a fictional character, created by Robert Kanigher and Carmine Infantino for DC Comics, deals with his own unique bereavement issues and disenfranchised grief. In the opening television pilot episode of The CW Network adaptation, appearing on Netflix, this synopsis describes The Flash and his primary bereavement issues: "Barry Allen was 11 years old when his mother was killed in a bizarre, terrifying incident and his father was falsely convicted of [her] murder. With his life changed forever by the tragedy, Barry was taken in and raised by Detective Joe West. Now, Barry has become a brilliant driven and endearing CSI assistant, whose determination to uncover the truth about his mother's strange death leads him to follow-up on every unexplained urban legend ... [Later] Barry is struck by lightning ... [and later, again he] awakens to find his life has changed once again – the accident has given him the power of super speed, granting him the ability to move through Central City like an unseen guardian angel ... Barry now has a renewed purpose – using his gift of speed to protect the innocent, while never giving up on his quest to solve his mother's murder and clear his father's name ..." ("The Flash", n.d.).

Imaginary characters like The Flash enable audiences to identify with themselves and to cope with their own real-life difficulties from within the safe and remote realm of the fantasy narratives (Langley, 2012; Fingerroth & Lee, 2013). The Flash character is a living embodiment of posttraumatic growth, having integrated the losses of his parents, his mother's own mysterious death, and his father's unjust incarceration into dealing with these issues and helping distressed others in society. If there is any single dominant, recurring theme occurring, across the span of over six seasons of *The Flash* TV series (Berlanti, Kreisberg, & Johns, 2014), it is the theme of The Flash helping people in distress. Thus, the saga is dedicated to highlighting Barry Allen's unwavering commitment toward posttraumatic growth.

Within the parallel realm of *The Flash* comic books ("The Fastest Man Alive", n.d.), which spawned the film series, we see many reference points to the character's real feelings and emotions. In the Year One storyline, Barry states,

"No matter how nice the day is I can always see when a storm is coming. Every day I stare down at crime scenes, and I'm reminded of the horror this life is capable of. And because of the crime in Central City, it's nearly impossible to look forward to the future and see anything positive" (Williamson, 2019, location 408). This hypervigilant behavior is symptomatic among the traumatically bereaved. Readers experiencing their own trauma and grief can identify with this expressed feeling and instantly feel an affinity that they and the character are one and the same. Throughout the dramas there are many other reference points to common emotions experienced by the viewers and readers.

In the first episodes of the series, before Barry is able to prove that his father did not kill his mother (familicide), Barry experiences associated pain for the stigmatized status of his father, accused of murdering his mother (Berlanti et al., 2014). He suppresses his grief and becomes a workaholic. There are many references to this stigmatization, although subtle. His grief is disenfranchised, especially for the loss of his father through his incarceration. And his father's grief over the death of his wife is not acknowledged because he is accused of her murder. Another close reference point to disenfranchised grief will be found at the end of the pilot film version, where Barry expresses an interest in further examining his mother's death, and his imprisoned father urges him to get on with his life instead and let this go. Within the vast realm of other superhero dramatizations, one will find other, perhaps even clearer, examples of this relatively common grief experience.

## 13.2 Conclusions

For most members of society, exposure to superhero sagas enable viewers to forget about their own personal troubles with grief and other adversities. As they focus their attention upon superhero dramas, they take a break from their everyday lives and troubles. For some, probably a small minority, the superhero dramatizations help them to understand themselves better, furnishing images of resilient strength to go forward, when others might be incapacitated from the aftereffects of their own tragic life circumstances. One member of our suicide survivors' support group spoke out at a meeting where he shared the feeling that he sometimes felt like he must be a superhero or "something like that". And then he elaborated on why he felt this way: he never thought he would be able to recover from the shattering suicide loss of his 19-year-old daughter, a promising artist and vibrant person. For many months afterwards, he had been deeply grieving, which is a natural response to loss; however, the continual persistence of the depth of hopeless suffering left him unable to focus on things, engaging in reckless behavior and uncaring about himself. But eventually an idea sprung up between he and his wife that it would be a good project for them to memorialize their daughter with creating a foundation in her name, dedicated to suicide prevention; to use the pain of their loss to making meaning of her life and death for the good of others – just like Barry Allen. Eventually, he and his family were able to raise hundreds of thousands of dollars earmarked for suicide prevention agencies that they had helped solicit. Both he and his wife also began to do some public speaking about suicide prevention at local schools, churches, and community groups. He never thought that he ever would have been capable of doing these things and also to resume his work as a practicing attorney. The superhero idea held firm in his mind as a guiding light leading him along the integration of the loss of his daughter into his life and making meaning of her death to help prevent future deaths by suicide – He is a true-life Flash.

## References


Berlanti, G., Kreisberg, A., & Johns, G. (Developers) (2014). *The flash*. Bonanza Productions and Warner Bros. Television.

Doka, K. (1989). *Disenfranchised grief: Recognizing hidden sorrow*. New York, NY: Lexington Books.

Doka, K. (2002) (Ed.), *Disenfranchised grief: New directions, challenges, and strategies for practice*. Champaign, IL: Research Press.

Fingerroth, D., & Lee, S. (2013) *Superman on the couch: What superheroes really tells us about ourselves and our society*. London: Bloomsbury Academic.

Guy, P. (2004). Bereavement through drug use: Messages from research. *Practice*, 16(1), 43–53.

Langley, T. (2012) *Batman and psychology: A dark and stormy night*. New York, NY: Wiley.

Neimeyer, R.A., & Jordan, J.R. (2002). Disenfranchisement as empathic failure: Grief therapy and the co-construction of meaning. In K. Doka (Ed.), *Disenfranchised grief: New directions, challenges, and strategies for practice* (pp. 95–118). Champaign, IL: Research Press.

The fastest man alive: The flash. (n.d.). *DC Comics, characters*. Retrieved from https://www.dccomics.com/characters/the-flash

The flash. (n.d.). Retrieved from http://www.atlanticbb.net/tv/3/series/series/The%20Flash/series_id/13789916

Williamson, J. (2019). *The flash, year one*. New York: DC Comics.

Worden, J.W. (2009). *Grief counseling and grief therapy: A handbook for the mental health practitioner* (4th ed.). New York, NY: Springer Publications.

# 14 Iron Man and Chronic Grief

*Rebecca S. Morse and Jacob Halbert*

Chronic/prolonged grief (C/PGD) refers to elevated or extreme symptoms of grief that extend past the initial or acute phase. Prolonged grief disorder (PGD) occurs in response to close relationship loss and is characterized by intense pain, longing, and persistent thoughts of the deceased, or the death. Further, there is a pattern of intense negative emotions (e.g., sadness, guilt, anger). The cognitive and emotional disturbances are present for a minimum of six months postloss and exceed the normative grief response for that individual's cultural expectations (World Health Organization [WHO], 2018). C/PGD is distinct from anxiety or depression (Golden & Dalgleish, 2010), with symptoms predictive of reduced mental health and quality of life (Boelen & Prigerson, 2007). While the *Diagnostic and Statistical Manual of Mental Disorders*, Fifth Edition (DSM-5) added Persistent Complex Bereavement Disorder (PCBD), PGD diagnosis remains clinically useful (Bonanno & Malgaroli, 2019; Malgaroli, Maccallum, & Bonanno, 2018). Recent meta-analysis estimates that 1 out of every 10 bereaved adults has experienced C/PGD (Lundorff, Holmgren, Zachariae, Farver-Vestergaard, & O'Connor, 2017).

## 14.1 Case Study: Iron Man

[Content for this case study is drawn from the following films: *Iron Man* (Arad, Feige, & Favreau, 2008); *Iron Man 2* (Feige & Favreau, 2010); *Avengers* (Feige & Whedon, 2012); and *Iron Man 3* (Feige & Black, 2013).]

Tony Stark is a white male in his mid-40s who presents with symptoms potentially related to C/PG. Stark has a significant history of trauma, including the loss of both parents. He has dealt with catastrophe – personal and global. Additionally, he has suffered depression, anxiety, nightmares, flashbacks, and conflictual interpersonal relationships. His case illustrates that impressive personal strengths and socially beneficial coping strategies can interfere with grief resolution in C/PG.

Stark's trauma history begins early, in an emotionally deprived home. During brief episodes when his father was present, Stark recalls him as cold, distant, and machine-like. Stark's mother was similarly absent, with Stark having few instances of positive interactions with her. When Stark was 21 years old, his parents were killed in a tragic hit-and-run accident. C/PGD is more likely to occur after a violent or sudden death (Kristensen, Weisæth, & Heir, 2012). Stark, already an accomplished engineer and inventor, began leading his father's company and spearheaded its dramatic growth into weapons technology and military hardware development (Arad et al., 2008). Superficially, Stark had "moved on" from the loss of his parents, channeling himself into industry. Preoccupied with reinventing himself and his company, Stark avoided processing the intense emotions associated with traumatic loss.

Stark would soon experience additional trauma. While in Afghanistan providing a demonstration of Stark Industries' latest weapon system, Stark was kidnapped by insurrectionists and forced to build a weapon for them for an impending terrorist attack (Arad et al., 2008). Throughout his incarceration, Stark observed the militants stockpiling crates filled with munitions – each labeled with the Stark Industries insignia. As his feelings of shame and guilt merged into a singular anger, Stark developed a plan to escape – and to ameliorate the harm he had indirectly facilitated. Pretending to build weapons for his captors, Stark constructed an automated armor-plated suit and detonated the munitions cases bearing his family name as he escaped. Stark thus re-created his identity in this origin story of Iron Man, the armored superhero and founding Avenger.

Stark's identity change represents accelerated processing of multiple death and nondeath losses, permitting minimal time for genuine reappraisal. After his return to the United States, Stark faced the harsh reality that his legacy was one of violence and destruction. The loss of this legacy compounded the loss of his parents and exacerbated his earlier emotional deprivation. Frequently those who have experienced loss incorporate the loss, and its meaning for them, into their self-narrative. Postloss psychopathology, e.g., C/PGD, is positively related to the centrality of the loss and the way in which the loss becomes an integral part of someone's life story, identity, and day-to-day experiences (Boelen, 2012). Consequently, Stark retreated into technological innovation. Perhaps to atone for the violent legacy he had confronted, the nascent Iron Man began to construct increasingly complex versions of his iconic armor.

Stark soon encountered another major loss: betrayal by Obadiah Stane. Stane had been a lifelong confidant of Stark's father and a key fixture of Stark Industries, but Stark learned that Stane was responsible for the attack and kidnapping in Afghanistan and again was forced to question his understanding of the world. Sense-making, the ability to reframe or contextually ground a traumatic loss, is helpful to prevent C/PGD and has been found to mediate the symptoms of complicated grief (Currier, Holland, & Neimeyer, 2006). Stark cemented himself into reality through violence. Subsequently, Stark came to the attention of recruitment operatives in the government agency S.H.I.E.L.D. Soon after, Stark announced to the world that he was the one behind the red-and-gold mask – he was Iron Man (Arad et al., 2008).

Stark's next experience of loss begins with Ivan Vanko (Feige et al., 2010), whose father had worked with Stark Industries decades prior on the first prototype of the arc reactor (the power source inside the Iron Man suit). The elder Vanko fell out of favor with the elder Stark and was deported to Russia and imprisoned. Ivan Vanko pursued revenge on the Stark family, and Stark was forced to confront yet another reality – his father was not the virtuous American hero he had believed.

Stark's story comes to a climactic midpoint after S.H.I.E.L.D. implemented the Avengers Initiative, which made Iron Man a founding member of the Avengers organization of "superheroes" (Feige et al., 2012). This latest aspect of his reframed Iron Man identity provided a relational component – connection to other Avengers – that further challenged Stark. Individuals who have been violently bereaved have been stripped of a sense of protection, and both their own internal response, and reactions of others toward them, lead to feelings of vulnerability (Currier, Holland, Coleman, & Neimeyer, 2008). Stark's orientation toward others was strained as a result; despite sharing repeated life-or-death experiences, Stark's attachment to the other Avengers was characterized by defensive avoidance and dry, often morbid, humor.

Compounding his experience of loss and related complex grief, Stark survived a near-death experience when attempting to save New York from an alien invasion (Feige et al., 2012). Although spared from death, Stark experienced flashbacks and nightmares. Facing his own demise left Stark with existential questions, anxiety, and comorbidity of posttraumatic stress disorder, but he continued to resist offers for assistance and support via sarcasm and witty retorts.

Struggling with chronic insomnia, Stark poured energy into his alter ego. He had significant relational difficulties with his romantic partner, Pepper Potts, whom he trusted with running Stark Industries. When Potts challenged him to determine whether the Iron Man persona was worth more to him than their relationship, Stark's actions seemed to show a differential preference for the superhero identity. Throughout the relationship, Stark attempted to isolate and protect Potts. Stark's behaviors are indicative of anxious attachment, consistent with research demonstrative that individuals with C/PGD have been found to be more likely to engage in anxious attachment-seeking behaviors (Stroebe, Schut, & van den Bout, 2013). Additionally, adults with chronic grief are more likely to exhibit marital dependency (Ott, Lueger, Kelber, & Prigerson, 2007), as evidenced when Stark focuses his expressed emotional attachment exclusively on Potts.

Dramatic circumstances forced Stark to address his relational and existential conflicts. Rival scientist Aldrich Killian was developing superhumans (Feige & Black, 2013). Killian embroiled Stark in battle and abducted Potts to use in his experiments. The danger to Potts forced Stark to confront his inner discernment between Tony Stark and Iron Man. At conflict's end, Stark detonated each suit, demonstrating to Potts (and himself) that he had chosen Tony Stark over Iron Man, his authentic and relational identity over his created identity as a super-defended hero. This denouement illustrates the fragmented sense of self often experienced by individuals who have survived trauma and how reintegrating of one's identity postloss can make it challenging to form secure attachments (Jobson & O'Kearney, 2008).

## 14.2 Conclusions

Stark's journey as Iron Man delineates several dimensions of psychological functioning, developmental growth, and posttraumatic recovery. This case focused on elements of Stark that exemplify C/PG. Recent research has established a qualitatively unique *network of connections* between quality of life for those with C/PGD and experiences of feelings of meaninglessness, difficulty establishing trust, bitter affect, and role confusion (Maccallum & Bryant, 2019). Stark's narrative exemplified these findings: a drive for meaning through work; repeated issues with trusting friends, colleagues, and romantic partner(s); negative cognitive appraisals moderated through sarcastic dialogue; and ultimately role confusion, as he experienced immense distress when removed from the role of Iron Man. It is important to note that not all of those who work through chronic grief will become armored superheroes (though this chapter should not deter anyone!). However, the Iron Man saga provides a clear, dramatic example of the ways that chronic grief can impact a person's life, from self-identity to relationship conflict.

*Thank you to our respective spouses, Jonathan and Haylea, as well as research assistants Maura McFadden and Lory Easton for their support with this chapter.*

## References

Arad, A., & Feige, K. (Producers), & Favreau, J. (Director). (2008). *Iron man* [Motion picture]. United States: Marvel Studios.

Boelen, P.A. (2012). A prospective examination of the association between the centrality of a loss and post-loss psychopathology. *Journal of Affective Disorders*, 137(1), 117–124. https://doi.org/10.1016/j.jad.2011.12.004

Boelen, P.A., & Prigerson, H.G. (2007). The influence of symptoms of prolonged grief disorder, depression, and anxiety on quality of life among bereaved adults. *European Archives of Psychiatry and Clinical Neuroscience*, 257(8), 444–452. https://doi.org/10.1007/s00406-007-0744-0

Bonanno, G. A., & Malgaroli, M. (2019). *Trajectories of grief: Comparing symptoms from the DSM-5 and ICD-11 diagnoses. Depression and Anxiety.* Advance online publication. http://dx.doi.org.mutex.gmu.edu/10.1002/da.22902

Currier, J.M., Holland, J.M., Coleman, R.A., & Neimeyer, R.A. (2008). Bereavement following violent death: An assault on life and meaning. In R.G. Stevenson & G.R. Cox (Eds.), *Death, value and meaning series: Perspectives on violence and violent death* (pp. 177–202). Amityville, NY: Baywood Publishing Co.

Currier, J.M., Holland, J.M., & Neimeyer, R.A. (2006). Sense-making, grief, and the experience of violent loss: Toward a mediational model. *Death Studies*, 30(5), 403–428. http://dx.doi.org.mutex.gmu.edu/10.1080/07481180600614351

Feige, K. (Producer), & Black, S. (Director). (2013). *Iron man 3* [Motion picture]. United States: Marvel Studios.

Feige, K. (Producer), & Favreau, J. (Director). (2010). *Iron man 2* [Motion picture]. United States: Paramount Pictures.

Feige, K. (Producer), & Whedon, J. (Director). (2012). *The avengers* [Motion picture]. United States: Marvel Studios.

Golden, A.-M.J., & Dalgleish, T. (2010). Is prolonged grief distinct from bereavement-related posttraumatic stress? *Psychiatry Research*, 178(2), 336–341. https://doi.org/10.1016/j.psychres.2009.08.021

Jobson, L., & O'Kearney, R. (2008). Cultural differences in personal identity in post-traumatic stress disorder. *British Journal of Clinical Psychology*, 47(1), 95–109. doi: 10.1348/014466507X235953

Kristensen, P., Weisæth, L., & Heir, T. (2012). Bereavement and mental health after sudden and violent losses: A review. *Psychiatry: Interpersonal and Biological Processes*, 75(1), 76–97. https://doi.org/10.1521/psyc.2012.75.1.76

Lundorff, M., Holmgren, H., Zachariae, R., Farver-Vestergaard, I., & O'Connor, M. (2017). Prevalence of prolonged grief disorder in adult bereavement: A systematic review and meta-analysis. *Journal of Affective Disorders*, 212, 138–149. https://doi.org/10.1016/j.jad.2017.01.030

Maccallum, F., & Bryant, R.A. (2019). *A network approach to understanding quality of life impairments in prolonged grief disorder. Journal of Traumatic Stress.* Advance online publication. http://dx.doi.org.mutex.gmu.edu/10.1002/jts.22383

Malgaroli, M., Maccallum, F., & Bonanno, G.A. (2018). Symptoms of persistent complex bereavement disorder, depression, and PTSD in a conjugally bereaved sample: A network analysis. *Psychological Medicine*, 48(14), 2439–2448. http://dx.doi.org.divinemercy.idm.oclc.org/10.1017/S0033291718001769

Ott, C., Lueger, R., Kelber, S., & Prigerson, H. (2007). Spousal bereavement in older adults: Common, resilient, and chronic grief with defining characteristics. *The Journal of Nervous and Mental Disease*, 195(4), 332–341. https://doi.org/10.1097/01.nmd.0000243890.93992.1e

Stroebe, M., Schut, H., & van den Bout, J. (Eds.). (2013). *Complicated grief: Scientific foundations for health care professionals* (pp. 190–203). New York, NY: Routledge/Taylor & Francis.

World Health Organization (WHO). (2018). International statistical classification of diseases and related health problems (11th Revision). Retrieved from https://icd.who.int/browse11/l-m/en

# 15 Avengers Infinity War and Avengers Endgame

## Cumulative and Collective Grief

*Mark de St. Aubin*

We live in a time when news of death – locally and on a global scale – has unfortunately become commonplace. With such daily exposure to tragedies in our world, we ourselves often suffer chronic, cumulative effects from these collective losses (Cabrera, 2012). Terms such as "cumulative grief" and "bereavement overload" (Kastenbaum, 1969; Neimeyer & Holland, 2004) describe one's response to such events. The generators of such grief may include a worldwide pandemic, multiple losses from crime or war, motor vehicle accidents with multiple fatalities, or a series of multiple deaths due to a variety of causes over a short period of time. Collective losses impact us, and this impact differs from that of a single-loss grief.

Multiple losses impacted over a short period of time give the bereaved less opportunity to process or adequately integrate these losses (Worden, 2018). In essence the bereaved are in a perpetual state of shock and disbelief, unable to move forward into the emotional processing of each loss due to the subsequent experiencing of one loss after another – essentially staying stuck in a state of shock (Mercer & Evans, 2006). This emotional numbness, normally a protective and insulating factor, becomes a straitjacket of sorts, constricting the bereaved from having the inner agility to navigate the emotional territory needed for healing, therefore postponing the mourning process (Tousley, 2013). Without time to heal, the losses become "layered," and the bereaved are unable to attend to each additional death with the attention that each loss demands. This grief, then, builds up and accumulates, hence the term "cumulative grief".

Additionally, if the bereaved experiences these deaths as traumatic, this presents further demands, as the sufferer must now approach the remembering of the deceased in their grief work with the accompanying challenge of triggering responses each time they move toward revising the continuing bond with the loved one. Such traumatic losses can critically undermine one's sense of self-efficacy in the world and be predictive of more severe persistent grief symptoms (Smith, Abeyta, Hughes, & Jones, 2015).

## 15.1 Case Study: Avengers: Infinity War (2018) and Avengers: Endgame (2019)

For the sake of this chapter, let's examine *Avengers: Infinity War* (Feige, Russo, & Russo, 2018) and *Avengers: Endgame* (Feige, Russo, & Russo, 2019) as a cinematic fictional case study. Through a portrayal of six colorful superheroes from the Marvel Cinematic Universe (MCU) film series – Iron Man, Captain America, Hawkeye, Thor, Black Widow, and The Hulk, the MCU has created a universe in which these superheroes experience the challenges we all face – how to live in a threatening world, protect those we most love, contend with adversity, and try to find balance between personal strengths and weaknesses. In the first movie, *Avengers: Infinity War* (Feige et al., 2018) the villain, Thanos, the personification of death, begins his murderous ambition to acquire six Infinity Stones. These stones will give him unlimited power by which he plans to bring his form of balance to the universe in ending the lives of half of its population, including those of the Avengers. He succeeds in obtaining these stones, and in the final battle scene, the Avengers make a futile attempt to defeat Thanos, but are themselves defeated. With the snap of his fingers, Thanos massacres half of the universe's inhabitants, leaving the superheroes to face, for the first time, their own powerlessness before the inevitable and to grieve those whose lives they were unable to save.

The sequel movie, *Avengers: Endgame* (Feige et al., 2019) begins with the superheroes simmering in the pain of their defeat, examining their decimated world, and all of them basking in their own unique grief response to their cumulative losses. Such a trouncing is not something such superheroes handle very easily, so accepting the full measure of these losses for them is close to impossible, and each superhero handles their grief differently. Let's now look at how they cope with the effects of their collective and cumulative grief.

**Tony "Iron Man" Stark:** At first Tony is journaling his grief into a recorder for his love, Pepper Potts, hoping against hope that someday she will be the recipient of his message. Alone and in despair, he finally "lets it all sink in" and allows his buried grief to surface. In his face is the new reality he is living, and his hopeless voice tone expresses his shattered worldview and sense of powerlessness. Shortly afterwards, at the Avengers' headquarters, Tony is angry and blaming the remaining Avengers for their failed mission, who collectively express a shared sense of guilt, "Guess what, Cap, we lost, and YOU weren't there! . . . Zero, Zip, Nada. No trust, liar!" (Feige et al., 2019, 0:11:36), all very expected grieving responses to cumulative losses, which have fragmented Tony's world and damaged his "Iron Man" sense of invulnerability.

**Steve "Captain America" Rogers:** Five years into the future, earth is still in postapocalyptic ruin, and its inhabitants are still in shock from the magnitude of the devastation. Captain America, now a grief group facilitator, spouts empty platitudes to attendees. "That's it. That's those little brave baby steps we gotta take to try and become whole again, try and find purpose . . . You gotta move on. Gotta move on" (Feige et al., 2019, 0:21:20). Later Steve tries hard to encourage another Avenger to look on the bright side of things to cope with it all. "Sorry, force of habit", he replies (Feige et al., 2019, 0:29:05). Trying to help others, but unable to help himself, Steve shows us how avoiding the pain of grief is one of the less-healthy ways of coping with loss.

**Clint "Hawkeye" Barton:** Early in the sequel, Clint saw his family vanish before his eyes at the snap of Thanos's fingers, and he is left to question why he deserved to live and his loved ones did not. In the first half of *Avengers: Endgame* (Feige et al., 2019), his survivor guilt comes to full expression as Hawkeye turns into a reckless vigilante, using his superpowers to hunt down and brutally murder those in the world, who, he feels (like himself) do not deserve to live. Only as other Avengers target him and rein him in, is he able to find community and the support of others grieving his shared losses.

**Thor:** The most colorful of the Avengers in his expression of unresolved cumulative grief is Thor, stuffing his anger and developing an episode of major depression – a deep sense of unworthiness, lethargy, constant drinking, and his excessive weight gain, distraction (PlayStation addiction), and self-isolation. Though it's played as comic relief, it definitely hits the mark as we perhaps see ourselves in his example and the destructive ways suppressed grief can wreak havoc on our physical bodies. Thor, hiding away in his "man cave" on the island of New Asgard is finally brought back, as was his fellow Avenger, Clint, by the support of his former community with his Avenger buddies.

**Bruce "The Hulk" Banner:** Presented in all previous Avenger films as a divided character, halfway through the film Bruce Banner now has finally embraced his inner shadow and rage, The Hulk, and though he is not yet addressing his grief wounds from the last battle as he is stuck in denial and disbelief, at least his inner congruence is one step in the right direction as the Smart Hulk.

**Natasha "Black Widow" Romanoff:** Having become a workaholic of sorts, Natasha tries to cope with her grief by busying herself in meetings with the remaining Avengers, finding distractions to keep herself from facing her pain, and, in being in denial, to pretend that things haven't changed (Blair, 2019). "All right. Uh, well, this channel's always active. So, if anything goes sideways, anyone's making trouble where they shouldn't, it comes through me" (Feige et al., 2019, 0:27:10). She is also, along with her fellow Avengers, stuck in her inability to accept the reality of their loss and wishing they could "undo the snap" of Thanos. "We can snap our own fingers. We can bring everybody back …" (Feige et al., 2019, 0:34:48). Ironically, the one adversary the Avengers seem to find most challenging is that of their own mortality.

## 15.2 Conclusions

As noted above, the Avengers experience myriad responses to their collective and cumulative grief that those affected in the real-world experience. The film illustrates through the characters the shattered world and traumatized sense of invulnerability of those bereaved in our nonfictional world. Fictionally, in their attempt to deal with this, they create a "time heist" and essentially undo

Thanos's "snap" and, in effect, cheat death (at least some of them). This is where our real world and fictional superhero worlds diverge – there are no time heists that we know of at least in this universe. As clinicians, we need to help the bereaved recognize and work through the potentially devastating effects of collective and cumulative grief. What *Avengers Endgame* (Feige et al., 2019) teaches us, is that despite their inability to fully accept what death had dealt them, our evolving superheroes engage in what truly heals grief – verbalizing one's pain, seeking community, connecting to remaining loved ones for support, making meaning from loss, reconstructing one's world view, and creating a new life narrative. We learn from them that devastating loss can be a vehicle through which to grow, reaffirm our place in the world, and continue to create meaning in ways that help us integrate the amazing lessons that love and loss have for each of us.

## References

Blair, S. (2019, May 14). The art of ending well: Grief, grieving and avengers: endgame. *Chaplains Report* [Blog post]. Retrieved from https://chaplainsreport.com

Cabrera, D., (2012) Additive trauma. In C.R. Figley (Ed.), *Encyclopedia of trauma: An interdisciplinary guide*. Thousand Oaks, CA: SAGE Publications, Inc.

Feige, K. (Producer), & Russo, A., & Russo, J. (Directors). (2018). *Avengers: Infinity war* [Motion Picture]. United States: Marvel Studios.

Feige, K. (Producer), & Russo, A., & Russo, J. (Directors). (2019). *Avengers: Endgame* [Motion Picture]. United States: Marvel Studios.

Kastenbaum, R., (1969). Death and bereavement in later life. In A. H. Kutscher (Ed.), *Death and bereavement* (pp. 27–54). Springfield, IL: Charles C Thomas

Mercer, D.L., & Evans, J.M. (2006). The impact of multiple mosses on the grieving process: An exploratory study. *Journal of Loss and Trauma*, 11(3), 219–227.

Neimeyer, R.A., & Holland, J. (2004). Bereavement overload. In N. Salkind (Ed.), *Encyclopedia of human development*. Thousand Oaks, CA; Sage.

Smith, A.J., Abeyta, A.A., Hughes, M., & Jones, R.T. (2015). Persistent grief in the aftermath of mass violence: The predictive roles of posttraumatic stress symptoms, self-efficacy, and disrupted worldview. *Psychological Trauma: Theory, Research, Practice, and Policy*, 7(2), 179–186.

Tousley, M. (2013, February 25). Coping with cumulative losses. *Grief healing* [Blog post]. Retrieved from: https://www.griefhealingblog.com

Worden, J.W. (2018). *Grief counseling and grief therapy: A handbook for the mental health practitioner* (5th ed.). New York, NY: Springer Publishing Company.

# Part IV

# Grief and Culture: Cultural Influence in the Superhero Universes

# 16 A Tale of Two Funerals

## Funeral Rites, Rituals, and Customs Across the Superhero Universes

*William G. Hoy*

Superman's persona is buried in Arlington Cemetery with the full military honors and fanfare of a fallen hero. Meanwhile, the simply coffined remains of Superman's alter ego, Clark Kent, are accompanied to Smallville's graveyard in the unmistakable simplicity of burial on the American frontier (Roven, Snyder, & Snyder, 2016). Befitting his "other galaxy" persona, Yondu is feted in death with an electric fireworks show, the symbols of which get mourners talking about their loss (Feige & Gunn, 2017). Such is the power of death rituals for superheroes and for ordinary humans, as well.

In the first edition of his landmark work on grief published in 1982 and in every edition since, Worden (2018) asserts that "the funeral, if it is done well, can be an important adjunct in aiding and abetting the healthy resolution of grief" (p. 120). In the same vein, Fulton (1994) suggests that funerals are powerful tools to engage entire communities in mourning and provide a socializing experience for mourners of all ages.

Ceremonies to mark the transition from life to death have been part of the human experience throughout history. More than a century ago, van Gennep (1909/1960) suggested that these rites articulate the acts of separation, transition, and reincorporation delimitating the space between life and death – both for the corpse and for the mourners. Ninety years later in reflection on the 9/11 terrorist attacks, Kastenbaum (2004) surmises that funerals assist in getting the mourners through this "betwixt" state of liminality on the way to the dead becoming "safely dead" (p. 7).

In the early decades of superhero existence, no readers likely entertained the thought that Superman, Batman, or any of the other mythical champions of justice could ever die (Alaniz, 2014), an ending that seemed out of concert with the created image of superhero immortality. The DC print comics of the 1990s first broached the subject, and then the silver screen followed suit: superhero death became more than a calculated risk as it moved from distinct possibility to actual occurrence. But the bereaved in these deaths, like mourners in virtually all cultural groups thus far studied, become active when faced with a loved one's death; "getting busy doing something seems to be a widespread natural human response to loss" (Hoy, 2013, p. 66).

This chapter focuses on funeral elements accompanying four death events in these films, all of which occur in traumatic circumstances. First, there are gravesite visits by Martha and Clark Kent to the grave of Jonathan Kent following his storm-related highway death in *Man of Steel* (Roven, Nolan, Thomas, Snyder, & Snyder, 2013). *Batman v Superman: Dawn of Justice* (Roven et al., 2016) both opens and closes with funeral scenes, beginning with the double-casket funeral procession for a young Bruce Wayne's murdered parents and ending with the dual-scene funeral for Clark Kent and his alter ego, Superman. Finally, *Guardians of the Galaxy, Volume 2* (Feige & Gunn, 2017) ends with a stirring 31st-century funeral for Yondu Udonta following his heroic and sacrificial death in an atmosphere without oxygen.

The funeral rituals depicted in the post-9/11 DC and Marvel superhero films provide rich examples of Hoy's (2013) five anchors of funeral rituals observed throughout history and around the globe. These funeral rituals depict the visceral ways humans (and nonhumans, as well) respond to the overwhelming emotional experience of loss through the use of (1) significant symbols, (2) gathered community, (3) ritual action, (4) connection to cultural heritage, and (5) transition of the corpse (pp. 4–5).

Taken together, these five anchors of funeral rituals seem to work in concert to help mourners accomplish the primary values of funerals in the grief process articulated by Worden (2018): to help make real the fact of the loss, to give people an opportunity to express thoughts and feelings about the deceased, to draw a social support network close to the bereaved family, and to affirm the life of the deceased. Perhaps all five funeral ceremony anchors working together create a synergy greater than the sum of the parts.

**Significant Symbols.** Whether in coffins, hearses, flowers, religious artifacts, or mourning colors, mourners have depended on symbols to express sorrow throughout history and around the globe. In *Man of Steel* (Roven et al., 2013), viewers are not definitively told of the death of Jonathan Kent, Clark's earthly father, even though viewers are exposed to the traumatic scene as he struggles to free himself from the family car as a deadly tornado approaches. While viewers do not see the elder Kent die, the graveyard and the tombstone with Jonathan Kent's name engraved remove all doubt as to the elder Kent's fate. Grave markers are important symbols of death and of life, generally commemorating at the very least the deceased's full name and dates of birth and death, but often also including epitaphs and other biographical tribute statements.

In the dual-scene funeral of Clark Kent and Superman at the conclusion of *Batman v Superman: Dawn of Justice* (Roven et al., 2016), viewers are bombarded with symbols, ranging from the simple pine coffin conveyed by buckboard and pasture horses in Smallville, Kansas, to the highly militaristic rites for Superman, staged at none other than the United States' highly symbolic hero burial ground, Arlington National Cemetery. The horse-drawn gun carriage transporting Superman's casket is draped with an American flag, which is folded with precision at the grave as howitzers fire the gun salute, all striking uses of symbolism that Alaniz (2014) suggests are reminiscent of the 1963 state funeral for President John F. Kennedy.

**Gathered Community**. Neither Clark Kent's mother, Martha, or his beloved Lois Lane are left to face his death alone; instead, they are surrounded by community members who solemnly join them in interring their dead. In the scene that begins *Batman v Superman: Dawn of Justice* (Roven et al., 2016), the young Bruce Wayne and his family are surrounded by concerned others as they mourn.

The final scene of *Guardians of the Galaxy, Volume 2* (Feige et al., 2017), however, may provide the best example in these films of gathered community in the face of death. After Yondu's sacrificial death, a small group gathers to place candles, flowers, and memorabilia around the fallen hero's corpse, and this gathering provides the space for remembrance and story-keeping. Peter Quill reflects on his life with Yondu and refutes earlier affirmations that Yondu was not a father-figure, but, rather, a kidnapper. As Peter and friends attend to Yondu's corpse, Quill admits to the depth of the father–son bond and then adds, "I had a pretty cool dad. What I am trying to say here is sometimes that thing you're searching for your whole life, it's right there by your side all along and you don't even know it" (Feige et al., 2017, 2:00).

In a final gesture to gathered community, viewers hear Rocket's voice simply declare, "They came" and then further explains, "I sent word to Yondu's old Ravager buddies and told them what he did." Quill replies, "It's a Ravager funeral" and then the colorful electronic fireworks ensue (Feige et al., 2017, 2:04).

**Ritual Action**. Words are often elusive in the face of loss; they can be especially hard-to-come-by when death comes unexpectedly and traumatically. One of the common hallmarks of death rituals throughout history is the trait of mourners engaging in the adaptive actions of planning and participating in ceremonies, raising money for important causes, and arranging the varied details of funerals.

Many of these ritual actions are also highly symbolic: lighting a candle, ordering flowers, preparing food for the bereaved, or selecting memorabilia for a life-honoring display at the funeral. The broad community grief for Superman is exemplified in the hundreds of mourners gathered for a candlelight vigil; the camera shot of a handmade sign speaks to the collective grief: "If you seek his monument, look around you" (Roven et al., 2016, 2:20).

In a gesture of irony at the Smallville graveyard ceremony, Bruce Wayne and Diana Prince engage in hushed conversation after other mourners have departed, a short distance from where Lois Lane continues her own private ceremony. Bruce notes, "All those circuses back east burying an empty box", to which Diana responds, "They don't know how to honor him except as a soldier" (Roven et al., 2016, 2:19). Lois Lane's private ceremony provides the setting for what is perhaps the most ubiquitous ritual action, also notable in its rich symbolism – shoveling soil onto the coffin. In her private observance, Lois grasps a handful of earth with her engagement ring-clad left hand and tosses it into the grave (Roven et al., 2016, 2:23). Words are not spoken at these ceremonies; symbols and actions in the presence of gathered community do all the "talking".

**Connection to Cultural Heritage**. Yondu's funeral differs; here, mourners speak about their loss and the deceased's life. Typical for these kinds of discourse, the gathered community engages in the adaptive task of *remembering*, a type of life-honoring storytelling that seems vital to the process of grief that leads to healthy integration of the loss "as the bereaved person shares stories and reflects on the values that underlie those stories" (Hoy, 2016, p. 27). While eulogy can become artificially positive, one value of this shared storytelling is that the gathered community affirms the character qualities it collectively observed exemplified in the life of the deceased, frequently describing this person with honorific terms such as compassionate, generous, kind, patriotic, and unselfish. Speaking aloud about these values seems to be an important way mourners both honor the life of the deceased and transmit the values heritage to other hearers.

In the gathered storytelling at Yondu's funeral, Rocket reflects more honestly than many eulogists in contemporary memorial gatherings: "He didn't chase them away" to which Quill replies simply, "No". Rocket continues: "… even though he yelled at them and was always mean, and stole batteries he didn't need" (Feige et al., 2017, 2:05). In cutaway scenes, other Ravager characters also reflect on the heritage of Yondu's life and in each setting, the remembrance concludes with a simple military salute.

Music and rhythm play vital roles in the cultural heritage of funeral rituals around the world and throughout history, as well. In the dual-scene funeral for Clark Kent and Superman, both ceremonies are accompanied by the strains of the Christian hymn, "Amazing Grace" on bagpipes, a ubiquitous cultural symbol common at the funerals for contemporary heroes – fallen military personnel, firefighters, and police officers. Befitting the theme of Peter Quill's acknowledgment of Yondu as father-figure, viewers hear the familiar strains of Cat Stevens' American folk song, "Father and Son" (Stevens, 1970, Side 2, track 5).

**Transition of the Corpse**. Humans do not generally leave the dead where they fall. At the close of the epic battle scene climaxing *Batman v Superman: Dawn of Justice* (Roven et al., 2016), viewers reach the uncomfortable conclusion that Superman has died. Batman slowly lifts Superman's lifeless corpse from the ledge where he perished, lowering it into the arms of a disbelieving Lois Lane. This event marks the beginning of death rituals for the "Man of Steel" as viewers recall a death pose eerily reminiscent of Michelangelo's 15th-century sculpture, *Pietà*.

In the same corpse-to-be-reckoned-with way, the funeral of Yondu features his body up close and personal. The corpse is "laid out" on a bier and lovingly attended to by friends bearing flowers, candles, and other personally meaningful items. In the presence of the body, family and friends are drawn to share stories; dead bodies seem to have a penchant for attracting storytelling in that they provide a point of focus around which experiences and events are recalled (Feige et al., 2017). This phenomenon is clearly evidenced by the custom of funeral "visitations" or "calling hours" in many communities. The mourners themselves then place Yondu's remains in the cremation retort-like receptacle, where his corpse is absorbed by light. In the superhero funeral, the dead body remains a part of the funeral ritual throughout the process until the rituals are sufficiently progressed so that community mourners can actually take leave of the corpse in a formal rite of separation.

## 16.1 Clinical Considerations

Smith (2012) suggests that the use of "borrowed narratives" has strong application in supporting and counseling bereaved individuals. It would seem that relying on the superhero films and a wide cultural awareness of superhero narratives might provide an important shared story with which many bereaved individuals can connect.

Moreover, superhero funerals provide a fitting model to remind mourners and professionals alike of the elements that seem vital to incorporate in funeral rituals. Because of the historical and cross-cultural presence of these anchors, it is likely also true that mourners will be best served when attention is paid to all five in creating rituals.

Superheroes are depicted as enjoying relationships with others so it is most appropriate that their deaths are acknowledged and their lives honored. Funeral rituals in these films provide fitting models for accomplishing these tasks in honoring the everyday superheroes in every family and community.

## References


Alaniz, J. (2014). *Death, disability, and the superhero: The silver age and beyond*. Jackson: University Press of Mississippi.

Feige, K. (Producer), & Gunn, J. (Director). (2017). *Guardians of the galaxy, volume 2* [Motion Picture], United States: Marvel Studios.

Fulton, R. (1994). The funeral in contemporary society. In R. Fulton & R. Bendicksen (Eds.), *Death and identity* (3rd ed., pp. 288–312). Philadelphia, PA: Charles Press.

van Gennep, A. (1960). *The rites of passage* (M.B. Vizedom & G.L. Caffee, Trans.). Chicago, IL: University of Chicago Press. (Original work published 1909)

Hoy, W.G. (2013). *Do funerals matter? The purposes and practices of death rituals in global perspective*. New York, NY: Routledge.

Hoy, W.G. (2016). *Bereavement groups and the role of social support: Integrating theory, research, and practice*. New York, NY: Routledge.

Kastenbaum, R. (2004). Why funerals? *Generations*, 28(2), 5–10.

Roven, C., Nolan, C., Thomas, E., & Snyder, D. (Producers), & Snyder, Z. (Director). (2013). *Man of steel* [Motion Picture]. United States: Warner Bros. Pictures.

Roven, C. & Snyder, D. (Producers), & Snyder, Z. (Director). (2016). *Batman v superman: Dawn of justice* [Motion Picture]. United States: Warner Bros. Pictures.

Smith, H.I. (2012). *Borrowed narratives: Using biographical and historical grief narratives with the bereaving*. New York, NY: Routledge.

Stevens, Cat (1970). Father and son. On *Tea for the tillerman* [Record]. London, UK: Morgan Studios.

Worden, J.W. (2018). *Grief counseling and grief therapy: A handbook for the mental health practitioner* (5th ed.). New York, NY: Springer.

# 17 Black Panther

## Exploring Grief, Ancestral Connection, and the Duty to Carry On

*Tashel C. Bordere and Marshall Allen*

Superheroes possess physical power and strength far exceeding that of human beings. Yet, traumatic loss and grief exerts its own power in ways that equalize and transform us all. In the superhero movie *Black Panther* (Feige & Coogler, 2018), themes of violent death and loss are pronounced. Within this film, we are able to witness the profound grief of two blood-related cousins of African heritage – T'Challa (King of Wakanda/Black Panther) and N'Jadaka (U.S.-born Warrior), who share the experience of father loss through violence. We see their humanity and unique transformations through loss as they navigate cultural expectations related to identity, including the "duty to carry on", in distinct familial, geographic, economic, and sociopolitical contexts.

The *Black Panther* film communicates the historical and contemporary richness of culture, land, and pride of African countries with a focus on the fictional country of Wakanda. It simultaneously highlights historical encounters with loss (e.g., loss of land, safety) and the continued economic repercussions for Black families of African heritage in the United States. The film masterfully addresses the centrality of understanding privilege, marginalization, and culture in grief and coping patterns for black male populations.

In this chapter, we discuss ways that patterns of violent death and coping in the film mirror patterns found among young black males in the United States. We address parallels and divergences between T'Challa and N'Jadaka in coping with loss within contexts and describe ways in which they are transformed through their loss and grief experiences. Clinical implications and suggestions for interventions are provided.

### 17.1 Patterns of Violent Death

The prominence of violent death for boys and men in *Black Panther* mirrors its pervasiveness among black males in the United States. As a young adult, T'Challa, of Wakanda, was faced with his father's (T'Chaka) sudden, violent death in an explosion. Similarly, N'Jadaka (Erik), T'Challa's U.S.-born cousin, was faced with the death of his father (N'Jobu) during childhood as a consequence of violence, literally and figuratively, occurring at the hands of T'Chaka (N'Jobu's older brother) (Feige et al., 2018).

atterns of death in the film are also similar to those in the /hich socioeconomic standing offers little protection for black , against a violent demise. T'Challa, the son of King T'Chaka d the Black Panther, was born into a life of economic privilege nation of Wakanda. Yet, both T'Chaka, who lived among wealth, n, N'Jadaka, who lived amid poverty, were conjointly faced with th deaths of their fathers.

Unlike T'Challa, N'Jadaka did not witness his father's death, but like his grief-stricken cousin, he was the first to arrive at his father's gruesome death scene. In N'Jadaka's case, he arrived to find his slain father lying on their living room floor with his Uncle T'Chaka's claws buried deeply in his father's chest. This, too, is similar to patterns in violent death in which the perpetrator is male and is often known to the victim (U.S. Department of Justice, 2019).

## 17.2 Loss in Context: T'Challa

*Black Panther* (Feige et al., 2018) provides a glimpse of the diversity in losses, grief expressions, and opportunity structures for two men of color, related by blood, but distinguished by social positionality (e.g., geographic region, financial status, ethnicity, race, gender, class, age) in assuming the "duty to carry on" amid their profound grief.

Within African culture, life is built around preparation for death with the knowledge that relationships do not end at death (Adkins, 2007). Although T'Challa had been prepared across his development to succeed his father at death, he experienced T'Chaka's death with sadness and anger. He felt guilt in his inability to protect his father and sought vengeance for his father's death both as a way of honoring his father and in keeping with his duty to carry on as the succeeding King and Black Panther.

T'Challa traveled to meet his mother and sister in preparation for the customary coronation rituals observed in transitioning the King of Wakanda and Black Panther. He solemnly asks his mother, Ramonda, about her well-being on this bittersweet day in which he would gain status and power as a consequence of his father's tragic death. Exemplifying strength, characteristic of African culture, she lifted her head high and exclaimed, "Proud! Your father and I would talk about this day all the time!" (Feige et al., 2018, 00:15:04). Continuing with an affirmation of T'Chaka's continued presence in his physical absence, she says, "He is with us and it is your time to be King" (Feige et al., 2018, 00:15:1). Ramonda's response represents African-centered values of pushing forward amid pain and struggle, present-time orientation, and recognition of eternal ancestral bonds in life and loss (Rosenblatt & Wallace, 2005).

T'Challa also experienced betrayal, anger, and a loss of trust upon learning a long-held family secret about his father and Uncle Zuri's (brother of T'Chaka & N'Jobu) involvement in the murder of N'Jobu (father of N'Jadaka) and their decision to leave N'Jadaka, a young child, alone and unprotected in an unsafe environment.

Amid his desire, initially, to seek revenge for his father's death and his anger around his father's unconscionable behaviors in the death of his uncle and cousin's abandonment, T'Challa was also able to observe the destructive behaviors and thoughts that manifest when individuals are consumed with vengeance. We see this in *Captain America: Civil War* (Feige, Feige, & Russo, 2016). In his encounter with the perpetrator responsible for his father's death, T'Challa learned that the perpetrator was a victim–survivor who spent years preoccupied with seeking revenge following the death of his wife, son, and father due to an Avenger's inadvertent destructive actions. T'Challa was changed, transformed through this encounter. "I am sorry about your father. He seemed a good man. With a dutiful son". Responding with empathy and pity, T'Challa says, "Vengeance has consumed you. It's consuming them" (i.e., Avengers). Retracting the claws he intended to use to kill his father's murderer, he exclaimed, "I'm done letting it consume me. Justice will come soon enough" (Feige et al., 2016, 02:08:45–02:09:15).

## 17.3 Loss in Context: N'Jadaka

Through Erik's lived experiences with disenfranchisement as a black male child and man in the United States and as a Wakandan of mixed heritage, we are exposed to numerous traumatic losses creating shifts and transformations in his identities – Erik, N'Jadaka, Killmonger, King, Black Panther – and coping mechanisms. We are also exposed to the suffocated grief or penalties (Bordere, 2016) that accompany life for him in the margins where resources are available but not easily accessible, where justice delayed was experienced as justice denied (see King – Letter from a Birmingham Jail, 1963).

Across Erik's development, he was faced with myriad significant death and nondeath losses. He lived in a poverty-stricken, low-resourced community, in which his mother was deceased. Erik was reared by his father, N'Jobu, in a single-parent household without the advantages and resources afforded by his Wakandan family, including those provided for his cousin, T'Challa. Thus, throughout his childhood and early adulthood, he lived with the loss of wealth, status, and security. As a consequence of discrimination from his Wakandan family about his parents' heterogamous union and his bicultural ethnicities, he lived much of his life with a loss of recognition as a Wakandan.

N'Jobu persisted in teaching N'Jadaka both about Black history in America and about life in Wakanda. In acknowledgment of his son's bicultural identities, N'Jobu provided him with two names – Erik (U.S. heritage) and N'Jadaka (Wakandan heritage). Erik was socialized with an awareness of the strengths of his African heritage and the social and economic disadvantages for people of African heritage living in the United States due to systemic oppression. He observed the tremendous energy that his father expended in his calculated social action efforts aimed at reducing inequities impacting Black communities. Erik's historical knowledge, acquired through his father's socialization practices (Livingston & McAdoo, 2007), is evidenced in his young adulthood when visiting a museum to reclaim the vibranium taken from Wakanda and inappropriately credited to a European nation. Erik corrects the curator, interjecting – "It [the referenced artifact] was taken by British soldiers but it's FROM Wakanda and it's made of vibranium!" (Feige et al., 2018, 00:16:22).

Although resources do not remove the pain of grief, they allow for greater opportunities for mental health support. T'Challa's loss experience was accompanied by significant gains in his social, economic, and political positionality and a wider support network. Similarly bereaved, Erik's experience of father loss created additional complex nondeath losses in economic security, safety, and identity for a child who already occupied intersecting positions (black, male, young) of marginality and vulnerability. Erik, disenfranchised and parentless, was prematurely placed in a position in which his decision making and actions revolved around surviving life and death (Bordere, 2014).

Lacking the social capital and securities afforded T'Challa, Erik's grief response is vastly different. Erik's grief, including his decision making, anger, and destructive behaviors, were fueled by multiple experiences with betrayal and trauma – "I found my daddy with panther claws in his chest!" (Feige et al., 2018, 01:15:46), unjust loss, and reinforcement of gendered expectations around male aggression. He was motivated by his basic needs to survive, to honor his father, and out of a sense of duty. He was also motivated by collectivist values within African culture to work for the good of the community by eradicating disparities and unjust losses in Black communities.

Marginalized individuals are often faced with resistance and swift consequences when speaking truth to power. This resistance is best illustrated when Erik embarks on his long-awaited journey to Wakanda and reveals his identity as N'Jadaka, son of N'Jobu, to the tribal elders. In lieu of embracing and making amends with N'Jadaka, Ramonda and the elders admonish him and collectively deny his identity, birthrights, and belongingness in the Wakandan family (Feige et al., 2018). This is tragic but unsurprising, given that privilege affords the unearned advantage of defining the reality of marginalized individuals even in the presence of contradictory information (Bordere, 2019), such as that provided by N'Jadaka to confirm his biological connection and associated rights to the throne as a Wakandan.

Ultimately, N'Jadaka is fatally injured in a violent battle with T'Challa for the throne. For N'Jadaka, solace would only come at death.

## 17.4 Culture and Healing Transformation

Cultural beliefs and practices offer opportunities for healing. The value and practice of ancestral connection allowed for both T'Challa and N'Jadaka to seek answers from their deceased fathers.

T'Challa's healing transformation was evidenced by his commitment to alliance formation in decreasing inequities following the death of his cousin, N'Jadaka. Influenced by N'Jadaka's desire to diminish economic oppression,

T'Challa (with his family) provides Wakandan resources to the impoverished community in which N'Jadaka was reared. T'Challa transformed his uncle's traumatic memorial site into a place for community connection, resource exchange, and enriching educational opportunities for marginalized youth and families. Through this act, T'Challa changed the course of Wakandan history and relationships with marginalized families existing outside of Wakanda. He was truly transformed to be the Black Panther.

## 17.5 Clinical Considerations

Black families are diverse and not monolithic/homogeneous. Individuals born in African countries outside the United States may appropriately define themselves based on their countries of origin. Although the Wakandans were similar in complexion, it is not surprising that they distinguished themselves from black people in the United States. Despite visible similarities in skin color, African individuals and families may not view themselves as African-Americans nor identify with the racialized experiences of African-Americans or Black individuals residing in the United States.

Further, a great deal of Erik/N'Jadaka's grief and sense of duty to carry on was related to *identity and quality of life losses* as a function of familial and social disadvantage.

N'Jadaka coped through maladaptive, destructive behaviors, which proved to be costly for society and contributed to his violent death. Thus, it is imperative for clinicians to be able to engage fully with clients who desire to address racialized or ethnocentric concerns and coping around everyday experiences with unjust loss and discrimination. In clinical work with oppressed populations, it is central that clinicians and counselors representing privileged statuses can remain present through active listening, free of distraction from fragility (e.g., see "white fragility" – DiAngelou, 2011, p. 54) or from vicarious trauma and collective grief among counselors representing intersecting marginalized statuses (e.g., female, Latino), so that candid discussions, resource allocation, and alliance formation are possible. Training in race-based trauma is particularly essential for Caucasian helping professionals both for increased clinician/counselor self-awareness, skill development and for engagement in ethically sound research and clinical practice with individuals and families occupying intersecting (race, sex, income) marginalized and privileged identities (Bordere, 2019; Bryant-Davis & Ocampo, 2005).

## 17.6 Intervention Strategies

Interventions with black male youth and families are experienced as enfranchising when they focus on the life of the deceased and continual ancestral connections. They are most effective when provided early and across children's development, and proactive measures are taken to avoid or limit future trauma and loss exposure. Interventions following homicide loss must include a focus on survivor safety, prosocial coping strategies valued within African culture (educational achievement, healthy human relationships, spirituality), acknowledgment of loss and trauma (see *Five A's of Culturally Conscientious Practice* – Bordere, 2016), and spaces and places for catharsis, support, and continuity of care.

## References


Adkins, E. (2007). Death in the family: Historical descriptions and funerary display of African American families. In H.P. McAdoo (Ed.), *Black families* (pp. 143–156). Thousand Oaks, CA: SAGE Publications.

Bordere, T. (2019). Suffocated grief, resilience, and survival among African American families. In M. H. Jacobsen & A. Petersen (Eds.), *Exploring grief: Towards a sociology of sorrow*. New York: Routledge.

Bordere, T.C. (2014). Adolescents and homicide. In K. Doka & A. Tucci (Eds.), *Helping adolescents cope with loss*. Washington, DC: Hospice Foundation of America.

Bordere, T.C. (2016). "Not gonna be laid out to dry": Cultural mistrust in end of life care and strategies for trust-building. In D. Harris & T. C. Bordere (Eds.), *Handbook of social justice in loss and grief: Exploring diversity, equity, and inclusion* (pp. 75–84). New York: Routledge.

Bordere, T.C. (2018). Grief and loss among First Nations and African American youth. In C. Arnold (Ed.), *Understanding child and adolescent grief: Supporting loss and facilitating growth* (pp. 135–146). New York: Routledge.

Bryant-Davis, T., & Ocampo, C. (2005). The trauma of racism: Implications for counseling, research, and education. *The Counseling Psychologist*, 33(4), 574–578.

DiAngelou, R. (2011). White fragility. *International Journal of Critical Pedagogy*, 3(3), 54–70.

Feige, K. (Producer), & Russo, A., & Russo, J. (Directors). (2016). *Captain America: Civil War* [Motion Picture]. United States: Marvel Studios.

Feige, K. (Producer), & Coogler, R. (Director). (2018). Black panther [Motion Picture]. United States: Marvel Studios.

Feige, K. (Producer), & Russo, A., & Russo, J. (Director). (2014). *Captain America: The winter soldier* [Motion Picture]. United States: Marvel Studios.

King, M.L. (1963). From the Birmingham Jail. *Christianity and Crisis*, 23, 89–91.

Livingston, J.N., & McAdoo, J.L. (2007). The roles of African American fathers in the socialization of their children. In H. P. McAdoo (Ed.), *Black families* (pp. 219–237). Thousand Oaks, CA: Sage Publications.

Rosenblatt, P.C., & Wallace, B.R. (2005). *African American grief.* New York, NY: Routledge

U.S. Justice Department: Federal Bureau of Investigation. (2019). Uniform Crime Report, Crime in the United States, 2018 (Released Fall 2019), Expanded Homicide Data. Retrieved from https://ucr.fbi.gov/crime-in-the-u.s/2018/crime-in-the-u.s.-2018/topic-pages/expanded-homicide

# Part V

# Grief and Family Systems: Superheroes and Relationship Types

# 18 Observations on a Hero's Response to Homicide

*Laura Takacs and Edward Rynearson*

When the life of someone loved is violated by a violent, volitional dying (the 3 V's of homicidal dying), grief can be overwhelmed by traumatic themes of helplessness and a retaliatory demand for retribution and justice. Could there be a more welcome time and space for the presence of a heroic figure? Someone to apprehend the killer, ensure punishment, and restore justice and honor is a vital figure in our oldest myths and scriptures. Unfortunately, only myths include such a figure after a homicide, and with the advent of Western law, there can be little promise of "heroic" involvement by the police or courts.

It was not always that way. In preliterate times when homicide was a trauma shared by the family's entire clan, grief-stricken family members had a more active role in seeking retaliation, retribution, and justice. Their leader met with the clan leader of the perpetrator to arrange an exchange of "blood" – in money or violence. The family was not helpless. While rare, justice killings continue to this day, but in 12th-century England Henry II (1154–1189) initiated a dramatic change (Green, 1976). He could no longer tolerate the social mayhem of multiple homicides, so he established homicide as a Capital Crime, a crime against the King, and appointed coroners to investigate each homicide and juries to establish guilt, punishment, and retribution. Since then, the family has never reestablished an active role in the criminal–judicial aftermath of homicide.

Without an active social role after homicide, the family must continue their own "heroic" and private inquest for retaliation, retribution, and justice. This inquest contains vivid themes of revenge and avenge.

*Revenge*, the act of committing a harmful action (retaliation) against a person or group, remains a timeless and ubiquitous psychological response after homicidal dying. We see this conflict in the comic superhero universes as the dark path to become a villain. Conversely, in modern times, *avenging* a loved one's honor is seeking justice or retribution rather than personal retaliation.

A desire to avenge is often something survivors seek for others rather than themselves. We see this woven throughout story arcs of most superheroes, as well as their conflict for revenge or justice.

When the death of a loved one is of one's own volition or suicide, survivors rarely feel revengeful but, like survivors of homicide, may be driven to avenge and restore the honor of the deceased by regulating social policies such as lenient gun laws or negligence within the health/mental health system that did not "protect" the deceased from dying.

Homicidal dying is a violation against the person who died. Not condoned by law or rule, homicide often produces fantasies of revenge. In clinical practice, most survivors with strong feelings of revenge do not seek support. Survivors with intense revenge perceive what is needed to be changed or "fixed" is not the revengeful impulse within the survivor but to be externally enacted – directed at the perpetrator.

For survivors experiencing a homicidal dying, Restorative Retelling (RR) can address feelings of both revenge and the desire to avenge the deceased. When thoughts of revenge surface, a turning point in healing can happen when it is realized that revenge, ultimately, will not bring back the deceased and could cause further harm to surviving loved ones. Evoking the voice of the deceased, bringing him or her into the conversation, which is often practiced in RR, can be a powerful neutralizer in revenge fantasies. When asking clients to reflect on how their loved one would help when difficult thoughts or feeling arise, such as, "How would *Bob* help you when you're feeling overwhelmed with anger and revenge?" the ability to reflect upon and identify words of encouragement and comfort from their loved one is restorative. Clients with a need to take action to prevent a similar fate for other families also find comfort and guidance when reflecting on what their loved one would say: "*Bob* would tell me he is proud of what I am doing to try to change things".

RR allows survivors to explore feelings of revenge and retribution, calling upon the deceased to help navigate such powerful emotions. By evoking a loved one's words, imagining expressions of support and guidance, difficult questions may find resolve, "I know Bob wouldn't want me to feel so much hate". The bond between the survivor and deceased continues as the survivor also has opportunities to say things not said before the death and to ask forgiveness, if needed (Rynearson, 2012).

The goal of RR cannot be the "heroic" rescue of the deceased or reversal of their dying; instead a retelling and reframing of the dying through RR establishes a role for the family member in the dying drama; a restorative presence rather than a helpless witnessing and rage – a more realistic and meaningful clinical goal (Rynearson & Salloum, 2011).

## References

Green, T.A. (1976). The jury and the English law of homicide. *Michigan Law Review*, 74, 413–499.

Rynearson, E.K. (2012). Invoking an alliance with the deceased after violent death. In R.A. Neimeyer (Ed.), *Techniques of grief therapy* (pp. 91–94). New York, NY: Routledge

Rynearson, E.K., & Salloum, A. (2011). Restorative Retelling: Revising the narrative of violent death. In R.A. Neimeyer, D.L. Harris, H.R. Winokuer, & G.F. Thornton (Eds.), *Grief and bereavement in contemporary society: Bridging research and practice* (pp. 177–188). New York, NY: Routledge

# 19 What Drax the Destroyer and Cable Help Us Understand About Grieving Fathers and Survivors of Familial Homicide

*Selin Santos and Louis A. Gamino*

When a child is murdered, the suffering specific to grieving fathers and their unique efforts to adapt may go unrecognized. Grief literature more often focuses on bereaved mothers, while the voices of grieving fathers may be underrepresented or misunderstood (Brown, 2017; Wickie and Marwit, 2001). In the United States, 1,208 children are murdered annually, leaving behind bereaved families and close others (U.S. Department of Justice, 2017). With much of our research and clinical attention focused on bereaved mothers, homicide-bereaved fathers are often an overlooked group who experience special pain and coping challenges associated with the violent death of a child.

Superhero characters are fictional. However, hero storylines portray important masculine characteristics pertaining to fatherhood grief. Superheroes' behavior can illuminate important compensatory strategies applicable to clinical work with bereaved fathers. Drax the Destroyer and Cable are both homicide-bereaved fathers whose grief responses and coping efforts are worth exploring as case examples to use as analogies for clinical considerations and intervention strategies.

## 19.1 Drax the Destroyer

Drax the Destroyer, born into a tribal and clan-like culture, was an intergalactic criminal seeking revenge on Ronan the Accuser for killing his wife, Hovat, and daughter, Kamaria, during a randomly perpetrated genocide on his home planet (Feige & Gunn, 2014). After the death of his family, Drax sought vengeance and went on a killing spree, which led to his eventual imprisonment. During his journey for revenge, he joined the Guardians of the Galaxy. Ultimately, he encountered Ronan after sending him a transmission about the Guardians' location. On arrival, Ronan dismissed Drax's claim that he murdered his family before subduing Drax with little effort. With the Guardians of the Galaxy, Drax has a second encounter with Ronan. Before the battle with Ronan, Drax understands that if he meets his demise in the fight, he will be able to be reunited with his wife and daughter. After Ronan's defeat, Drax found that Ronan was merely a lackey for Thanos, whom he declared as his next target (Feige & Gunn, 2014).

## 19.2 Cable

Cable was part of a task force charged with eradicating mutants vying for supremacy on Earth. He became embroiled in a feud with one of the mutants, Russel Collins (Kinberg, Reynolds, Donner, & Leitch, 2018). Caught in the middle of the feud were Cable's wife, Aliya, and his daughter, Hope, who were both murdered by Russel. After finding his home scorched, Cable sought retribution. He went back in time intending to kill young Russel before he becomes war driven and murders thousands of others. After multiple attempts to kill Russel as a child, Cable befriends Deadpool and joins the X-Force, heroes intent on saving young Russel. Cable ultimately decided to join them and allow Deadpool one chance to convince Russel of not committing his first murder, so that Cable would not break his own moral code against killing a young child (Kinberg et al., 2018). In a turn of events, Cable felt that Deadpool had taken his one chance and shoots Russel. Deadpool threw himself into the bullet's path, sacrificing himself to save Russel. Remorseful over witnessing Deadpool's sacrifice, Cable went back in time a few moments to use a token as a bullet shield and prevent Deadpool's death. Deadpool's selflessness inspired Russel not to turn down the path of murderous destruction and join the X-Force as well as convinced Cable to stay in the present timeline to prevent a war-driven future with a selfless sacrifice of not using his time-traveling device to return to the future to be with his family (Kinberg et al., 2018).

## 19.3 Clinical Considerations

Fear and Anger. The homicide of a child breeds fear and anger in bereaved parents, as in the case of Drax and Cable (Rynearson, 1988; Seymour, Gaboury, & Harrold, 2012). Fear arises from parents engaging in continuous recollections of the murder and ruminative worry about the safety of themselves and other family members. The fear can last for several years and lead to a worldview of unkindness and malevolence (Peach & Klass, 1987). Also, homicide-bereaved parents commonly experience anger toward the murderer and may fantasize about exacting revenge or engaging in retribution (Boelen, van Denderen, & de Keijser, 2016; Rynearson, 1984). According to Rynearson, these feelings represent normative clan-type responses to perpetration and the taking of human life that predate the Western legal system.

Peach and Klass (1987) and Rynearson (1988) posit that anger can morph into a quest for personal vengeance and retaliation. For some homicide-bereaved families, these feelings may never be present, or the feelings may diminish over the course of lengthy judicial proceedings and transform into seeking justice through sentencing and advocacy to prevent future criminal violations from the perpetrator. Drax's and Cable's responses to their families' violent deaths are similar in that the fear and anger propelled them to try preventing the perpetrators from harming other families. The superheroes appear to combat their own fears with a riveting focus on pursuing the perpetrators and exacting preventative revenge. Contemporary clinical interventions focus on redirecting such rage so as not to perpetuate a cycle of violence.

Parental Competence. Fathers, like Drax and Cable, may feel they failed to protect their child, which can be experienced as a deficiency in parental competence. Klass and Marwit (1989) define parental competence as a sacred obligation to protect the security and viability of the parent–child attachment bond. When fathers experience the murder of their child, the adequacy of their parental competence is threatened. Both Drax and Cable manifest shame and remorse over their inability to prevent the deaths of their family members and spring into action to compensate for these painful feelings as a way of restoring their parental competence.

Drax's and Cable's rageful anguish is intensified by the additional murder of their wives. The double murders enhanced their desperation and stoked disregard for their own mortality. Similar to Drax and Cable, Rynearson (1984) found that the retribution behaviors exhibited by homicide survivors were likely to be intensified due to the intentionality of the death, disproportionately light consequences for the perpetrator, and perception of a weak judicial system, which fails to meet their standards of punishment.

Warrior Archetype. According to Moore and Gillette (1990), the Warrior archetype represents purposeful aggression, decisive skill, loyalty, discipline, emotional detachment, and creative destroying. Aggression in the context of mature masculinity means having an internal force or motivation that propels an individual to fight for salutary goals. Similarly, creative destroying is focused on eradicating evil to supplant it with good (Moore & Gillette, 1990). The Warrior's loyalty centers on either a cause, higher power, or community of people that are perceived to be more than themselves (Moore & Gillette, 1990). Drax and Cable personify this Warrior archetype in their respective storylines and cultures in which they are depicted. Mindfulness encompasses an overall awareness of life and death as the understanding that life is brief and allows the Warrior to understand the importance of making decisions (Moore & Gillette, 1990). In terms of emotional detachment, the Warrior focuses on the missions at hand and rids himself of all fear and doubt. Drax and Cable both maintain a Warrior mindset with their belief in creative destroying, after the violent murder of their children. Their goal is revenge and punishment of their child's murderer, maintaining loyalty to their own cause and idea of righteousness – to "save the world" from villains.

Eradicating Death. Through seeking vengeance and retribution, both Drax and Cable seem to carry an unconscious mission of eradicating death itself. Intrapsychically speaking, Drax and Cable are attempting to kill murderers – villains who have killed their families and many others as well. In a way, these heroes are attempting to kill killing. However, despite their futile attempts, it is not possible for them to reverse the murders of their children and wives due to the finality of death. A common trend among homicide-bereaved fathers is attempting to bring order to a world that is chaotic, disrespectful, and unpredictable. Sudden homicide shatters any assumption that the world is a safe and secure place. Bereaved fathers' redoubled efforts to make the world "safe" imply a wish to defeat death entirely.

Forgiveness. Alternative models to retribution and revenge killing do exist. In the case of the mass murder in West Nickel Mines, Pennsylvania, where an assailant shot and killed 10 young Amish girls in their one-room schoolhouse, the Amish response involved prayer, mourning, and burial, while blaming, second-guessing, or revenge were conspicuously absent (Smoyak, 2006). The spiritual beliefs of this traditional religious sect endorsed the principle of redemptive suffering – absorbing the anguish of the murders in an effort to transform homicidal hate into brotherly love. Superhero Cable's metamorphosis from revenge-minded bounty hunter to X-Force member who foregoes his quest for retribution and spares the life of his nemesis for the sake of peace shows some parallels to this Amish way.

## 19.4 Intervention Strategies

Social Support. Being the parent of a murdered child is an unwanted, isolating role. Family and friends are often confused about how to engage with parents of murdered children and may withdraw their support at the very moment when it is most needed (Wickie & Marwit, 2001). Also, child murder shatters the expectation that parents outlive their children (Peach & Klass, 1987), an expectancy bolstered by modern medicine, where child mortality in developed countries is seen as mostly preventable (National Organization of Parents of Murdered Children [NOPMC], 2019). With the shock of the murder of one's child, parents become disillusioned and have more negative views of the world (Wickie & Marwit, 2001). The murder of a child violates parents' and survivors' perceptions of childhood as an age of innocence. Consolidating social support for bereaved fathers is a potential antidote to isolative feelings of victimization and rogue revenge fantasies. Suggested resources at the conclusion of this chapter offer many avenues for bereaved fathers to connect with others who have experienced a similar tragedy.

Overcoming Gender Stereotypes. Differences between male and female reactions in parental grief may be gender linked (NOPMC, 2019). Fathers often carry their grief silently, remain less verbal to protect their sense of vulnerability, and actively suppress uncomfortable feelings of helplessness and guilt. Stoicism may be interpreted as being "strong" in the interest of supporting and protecting his family. Many fathers exhibit instrumental patterns of grieving (Doka & Martin, 2010), whereby doing the activities required by a death in the family, e.g., finalizing funeral arrangements, filing insurance claims, or even washing the cars, gives them an avenue for "working out" their grief. However, it is important to provide fathers with alternative ways to grieve and cope, including the liberty to verbalize their deepest thoughts and feelings and/or to outwardly express emotions of sadness and loss.

Drax and Cable show traditional male grief responses when they maintain silence about their internal emotional turmoil, suppress feelings of helplessness and guilt, and go directly into action. Clinicians working with bereaved fathers need to respect the integrity of traditional pathways for instrumental grieving while at the same time providing psychoeducation and support for fathers about how they can broaden their coping armamentarium. Permission-giving and gentle guidance can help reluctant fathers safely discharge some of their emotional turmoil in a secure and nonjudgmental space within the therapeutic milieu.

Defusing Revenge. Fathers who experience strong feelings of revenge, like Drax and Cable, may experience decreased levels of positive emotion and overall lower well-being. According to van Denderen, de Keijser, Gerlsma, Huisman, and Boelen (2014), high levels of revenge undermine a person's effort to cope with the traumatic death of a child. Similarly, McCullough, Bellah, Kilpatrick, and Johnson (2001) found that feelings of revenge, albeit in other nonhomicide crime victims, was associated with more intense rumination, less life satisfaction, and more negative affect. Revenge may block grief processing for homicidally bereaved fathers as they tend to ruminate and focus on why and how the murder occurred and which punishment the perpetrator deserves. These preoccupations, coupled with vengeful thoughts and feelings, may constitute a defensive avoidance of accepting the death and trauma, which leads to prolonged or complicated grief (Rynearson, 1984).

Rynearson, Correa, and Takacs (2015) developed a group treatment protocol to help survivors of violent death accommodate to their loss(es) via a process called Restorative Retelling. Particularly for survivors plagued with frequently occurring "reenactment imagery" fixated on the murdered victim's agonal distress and suffering (Rynearson, 2018), this program teaches homicide survivors three essential skills: how to calm themselves effectively so as not to become overwhelmed; how to create a healthy boundary between themselves and the actors or actions in the murder scenario to avoid psychological/emotion fusion; and how to alter the role and perspective of the survivor by reconstructing the story of loss through imaginal retelling.

Therapeutic Strategies. From the nursing literature, Kashka and Beard (1999) described a series of therapeutic strategies for survivors of murdered children authenticated by their personal experiences as homicide-bereaved parents. Their list can help clinicians see a range of interventions that could be incorporated in psychotherapy with homicide-bereaved parents, as illustrated by the following excerpts.

- Helping survivors decide whether to view the body, then preparing and debriefing with them.
- If the homicide occurred at home, providing resources to cleaning services after receiving permission from investigators.
- Coaching survivors on how to handle inquiries from media and filter their exposure to television news about the murder.
- Referring survivors to victim assistance programs or a victims' advocate office.

- Educating bereaved parents about support organizations such as Parents of Murdered Children (POMC).
- Connecting survivors with spiritual support, if needed, when questions pertaining to spirituality emerge.
- Assisting parents in rebuilding their own inner representation of their deceased child, including positive memories as well as other recollections.
- Preparing survivors for their long-term interface with the criminal justice system through arrest, arraignment, trial, conviction, punishment, appeals, and parole requests.
- Facilitating homicide-bereaved parents in healing and rebuilding their lives through community action and/or helping other survivors.

Finding Meaning. Ultimately, finding meaning in life can be a key to grief integration and resiliency in the face of profound loss (Rogers, Floyd, Seltzer, Greenberg, & Hong, 2008). Neimeyer (2001) also stressed the importance of purpose as a predictor of better overall life functioning, especially among bereaved fathers. One way that a sense of purpose can create meaning is through compensatory altruism, which promotes restoration of parental competence by joining survivor organizations, forming a neighborhood watch, donating time and resources to other survivors, facilitating support groups, or speaking out publicly against violence (a constructive way to enact the warrior archetype through social leadership). When homicide-bereaved fathers find personal meaning and take authorship of their survivor narrative, they can experience a renewed sense of purpose, and hope, which can reduce subjective grief and promote adaptation to loss.

## 19.5 Conclusions

Antiheroes Drax and Cable are homicide-bereaved fathers. In the story arcs of their personal journeys through incomprehensible grief and trauma, intense feelings of revenge turn to creative destroying as a way to seek personal revenge as well as prevent further murders by the perpetrators. Understanding their fear and anger, their perceived failure to protect their families, and their warrior mentality explains many of Drax's and Cable's actions. Similar themes may emerge in the grief trajectory of homicide-bereaved families. Borrowing from these storylines, contemporary grief professionals may better understand the psychology of homicide-bereaved fathers and assist them in alternatives to revenge violence while providing a safe place for emotional expression. Informed therapists can help bereaved fathers mobilize social support, overcome gender-based stereotypes, defuse revenge, manage their grief, and find compensatory meaning and purpose.

## References

Boelen, P.A., van Denderen, M., & de Keijser, J. (2016). Prolonged grief, posttraumatic stress, anger, and revenge phenomena following homicidal loss: The role of negative cognitions and avoidance behaviors. *Homicide Studies*, 20(2), 177–195.

Brown, A.D. (2017). The loss of a child – Surviving emotionally. *Psychology Today*. Retrieved from https://www.psychologytoday.com/us/blog/towards-recovery/201706/the-loss-child

van Denderen, M., de Keijser, J., Gerlsma, C., Huisman, M., & Boelen, P.A. (2014). Revenge and psychological adjustment after homicidal loss. *Aggressive Behavior*, 40(6), 504–511.

Doka, K.J., & Martin, T. (2010). *Grieving beyond gender: Understanding the ways men and women mourn*. New York, NY: Routledge.

Feige, K. (Producer), & Gunn, J. (Director). (2014). *Guardians of the galaxy* [Motion picture]. United States: Marvel Studios.

Kashka, M.S., & Beard, M.T. (1999). The grief of parents of murdered children: A suggested model for intervention. *Holistic Nursing Practice*, 14(1), 22–36.

Kinberg, S., Reynolds, R. & Donner, L.S. (Producers), & Leitch, D. (Director). (2018). *Deadpool 2* [Motion picture]. United States: 20th Century Fox.

Klass, D., & Marwit, S.J. (1989). Toward a model of parental grief. *Omega: Journal of Death and Dying*, 19(1), 31–50.

McCullough, M.E., Bellah, C.G., Kilpatrick, S.D., & Johnson, J.L. (2001). Vengefulness: Relationships with forgiveness, rumination, well-being, and the Big Five. *Personality and Social Psychology Bulletin*, 27(5), 601–610.

Moore, R., & Gillette, D. (1990). *King, warrior, magician, lover: Rediscovering the archetypes of the mature masculine*. New York, NY: HarperCollins Publishers.

National Organization of Parents of Murdered Children (NOPMC). (2019). Survivors of homicide victims. Retrieved from https://www.pomc.com/survivors.html

Neimeyer, R.A. (2001). *Meaning reconstruction and the experience of loss*. Washington, DC: American Psychological Association.

Peach, M.R., & Klass, D. (1987). Special issues in the grief of parents of murdered children. *Death Studies*, 11(2), 81–88.

Rogers, C.H., Floyd, F.J., Seltzer, M.M., Greenberg, J., & Hong, J. (2008). Long-term effects of the death of a child on parents' adjustment in midlife. *Journal of Family Psychology*, 22(2), 203.

Rynearson, E.K. (1984). Bereavement after homicide: A descriptive study. *The American Journal of Psychiatry*, 141(11), 1452–1454.

Rynearson, E.K. (1988). The homicide of a child. In F. M. Ochberg (Ed.), *Post-traumatic therapy and victims of violence* (pp. 213–224). New York, NY: Brunner/Mazel.

Rynearson, E.K. (2018). Disabling reenactment imagery after violent dying. *Death Studies*, 42(1), 4–8.

Rynearson, E.K., Correa, F., & Takacs, L. (2015). Accommodation to violent dying: A guide to restorative retelling and support. Retrieved from http://www.vdbs.org/docs/RR-MANUAL-REVISION-FINAL-1.pdf

Seymour, A., Gaboury, M., & Harrold, D.B. (2012). Office for Victims of Crime – Training and Technical Assistance Center. Retrieved from http://www.ncdsv.org/images/OVCTTAC_HomicideResourcePaper_2012.pdf

Smoyak, S.A. (2006). The Amish way: Coping with tragedy. *Journal of Psychosocial Nursing and Mental Health Services*, 44(12), 6–7.

U.S. Department of Justice, Federal Bureau of Investigation, Criminal Justice Information Service Division. (2017). Murdered victims by age, sex, race, and ethnicity. Retrieved from https://ucr.fbi.gov/crime-in-the-u.s/2017/crime-in-the-u.s.-2017/topic-pages/tables/expanded-homicide-data-table-2.xls

Wickie, S.K. & Marwit, S.J. (2001). Assumption world views and the grief reactions of parents of murdered children. *Omega: Journal of Death and Dying*, 42(2), 101–113.

# 20 Parents and Caregivers

## The Everyday Heroes Behind Superheroes

*Irwin Sandler and Donna Gaffney*

Although the stories of superheroes are fantasy, they bring to life real scientific evidence that the quality of caregiving is one of the most powerful resilience resources for bereaved children. By resilience resources we mean factors that strengthen children's healthy development, enabling them to lead meaningful and satisfying lives and avoid developing problems such as long-term complicated grief and depression. The stories of emerging superheroes provide a glimpse of the everyday heroism of caregivers as they support their bereaved children.

### 20.1 Parents and Caregivers: The Everyday Heroes for Bereaved Children

We refer to caregivers as heroes because, while parenting is a normative developmental task of adulthood, it takes on heroic proportions in the context of a caregiver's grief, their changed life circumstances, and the needs of their bereaved children. A major epidemiological study of 2,823 adults illustrates the importance of parenting bereaved children. Nickerson et al. (2013) found that higher-quality parenting postdeath related to a lower likelihood of children developing mental health problems in adulthood. Other studies have identified aspects of caregiving associated with resilient outcomes of bereaved children. Lin, Sandler, Ayers, Wolchik, and Luecken (2004) found that caregiver warmth (including positive family routines, listening to feelings) and consistent discipline differentiated bereaved children who had serious behavioral health problems from those who were free from such problems. Another study (Shapiro, Howell, & Kaplow, 2014) found that when surviving mothers sensitively communicated with their children about their deceased father, their children experienced fewer maladaptive grief and depression symptoms. Wolchik, Coxe, Tein, Sandler, and Ayers (2009) found that higher levels of support from surviving parents or caregivers predicted posttraumatic growth in positive relationships and personal strengths six years later. Based on interviews with 41 bereaved spouses Saldinger, Porterfield, and Cain (2004) identified aspects of what they termed "child-centered" parenting of bereaved children: parent–child interaction around the death (e.g., facilitating continued attachment to the deceased parent), emotional support (e.g., communication around feelings), maintaining a stable family environment, and helping the child develop a sense of purpose in life. Although these studies illustrate ways parenting can promote resilience of bereaved children, a parent's own grief and depression following the death make providing positive parenting particularly challenging (Kwok et al., 2005; Silverman & Kelly, 2009). Indeed, working through the challenges to parenting while grieving takes a heroic effort.

Superheroes are complex individuals with characteristics that reflect their ongoing grief, their positive adaptations following the death, and a full range of adjustments to adult life tasks. Kaplow, Layne, Pynoos, Cohen, and Lieberman (2012) describe multiple dimensions of childhood grief: an ongoing sense of missing the deceased, existential distress over one's identity and meaning, and distress around the circumstances of the death. Positive adaptation following parental death has been found to include posttraumatic growth, including finding personal strength; appreciation for life; and positive relationships with others (Calhoun & Tedeschi, 2006). Multiple factors can influence the development of all aspects of a bereaved child's future well-being, including the course of their grief, their development of mental health problems, and of satisfying and meaningful adult life roles. Parenting shapes how the developing superhero navigates these influences; buffering the pain of stressors, helping to make sense of the inexplicable, and providing a secure base from which the superhero is able to cope with the stressors of life.

## 20.2 Superman: Caregivers Help Children Cope with Challenges

As depicted in the film *Man of Steel* (Roven, Nolan, Thomas, Snyder, & Snyder, 2013), Superman's parenting exemplifies multiple ways in which caregivers can promote resilience in bereaved children. The movie tells how Superman's father and mother send him to earth to save him from the destruction of the planet Krypton. The baby Superman falls to earth in rural America and is raised by John and Martha Kent. Although they know he is different, they raise him as their own. The film implies that the Kents provide a stable, supportive environment in which he becomes securely attached to them as their son, Clark Kent. As Clark grows, he begins to experience physical powers that he does not understand. Several moving scenes reveal that the Kents are supportive and empathic parents. They listen to his concerns and validate them. When Clark is bullied by taunting peers who dare him to fight, his father provides a listening ear and asks, "Did he hurt you?" Clark answers truthfully, "No, they can't hurt me". His father shows a deep level of empathy when he responds, "I don't mean physically" (Roven et al., 2013, 01:08:18). Superman's earthly parents provide meaning in his life and help him make sense of his unique circumstances, "You were sent here for a reason and you owe it to yourself to find out what that reason is" (Roven et al., 2013, 00:31:28). Although Clark confronts them, "You are not my dad, you're just someone who found me in a field", they respond in a very honest and humane way assuring him of their love, and that they are "doing the best they can" (Roven et al., 2013, 00:54:50). They share Clark's secret. They let him know that he is not alone.

## 20.3 Spider-Man: Caregivers Do the Everyday Work of Providing a Stable, Supportive Home

The story of Spider-Man's childhood is a testament to the magic of day-to-day parenting. In the film *Spider-Man* (Ziskin, Bryce, & Raimi, 2002), Peter Parker, who becomes Spider-Man after being bitten by a biologically engineered super-spider, is raised by Aunt May and Uncle Ben following the death of his parents. Although Aunt May and Uncle Ben receive little attention in the Marvel comics *Spider-Man* franchise, the executive editor of Marvel Comics, Nick Lowe, stated that May and Ben made Peter Parker the superhero Spider-Man (Mejia, 2017). Aunt May and Uncle Ben are portrayed as ordinary, unpretentious people. They create a stable, caring home for Peter, encouraging him to participate in family chores and hosting warm family dinners for his friends and aspirational girlfriend. They listen to Peter when he needs them. Peter shares his romantic feelings for MaryJane (M.J.) with Aunt May, who patiently listens and encourages him to tell M.J. how he feels. She comforts Peter in his grief for Uncle Ben, who was murdered and was not at Peter's graduation. Although Peter feels guilty that his last interaction with Uncle Ben was an unpleasant one, Aunt May consoles him. She cries with him and lets him know that he is not alone in his grief. May tells him, "You loved him and he loved you. He never doubted the man you'd grow into" (Ziskin et al., 2002, 00:51:14). Peter remembers Uncle Ben's powerful words, "With great power comes great responsibility" (Ziskin et al., 2002, 00:52:03), giving Peter's life meaning. Aunt May and Uncle Ben work diligently at parenting despite their challenges with Peter. Uncle Ben and Aunt May persist even when Uncle Ben says to Peter, "I know I'm not your father", and Peter responds, "Then stop pretending to be" (Ziskin et al., 2002, 00:34:31). The movie *Spider-Man*, gives us a glimpse of the specialness of everyday parenting by introducing an alternative destructive parent figure, Norman Osborn (aka The Green Goblin), who seeks to develop a parental relationship and lure Peter down a path of evil. The loving, empathic, routine everyday parenting of Aunt May and Uncle Ben doesn't seem so ordinary in comparison to the alternative.

## 20.4 Batman: Heroic Caregiver Provides Stability, Continuity, Wise Counsel, and Supports Coping Efficacy – But Where Is the Self-Care?

Batman's story illustrates how effective caregiving can sometimes arise from an unlikely source. It also raises the important question regarding self-care for caregivers of bereaved children. In the movie *Batman Begins* (Roven, Thomas, Franco, & Nolan, 2005), Bruce Wayne, who becomes Batman, is the child of a loving, prominent, and wealthy family. He experiences a trauma as a young boy when he falls down a well and is attacked by bats. His father rescues him and teaches him a lesson about resilience. This lesson will be repeated by Bruce's caregiver after his parents' deaths, "Why do we fall? So we can learn to pick ourselves up" (Roven et al., 2005, 00:10:41). Bruce witnesses his parents' murders, and in a matter of hours, their butler, Alfred, begins to take on a caregiving role. He listens to Bruce's concern that he is to blame and reassures him that he is not at fault for the deaths. Later when Bruce pushes him away by saying: "Why do you give a damn? It's not your family", Alfred asserts the legitimacy of his role: "A good man once made me responsible for what was most precious to him". When Bruce responds: "You haven't given up on me yet", Alfred maintains his long-term commitment, saying: "Never" (Roven et al., 2005, 0:21:42). Although Alfred's caregiving relationship with Bruce is unusual, he assumes several critical caregiving roles over time. He maintains the family home, providing continuity with the family legacy to which he is fiercely loyal. He becomes a confidant with whom Bruce shares his plans and provides both emotional support and advice. When Bruce experiences setbacks, Alfred reminds him of his fathers' words: "Why do you fall? So you can learn to pick yourself up" (Roven et al., 2005, 01:51:12). When Bruce is consumed by anger and the need for revenge, Alfred guides Bruce, bringing him back to his family values, "For Thomas Wayne helping others wasn't about proving anything to anyone, including himself. What you're doing needs to be beyond that. It can't be personal or you're just a vigilante". When Bruce says, "I don't care about my name", Alfred brings him back to his family identity, "It's your father's name. And it's all that's left of him" (Roven et al., 2005, 01:40:20). While Alfred provides Bruce with stability, guidance, support, and caregiving continuity, we ask how does Alfred take care of himself? Although he also grieves the loss of Bruce's parents, we learn little of how Alfred copes with his grief and meets his own life needs.

## 20.5 Implications for Strategies to Promote Resilience of Parentally Bereaved Children

How can the stories of superheroes be used to promote resilience of bereaved families? For children, the approach can be to directly introduce them to the superhero origin stories in a setting in which they can process their own loss, grief, and coping. A randomized trial of group bibliotherapy with bereaved children and adolescents found that focusing specifically on superhero stories and videos led to greater reduction in mental health problems of bereaved children as compared to bibliotherapy, which focused on other affective themes, or receipt of no bibliotherapy (Betzalel & Shechtman, 2017).

But what resources are there to promote resilience of bereaved caregivers? Although there are some excellent books for bereaved caregivers (e.g., Silverman & Kelly, 2009), the struggles of the caregivers are kept in the background of superhero stories; as a result they do not provide a strong resource for bereaved caregivers. However, there is evidence of the effectiveness of a more direct approach in which caregivers are taught practical tools to promote resilience in their children. The Family Bereavement Program taught many of these practical tools to bereaved parents as part of a 12-meeting group program that also included child and adolescent groups (Sandler, Wolchik, Ayers, Tein, & Luecken, 2013). The randomized trial of this program found a number of benefits, including reduced long-term distressing grief and fewer mental health problems for both bereaved children and parents up to 15 years later (Sandler et al., 2010; Sandler, Tein, Cham, Wolchik, & Ayers, 2016). An adaptation of the caregiver component of this program is structured around five "building blocks" for resilient parenting: tools for self-care, building strong family bonds between parents and children, active listening to children, using effective discipline, and promoting children's effective coping (Resilient Parenting for Bereaved Families, https://reachinstitute.asu.edu/programs/resilientparent). The tools of active and empathic listening and providing a stable, positive and caring home are similar to those used by caregivers of superheroes. Missing from these superhero films is the deeper story of how caregivers find the strength and courage to parent their bereaved child, to understand their pain and help them cope with the multiple stressful challenges they face, and to do this while caring for their own needs. There would be no superheroes without the everyday heroism of the caregivers. Their stories need to be told.

## References


Betzalel, N., & Shechtman, Z. (2017). The impact of bibliotherapy superheroes on youth who experience parental absence. *School Psychology International.* 38(5), 473–490.

Calhoun, L, & Tedeschi, R. (2006). *Handbook of posttraumatic growth: Research and practice*. Mahwah, NJ: Erlbaum.

Kaplow, J.B., Layne, C.M., Pynoos, R.S., Cohen J.A., & Lieberman, A. (2012). DSM-5 Diagnostic criteria for bereavement-related disorders in children and adolescents: Developmental considerations. *Psychiatry*, 75 (3), 243–266.

Kwok, O.-M., Haine, R., Sandler, I.N., Ayers, T.S., & Wolchik, S.A. (2005). Positive parenting as a mediator of the relations between parental psychological distress and mental health problems of parentally-bereaved children. *Journal of Clinical Child and Adolescent Psychology*, 34, 261–272.

Lin, K., Sandler, I., Ayers, T., Wolchik, S., & Luecken, L. (2004). Resilience in parentally bereaved children and adolescents seeking preventive services. *Journal of Clinical Child and Adolescent Psychology*, 33, 673–683.

Mejia, C. (2017, July). "Spider-Man Homecoming" Has an Uncle Ben Problem. *Fatherly*. https://www.fatherly.com/play/spider-man-homecoming-uncle-ben-problem/

Nickerson, A., Bryant, R., Aderka, I., Hinton, D., & Hoffman, S. (2013). The impacts of parental loss and adverse parenting on mental health: Findings from the National Comorbidity Survey-Replication. *Psychological Trauma: Theory, Research, Practice and Policy*, 5, 119–127. Doi: 10.1037/0025695

Roven, C., Nolan, C., Thomas, E., & Snyder, D. (Producers), & Snyder, Z. (Director). (2013). *Man of steel* [Motion Picture]. United States: Warner Bros. Pictures.

Roven, C., Thomas, E., & Franco, L. (Producers), & Nolan, C. (Director). (2005). *Batman begins* [Motion picture]. United States: Warner Bros. Pictures.

Saldinger, A., Porterfield, K., & Cain, A. (2004). Meeting the needs of parentally bereaved children: A framework for child-centered parenting. *Psychiatry*, 67 (4), 331–352.

Sandler, I., Ayers, T.S., Tein, J.Y., Wolchik, S., Millsap, R., Khoo, S.T., Kaplan, D., Ma, Y., Luecken, L., Schoenfelder, E., & Coxe, S. (2010). Six-year follow-up of a preventive intervention for parentally-bereaved youth: A randomized controlled trial. *Archives of Pediatrics and Adolescent Medicine*, 164 (10), 907–914.

Sandler, I., Tein, J.Y., Cham, H., Wolchik, S., & Ayers, T. (2016). Long-term effects of the Family Bereavement Program on spousally-bereaved parents: Grief, mental health, alcohol problems and coping efficacy. *Development and Psychopathology*, 28 (3), 801–818. doi:10.1017/S0954579416000328

Sandler, I.N., Wolchik, S.A., Ayers, T.S., Tein, J.Y., & Luecken, L. (2013). Family Bereavement Program (FBP) approach to promoting resilience following the death of a parent. *Family Science*, 4 (1), 87–95.

Shapiro, D.N., Howell, K.H., & Kaplow, J. (2014). Associations among mother–child communication quality, childhood maladaptive grief, and depressive symptoms. *Death Studies*, 38 (1–5), 172–178. DOI: 10.1080/07481187.2012.738771.

Silverman, P., & Kelly, M. (2009). *A parent's guide to raising grieving children: Rebuilding your family after the death of a loved one*. New York, NY: Oxford University Press.

Wolchik, S. A., Coxe, S., Tein, J.Y., Sandler, I.N., & Ayers, T. (2009). A longitudinal study of predictors and outcomes of growth through grief in parentally bereaved children. *Omega: The Journal of Death and Dying*, 58(2), 107–128.

Ziskin, L., & Bryce, I. (Producers), & Raimi, S. (Director). (2002) *Spider-man* [Motion Picture]. United States: Columbia Pictures, Marvel Enterprises and Laura Ziskin Productions.

# 21 Katana

## Spousal Bereavement and Continuing Bonds

*Kathleen R. Gilbert and Andy H.Y. Ho*

*Katana began life as an ordinary girl, Tatsu, except for her proficiency in martial arts. As she matured, she drew the attention of twin brothers, Maseo and Takeo Yamashiro. Both professed their love for her but, having to make a choice, she chose to marry Maseo, alienating and enraging Takeo. Maseo and Tatsu settled into a happy marriage with Tatsu giving birth to twins. Meanwhile, Takeo joined the organized crime syndicate, Yakuzu, moving up through the ranks. For his excellent service, his crime lord awarded him with a set of matching antique samurai swords, known as "katanas". The only difference between these katanas is that one, Soultaker, possessed the ability to capture the souls of people killed by its blade (Barr, 1983).*

*Jealous of Maseo and Tatsu's happiness, Takeo brought both swords to Tatsu and Maseo's home. After knocking Tatsu unconscious, he challenged Maseo to a duel, keeping Soultaker for himself and giving Maseo the identical-appearing sword. During their fight, a fire started, ultimately consuming the house with the children in it. Maseo, distracted by his trapped children's cries, was slain by his brother. Tatsu regained consciousness, saw her husband lying dead, and, using her superior martial arts skills, overwhelmed Takeo and took his sword. He fled the scene, and Tatsu, still carrying Soultaker, tried to reach her children. Tatsu heard Maseo call out to her from the sword, telling her the children were lost and she should save herself. Shocked, Tatsu realized her husband's spirit was trapped within the sword (Barr, 1983).*

*Grieving her losses, Tatsu determined she would seek out the people responsible for her family's deaths and kill them. She underwent further training from a master samurai so she could expertly wield Soultaker. She took on the alter ego of "Katana" and set out to avenge her family's deaths. Meeting Batman and with encouragement from her husband's spirit, still trapped in Soultaker, she joined Batman's Outsiders team and took on their quest to fight for justice and against evil (Barr, 1983).*

### 21.1 Katana and Grief after Traumatic Loss

In her origin story, Katana's identity shifts from that of a young, happily married wife and mother to that of a young, bereaved mother and a widow, who was present at the scene of the brutal deaths of her family. More than the identity she held and the roles she carried out, her entire worldview would be assaulted by the deaths of her children and husband (Janoff-Bulman, 1992). The death of one's child is a death out of sequence as is widowhood at an early age. The inability to protect one's child, the pressure from others to "get back to normal", and the overwhelming intensity of their grief all feed the experience of parents after their child has died (Price & Jones, 2015). Becoming a widow in young adulthood challenges assumptions about how life ought to be and to complicate grief after the loss (Jones, Oka, Clark, Gardner, Hunt, & Dutson, 2019). In both cases, a continuing bond follows long after the death. Every aspect of Katana's loss, including the deaths of her children and young widowhood, as well as witnessing traumatic death when she was present and powerless, likely would cause us to question the long-standing and common belief that the purpose of grief is to quickly seek closure and move on (Silverman & Klass, 1996).

Beginning with Freud, a belief has existed that we need to emotionally disengage from the lost loved one and move on to form other relationships. Retaining a connection to the deceased was seen as unhealthy, even pathological. The commonly stated ideas of achieving closure and leaving the past behind comes from this perspective (Klass & Steffen, 2018; Klass & Walter, 2001; Silverman & Klass, 1996).

This belief not only that relationships were to be ended with a death and that not doing so was unhealthy was confronted in *Continuing Bonds: New Understanding of Grief* (Klass, Silverman, & Nickman, 1996). Rather than ending their relationship with the deceased, the chapter authors of this edited volume acknowledged that the living often maintain a relationship with the deceased and that although this ongoing relationship has the potential to be negative, it can also be positive for the living (Klass et al., 1996). The meaning attributed to this altered relationship in which one person is no longer alive as well as how it impacts the ability of the living person to function in the world are important considerations with regard to how positive or negative the continued ties are (Klass, 2006).

Continued connections between the bereaved and the deceased loved one are maintained in various ways: the bereaved may sense the presence of the deceased (Epstein, Kalus, & Beger, 2006; Klass & Walter, 2001; Silverman & Klass, 1996). They may experience vivid dreams of the deceased or feel as though the deceased is watching them (Silverman & Klass, 1996). These experiences may go on for years after the loss, in some form or another, and may be labeled as hallucinations and seen as dysfunctional (Epstein et al., 2006). This labeling of dysfunction was implied by another character with regard to Katana in a scene from *Suicide Squad* (Roven, Suckle, & Ayer, 2016), when she was seen holding Soultaker and talking with her husband.

Bonds are also continued through ongoing conversations with the dead (Klass & Walter, 2002; Silverman & Klass, 1996). The dead acting as moral guides is also identified by Klass and Walter (2001), serving as both role models for the living and guides for making decisions. After Katana has killed

Takeo, Maseo tells her that she must keep Soultaker because she can be trusted to use the sword in the service of good (Barr, 1983).

The living retain a connection by talking with others about the dead (Klass & Walter, 2002). This can be seen at funerals and memorial services as the bereaved come together to share stories about the deceased. In doing this, they engage in an ongoing construction and reconstruction of a meaningful biography for the deceased.

Finally, through meaningful objects or activities, an ongoing connection to the deceased is maintained (Epstein et al., 2006), a connection that contributes to their own evolving identity. In everyday life, this is seen in a young widow choosing to sleep in her husband's nightshirt, a sibling making a quilt out of her deceased brother's t-shirts, or a parent creating a memory box that includes her child's favorite toys.

Katana's experience of continuing bonds is most clearly demonstrated in her ongoing connection to her husband through Soultaker. After initially hearing his voice as she attempted to save their children, Katana maintains ongoing communication with Maseo through Soultaker. Maseo served as a moral guide in her evolution from a mission to avenge her family's deaths into one in which she was fighting for justice and against evil. Soultaker acts both as a literal conduit for communication between the two and as a linking object, an item that is symbolic of what she has lost (Barr, 1983).

## 21.2 Clinical Considerations

There are a number of things that we should consider when we think about the relationship between the bereaved and their experiences with continuing bonds.

**Nature of the Death.** The death of a spouse is deeply recognized as a heartbreaking and distressing event, in which one's pledged lifelong companion is taken and exchanged for a cruel collection of losses; thereupon the grief suffered by one whose spouse has been murdered in a familial homicide is certainly unparalleled to some of the most tragic human experiences. The emotional tasks of a normal grieving process are often unavoidably compounded by the intensity and complexity of the bereavement due to the sudden and violent nature of the death (Currier, Holland, & Neimeyer, 2006). While it is never really quite discussed in the comics or films, Katana, having been racked with the anguish of such traumatic loss, would have been at a high risk for developing posttraumatic stress disorder (PTSD) or complicated grief (Kaltman & Bonanno, 2003).

**Culture of the Bereaved.** While one may be quick to wonder if Katana's expressions of continuing bonds are really unhealthy manifestations of PTSD or complicated grief, it is important to consider her culture in Japan. The Japanese in general do not regard death as the finality of one's existence and have many complex rituals and traditions that focus on continuity after death. Serious considerations are placed on posthumous security and comfort, even as myriad changes are being made to traditional rituals. The Japanese hold strong to the belief that the living and the dead continue to be connected, with special festivals dedicated to specific days in which the dead return to visit the living (Tsuji, 2011). With this understanding of the Japanese people's attitudes toward dying and the deceased, it is then perhaps not particularly alarming that Katana accepts the notion that her husband's soul is trapped in a sword and communicates regularly with her.

**Social Context of the Loss.** While the loss of a spouse is recognized as something deeply painful, many such losses often occur later in life, and grief processes are traditionally discussed with respect to older spouses. However, losing a partner at a younger age could result in further long-term and complex losses, such as a financial burden due to a loss of income, having to raise children alone, and unanticipated loneliness, which can exacerbate grief processes. Young bereaved spouses could also sometimes experience disenfranchised grief, with society expecting them to move on, enter new relationships, and eventually remarry (Bar-Nadav & Rubin, 2016). They may also experience social judgments about whether they do or do not, how long after the death, and to whom. On the other hand, social norms in certain societies strongly oppose a second marriage, expecting the bereaved spouse to complete grieving in a stipulated amount of time and continue to fulfill their duties to the household of the deceased, thus effectively cutting off any expressions of personal suffering or needs (Yasien-Esmael & Rubin, 2005).

## 21.3 Intervention Strategies

Working with clients who have experienced a homicide of a loved one or something similarly traumatizing is a slow and challenging process. Adams (in Thompson, Cox, & Stevenson, 2017) recommends that to avoid triggering sudden pain and anxiety in clients, techniques that focus on the cognitive thought processes could be used first through narrative sharing, with clients allowing themselves to delve into the emotional perspectives once they feel comfortable enough.

Neimeyer, Baldwin, and Gillies (2006) describe the death of a loved one as an attack on the bereaved's meaning system and worldview, setting into motion the process in which the bereaved attempts to reestablish his or her new life circumstances. As such, the adaptiveness of continuing bonds are highly dependent on whether it is complemented with reaffirming or reconstructing meaning after the loss; if one should remain strongly bonded to the deceased but unable to make sense of the loss, greater complications in grieving can be anticipated. At the same time, continuing bonds are seen as beneficial to the bereaved by providing a source of comfort in the midst of distressing changes (Klass, 1993) and may act as effective coping strategies to help ease the pain associated with death (Asai et al., 2010).

Intervention strategies can take the form of finding creative ways for the bereaved to tell their stories and talk about their expressions of continuing bonds, while simultaneously making meaning out of these experiences. Besides talk therapy, interventions can include art-making, poetry, rituals, and memorialization activities, in the context of both the individual and group settings. Torres and García-Hernández (in Harris & Bordere, 2016) suggest that the bereaved deciding which personal traits and values of the deceased they want to be inspired and guided by is an important process in coping with grief and maintaining adaptive continuing bonds. With Katana, we see that she often seeks guidance from her husband's soul in the sword on whether she should join certain teams on adventures. She draws on her continued relationship with him to help her navigate a new world without him.

## References

Asai, M., Fujimori, M., Akizuki, N., Inagaki, M., Matsui, Y., & Uchitomi, Y. (2010). Psychological states and coping strategies after bereavement among the spouses of cancer patients: A qualitative study. *Psycho-oncology*, 19(1), 38–45.

Bar-Nadav, O., & Rubin, S.S. (2016). Love and bereavement: Life functioning and relationship to partner and spouse in bereaved and non-bereaved young women. *Omega: Journal of Death and Dying*, 74(1), 62–79.

Barr, M. (August, 1983). The truth about Katana, part II: ... To love, honor and destroy! In D. Giardano (Exec. Ed.), *Batman and the Outsiders: Vol. 1*. Issue #12. New York, NY: DC Comics.

Currier, J.M., Holland, J.M., & Neimeyer, R.A. (2006). Sense-making, grief, and the experience of violent loss: Toward a mediational model. *Death Studies*, 30, 403–428.

Epstein, R., Kalus, C., & Beger, M. (2006). The continuing bond of the bereaved towards the deceased and adjustment to loss. *Mortality*, 11, 253–269.

Harris, D.L., & Bordere, T.C. (2016). *Handbook of social justice in loss and grief: Exploring diversity, equality and inclusion*. New York, NY: Routledge.

Janoff-Bulman, R. (1992). *Shattered assumptions*. New York, NY: Free Press.

Jones, E., Oka, M., Clark, J., Gardner, H., Hunt, R., & Dutson, S., (2019). Lived experience of young widowed individuals: A qualitative study, *Death Studies*, 43, 183–192.

Kaltman, S., & Bonanno, G.A. (2003). Trauma and bereavement: Examining the impact of sudden and violent deaths. *Anxiety Disorders*, 17, 131–147.

Klass, D., & Steffen, E.M. (Eds.). (2018). *Continuing bonds in bereavement: New directions for research and practice*. New York, NY: Routledge.

Klass, D. (1993). Solace and immortality: Bereaved parents' continuing bond with their children. *Death Studies*, 17, 343–368.

Klass, D. (2006). Continuing conversations about continuing bonds. *Death Studies*, 30, 843–858.

Klass, D., Silverman, P.R., & Nickman, S. (Eds.). (1996). *Continuing bonds: New understanding of grief*. Washington, DC: Taylor & Francis.

Klass, D., & Walter, T., (2001). Processes of grieving: How bonds are continued. In M.S. Stroebe, R.O. Hansson, W. Stroebe, & H. Schut (Eds.), *Handbook of bereavement research: Consequences, coping, and care* (pp. 431–441) Washington, DC: American Psychological Association.

Neimeyer, R.A., Baldwin, S.A., & Gillies, J. (2006). Continuing bonds and reconstructing meaning: Mitigating complications in bereavement. *Death Studies*, 30, 715–738.

Price, J.E., & Jones, A.M. (2015). Living through the life-altering loss of a child: A narrative review. *Issues in Comprehensive Palliative Nursing*, 38, 222–240.

Roven, C., & Suckle, R. (Producers), & Ayer, D. (Director). (2016). *Suicide squad* [DVD]. United States: DC Entertainment.

Silverman, P.R., & Klass, D. (1996). Introduction: What is the problem? In D. Klass, P.R. Silverman, & S. Nickman (Eds.), *Continuing bonds: New understanding of grief* (pp. 73–86). Washington, DC: Taylor & Francis.

Thompson, N., Cox, G.R., & Stevenson, R.G. (2017). *Handbook of traumatic loss: A guide to theory and practice*. New York, NY: Routledge.

Tsuji, Y. (2011). Rites of passage to death and afterlife in Japan. *Journal of the American Society on Aging*, 35(3), 28–33.

Yasien-Esmael, H., & Rubin, S.S. (2005). The meaning structures of Muslim bereavement in Israel: Religious traditions, mourning practices and human experience. *Death Studies*, 29, 495–518.

# 22 Sibling Grief and Complex Relationships

## Thor and the Death of Loki

*Rayna Vaught Godfrey*

The sibling relationship is forged before we meet our spouses and have children; it continues after our parents die. If not for death, our siblings would be with us longer than anyone else on this earth. Siblings have the opportunity to know one another from childhood into adulthood and old age. No other person encompasses our lives to such an extent.

Siblings are friends and rivals, companions and competitors, confidants and betrayers. The sibling relationship contains the entire range of human emotion and experience. This relationship is too complex to have one standard definition or model (Bank & Kahn, 1982).

Sibling influence is significant across the lifespan (Sandmaier, 1994). Into adulthood, siblings act as a "mirror for the other as he or she meets developmental milestones" (Moss & Moss, 1986, p. 405) and have a major impact on one another's behavior and development (Cicirelli, 1995). They are instrumental in the development of our sense of self.

Siblings provide companionship and support, play a prominent role in our development, and constitute a significant part of our sense of self (Godfrey, 2002). As such, the death of a sibling is a profound loss (Godfrey, 2002). Siblings experience tremendous pain and suffering after the death of a sibling (Marshall, 2013). The death of a sibling impacts who we are, what we hold dear, and how we relate to others. For better or for worse, we are never the same (Godfrey, 2006).

Not all siblings are close; some are estranged or in constant battle with one another, but "closeness is not a prerequisite for connection, and the story of 'intimate' relationships is not always a happy one" (DeVita-Raeburn, 2004, p. 5). In my research, even those who weren't as close to their siblings still described "a sense of understanding, an enrichment of relationship, and a connection that was unique to siblings" (Godfrey, 2002, p. 121). Berman (2009) found that even those who describe difficult and problematic sibling relationships still feel deep pain after their death.

## 22.1 Thor and Loki

One such complicated sibling relationship is that of Thor (God of Thunder, son of Odin the King of Asgard) and Loki (God of Mischief, abandoned son of the Frost Giant King, adopted by Odin as an infant).

Thor and Loki are typical siblings in childhood – companions and natural rivals who move back and forth along the spectrum of normal sibling behavior. As they become adults, Loki's jealousy and Thor's arrogance elicit behaviors with greater consequences for one another. This impacts their development as individuals and in relation to one another. They move into a complicated pattern of connecting and retreating, of assistance and betrayal.

A significant factor in this is Loki's shattered sense of identity when he finds out that he is a Frost Giant (Feige & Branaugh, 2011, 0:39:40–0:41:50). Loki continually uses Thor in his quest to regain a sense of identity, to answer the question, "Who am I now?" At times, this quest includes embracing their familiarity and reveling in their shared bond. At others, it begets massive betrayal and violence.

Throughout it all, the sibling influence on their individual development continues. Thor is arrogant and self-centered. He doesn't see the value in others. Because of Loki's manipulations and lies, Thor is banished to Earth, where he learns a great deal about himself in relation to others (Feige & Branaugh, 2011). Loki comes to Earth, and his act of betrayal facilitates Thor's act of self-sacrifice, deeming him worthy of his powers and restoring him to the God of Thunder (Feige & Branaugh, 2011, 01:26:06–01:34:18). It is because of Loki that Thor's arrogance is turned into humility, and Thor begins to grow into his true self.

As their individual identities diverge further, the competition between them grows, increasing their conflicts. In a violent fight, Loki falls into an abyss and dies when he lets go of the scepter connecting him to Thor as they hang off the Bi-Frost bridge (Feige & Branaugh, 2011, 01:36:22–01:40:44). Thor "mourns for his brother" (Feige & Branaugh, 2011, 01:43:08), but it will not be the first time.

When Thor is reunited with Loki in *Avengers* (Feige & Whedon, 2012), he implores Loki to remember their sibling bond. "We were raised together! We played together, we fought together! Do you remember none of that?" (Feige & Whedon, 2012, 0:45:33). Loki replies, "I remember a shadow. Living in the shade of your greatness" (Feige & Whedon, 2012, 0:45:41). Thor shakes Loki by the shoulders and begs him to give up his poisonous dream and to "come home!" (Feige & Whedon, 2012, 0:46:56). The emotion in Thor's voice speaks to a continued mourning for the brother Loki used to be, for the brother Thor still wants him to be.

We return to our siblings time and again, for the support and understanding that this unique relationship can provide. Thor keeps trusting Loki, betrayal after betrayal, because he loves Loki and wants a relationship with him. While it seems that Loki takes advantage of this trust, he too loves his brother and is bonded to him. There is this back and forth of working together and fighting one another, as only siblings can do.

Thor must return to Loki and ask for his help in escaping Asgard in *Thor: Dark World* (Feige & Taylor, 2013). "You should know that when we fought each other in the past, I did so with a glimmer of hope that my brother was still in there, somewhere. That hope no longer exists to protect you. You betray me, I will kill you", Thor tells Loki (Feige & Taylor, 2013, 0:59:50). It seems Thor has come to terms with the loss of his brother.

Yet in the escape scene that follows (Feige & Taylor, 2013, 01:05:00–01:08:14), we see their indelible history as they lob insults at one another with the tender familiarity of siblings. They come together as brothers once more, and Loki helps Thor escape. They enact a brilliant ruse to foil Malekith, the king of the dark elves (Feige & Taylor, 2013, 01:13:53–01:16:24). They fight in alliance, and Loki saves Thor's life by stabbing a dark beast from behind. But the beast grabs Loki and pulls him into the other end of the knife, mortally wounding Loki (Feige & Taylor, 2013, 01:19:30–01:19:36). Thor screams, "No!" and runs over to the dying Loki pulling him into his arms. It is an emotional scene between the two brothers as Loki dies (Feige & Taylor, 2013, 01:20:06–01:20:39). Thor screams in rage and grief, tears streaming down his face. He mourns his brother once more. It will not be the last time.

After another round of resurrection and betrayal, Thor and Loki come together to escape Planet Sakaar in *Thor: Ragnarok* (Feige & Waititi, 2017). They have a heart-to-heart conversation in the elevator. "Loki, I thought the world of you. I thought we were going to fight side by side forever. But at the end of the day, you're you and I'm me. I don't know, maybe there's still good in you, but let's be honest, our paths diverged a long time ago" (Feige & Waititi, 2017, 01:29:29–01:29:58). Loki looks hurt and says, "Yeah, it's probably for the best that we never see each other again". Thor claps him on the back affectionately and says, "That's what you always wanted". Loki nods, but he's frowning, suggesting it's not really what he's always wanted (Feige & Waititi, 2017, 01:29:59–01:30:41). Again, it seems that Thor has resolved the loss of his brother, yet within seconds of this serious exchange, they are back to their lighthearted brotherly banter and doing their "Get Help" routine to trick their common enemies (Feige & Waititi, 2017, 01:29:59–01:30:05).

After more cycles of betrayal and cooperation, their relationship evolves yet again (Feige & Waititi, 2017). We see Thor looking at himself in the mirror, wearing an eye patch as Odin once did, contemplating the development in his identity as Asgard's leader now. Loki appears behind him and says softly, "It suits you", finally accepting this piece of Thor's identity that he has fought against for so long. In doing so, it seems Loki has come to a sense of peace with his own identity. Thor recognizes this and says, "You know, maybe you're not so bad after all, brother". Loki smiles and replies, "Maybe not". Thor says he would give Loki a hug, "if you were here", assuming that Loki is an illusion, a form he often takes with Thor. But Loki isn't an illusion. "I'm here", he says (Feige & Waititi, 2017, 01:58:59–01:59:14). Loki has returned to Thor once more, for real this time.

In the opening to *Avengers: Infinity War* (Feige, Russo, & Russo, 2018), Thanos has Thor, beaten and bloodied, by the scalp and offers Loki the chance to save him. Initially Loki tells Thanos to "kill away!" and Thanos begins to crush Thor's skull. Loki tries to hold a straight face, but when he looks at Thor, he becomes visibility distraught, eyes filling with tears. He can't take his brother's suffering and yells out, "Alright, stop!" (Feige et al., 2018, 0:02:53–0:03:26). Loki tries to trick Thanos, but his attempt to stab Thanos is thwarted. Thanos takes Loki by the throat and chokes him to death (Feige et al., 2018, 0:08:23–0:09:06). Thor watches on his hands and knees, chained and gagged, helpless to save his little brother. Thanos deposits Loki's lifeless body in front of Thor, declaring, "No resurrections this time!" When Thanos and his forces leave, Thor's chains fall away, and he crawls to Loki. He rests his head on Loki's chest and sobs (Feige et al., 2018, 0:09:07–0:09:48). This death is for real, and Thor's identity is impacted by Loki once again: Thor is now and forever a bereaved sibling.

## 22.2 Clinical Considerations

It is tantamount for clinicians to recognize the importance of the sibling relationship across the lifespan and to understand that the death of a sibling can be a profound loss, regardless of the closeness of the relationship. Siblings are often the forgotten mourners (Marshall & Winokuer, 2017). Those in a complicated relationship may be even more forgotten. "Grieving siblings must not be ignored, but rather supported on their lonely journey" (Marshall & Davies, 2011).

Because the sibling relationship is unique, it is important to approach the loss without assumptions. Clients may enter therapy for a loss or concern other than sibling loss, and it's not until then that they themselves realize the impact of the loss. It is important to ask about siblings and allow the client to explore their relationship as it was or how they wished it could have been. Recognize that "troubled relationships are not the ones we expect to miss – but it's different with siblings" (DeVita-Raeburn, 2004). People who weren't that close with a sibling may struggle with their intense grief reaction because it wasn't expected (Sandmaier, 1994).

## 22.3 Interventions

Although many interventions can be used with the bereaved (Neimeyer, 2012, 2016), an important aspect of working with bereaved siblings is giving them permission to grieve and a place to tell their story. "Bereaved siblings do not have the opportunity to tell their stories because their loss is not recognized" (Godfrey, 2006, p. 7). Providing this opportunity can be "enormously helpful" (Marshall & Davies, 2011, p. 115). It is imperative to create a validating and safe space for the client to talk about their sibling and integrate the loss into their life story. Being able to construct a coherent narrative with all of its unique characteristics and complexities is a powerful intervention for bereaved siblings. Constructing this narrative in complicated sibling relationships can be more difficult, but it is no less important.

## References

Bank, S.P., & Kahn, M.D. (1982). *The sibling bond*. New York, NY: Basic Books.

Berman, C. (2009). *When a brother or sister dies: Looking back, moving forward*. Westport, CT: Praeger.

Cicirelli, V. (1995). *Sibling relationships across the lifespan*. New York, NY: Plenum Press

DeVita-Raeburn, E. (2004). *The empty room: Understanding sibling loss*. New York, NY: Scribner.

Feige, K. (Producer), & Branaugh, K. (Director). (2011). *Thor* [Motion picture]. United States: Marvel Studios.

Feige, K. (Producer), & Russo, A., & Russo, J. (Directors). (2018). *Infinity war* [Motion picture]. United States: Marvel Studios.

Feige, K. (Producer), & Taylor, A. (Director). (2013). *Thor: Dark world* [Motion picture]. United States: Marvel Studios.

Feige, K. (Producer), & Waititi, T. (Director). (2017). *Thor: Ragnarok* [Motion picture]. United States: Marvel Studios.

Feige, K. (Producer), & Whedon, J. (Director). (2012). *Avengers* [Motion picture]. United States: Studios.

Godfrey, R.V. (2002). Losing a sibling in adulthood. (Doctoral dissertation, University of Denver, 2002). *Dissertation Abstracts International*, 63, 3459.

Godfrey, R.V. (2006). Losing a sibling in adulthood. *ADEC: The Forum*, 32(1), 6–7.

Marshall, B., & Winokuer, H. (Eds.). (2017). *Sibling loss across the lifespan: Research, practice, and personal stories*. New York: Routledge.

Marshall, B. J. (2013). *Adult sibling loss: Stories, reflections and ripples*. New York: Routledge.

Marshall, B.J. & Davies, B. (2011). Bereavement in children and adults following the death of a sibling. In R.A. Neimeyer, D.L. Harris, H.R. Winokuer, & G.F. Thornton (Eds.), *Grief and bereavement in contemporary society: Bridging research and practice* (pp. 107–116). New York: Routledge.

Moss, S., & Moss, Z. (1986). Death of an adult sibling. *International Journal of Family Psychiatry*, 7, 397–418.

Neimeyer, R.A. (Ed.). (2012). *Techniques in grief therapy: Creative practices for counseling the bereaved*. New York, NY: Routledge.

Neimeyer, R.A. (Ed.). (2016). *Techniques in grief therapy: Assessment and intervention*. New York, NY: Routledge.

Sandmaier, M. (1994). *Original kin: The search for connection among adult sisters and brothers*. New York, NY: Penguin Books.

# Part VI
# Challenges in Bereavement: Facing Adversity

# 23 Deadpool 2 and Suicide After Bereavement

## Lessons Learned from the Merc with a Mouth

*Jill A. Harrington, Kim A. Ruocco and John R. Jordan*

Suicide after the death of a loved one is a serious issue and has been identified as an overlooked problem (Ajdacic-Gross et al., 2008), as grieving individuals are "expected" to be sad and long for reunion with the deceased; after all, these are a natural part of the process and can be especially intense for those newly bereaved. Because of this, suicidality is often dismissed or overlooked. Parkes (1982) addressed the gravity of the risk of suicide after bereavement to practitioners, stating that "many bereaved people at the height of their grief would agree that life is not worth living, or I wouldn't care if I died tomorrow" (p. 4). This is illustrated most poignantly by the character Deadpool in the film *Deadpool 2*, when he begs Russell, "Just let me die in peace … there's only one person in this world that I care about, and she's gone" (Kinberg et al., 2018, 0:40:54–0:41:20).

Deadpool's pain is often dismissed by friends throughout the film as a "self-pitying mess" (Kinberg et al., 2018, 0:24:07); however, for those who work in the field of suicide prevention and postvention, this fictional character's words provide a "steaming bowl of foreshadowing" (Kinberg et al., 2018, 0:37:41) for a man with unbearable psychache (Shneidman, 1993), perceived burdensomeness, capability, and a thwarted sense of belongingness (Joiner, 2005).

So, what can we learn about bereavement from this graphically violent, profanity-filled, definitely "R" rated, sexually explicit, hugely sarcastic, yet endearing film filled with so many themes about love, relationships, family, trauma, loss, grief, and bereavement? Don't get us wrong, the "merc with a mouth … least Canadian person ever … with great power comes no responsibility" ("Deadpool", 2020, para 1), Deadpool, and his genre is an antihero who is right up our alley. But, he is not your typical hero, and getting past some of the violence to attune yourself to the lessons of loss may be difficult. Nevertheless, this film, laden with sarcasm, filtering pain "through the prism of humor" (Kinberg et al., 2018, 1:18:20), addresses one of the most serious issues in bereavement – the presence of both passive, and sometimes active suicidality in people who are grieving, especially loved ones' deaths that are traumatic. *Deadpool 2* is a film rich with teaching moments; however, due to limited space and not "lazy writing" (Kinberg et al., 2018, 1:17:28), this chapter will succinctly explore *Deadpool 2,* highlighting some important lessons on the issue of suicide after bereavement.

## 23.1 Deadpool Background

Death is inevitably a part of life. Unless, that is, you are Deadpool, whose origin in the first film *Deadpool* (Kinberg, Reynolds, Donner, & Miller, 2016) begins with Wade Wilson, seeking a cure from terminal cancer, to avoid death and stay with Vanessa Carlysle, a woman with whom he has found true love and a sense of belonging. He is a former dishonorably discharged Special Forces operative turned mercenary, with a history of child abuse (and implied sexual abuse), who contracts himself out for hire to help abused children. Wade pursues a cure from an organization whose leader, Ajax, exposes his latent mutant abilities – giving Wade the superpower of regeneration (healing). He is betrayed by Ajax, who enslaves his mutants and sells them as weapons. Deadpool eventually escapes, forms bonds with others, eliminates Ajax, and rejoins Vanessa. The obvious crux of the film is about Wade's physical transformation into the red-suited antihero, Deadpool, who uses a lifelong dark and sarcastic sense of humor to often push away others or mask emotional pain. However, underscoring his physical transformation is also an emotional one – as Wade discovers healing through developing secure and safe attachments with others, especially Vanessa.

Fast forward to *Deadpool 2*, where, right from the opening scene, we are drawn into Wade's intense suicidality after thugs he had been contracted to kill break into his apartment and murder Vanessa while he tries to save her. This murder occurs after the couple spent a warm evening together contemplating a baby and their new beginnings together as a happy family – something that Wade has never previously experienced. *It is important to note here that the murder of Vanessa truly leaves Wade a sudden, traumatic loss survivor – someone who has, in the blink of an eye, had his source of meaning, purpose, and happiness stolen away by the brutal and intended death of the most important person in his life.* From this point forward, this violent amputation from Vanessa, coupled with an intense sense of guilt and responsibility for her death, fuel Wade's powerful desire to die, as well as seek revenge – even on himself, who he also holds responsible. Cue the music to Air Supply's "All Out of Love" (Russel & Davis, 1979, track 2), as Deadpool first attempts to kill himself by taking "a cat-nap on 1,200 gallons of high-test fuel" (Kinberg et al., 2018, 0:02:38), but discovers to his great frustration that his superpowers of regeneration prevent him from ending his life.

Early in the film, Wade shows us most of the characteristics of people who are suffering from the sudden/violent death loss of a loved one: deep preoccupation with the deceased; a traumatic and repetitive reliving of the death scene; intense yearning for reunion with the loved one; a profound sense of loss of meaning or purpose in life; and great feelings of failure and responsibility for the death that contribute to significant suicidality. While we will discuss some additional suicide risk factors for Wade, as with many who are suddenly/violently bereaved, *this one, shattering death by itself is sufficient to make Wade suicidal.* Additionally, the vulnerability of separation distress combined with Wade's early attachment experiences also significantly contributes to his suicidality.

## 23.2 Attachment and Separation Distress

Bowlby (1958) suggested that at the moment we are born, we have an adaptive, survival instinct to attach. Our early attachment figures affect our attachment systems in childhood, which drive attachment styles in adulthood and are thought to result from the internalization of the individual's unique history of attachment experiences (Kosminsky & Jordan, 2016). They affect a person's sense of self, shaping their ability to regulate emotion, form relationships, and influence how we behave within them – especially how one approaches closeness and intimacy.

Bowlby also investigated the interplay of attachment and loss and how we use our developed attachment styles to cope with the pain of loss, process grief, and regain a sense of security (Kosminsky & Jordan, 2016). In times of death-related loss, our attachment system is fully galvanized against the separation; otherwise known as separation distress, this distress produces an intense desire for a reunion with our loved one. It is activated because death not only permanently bars a physical connection to our loved one, but a psychological barrier as well (Rubin, Malkinson, & Witztum, 2016). Thus, we respond with a physical and/or psychological "search behavior" called proximity-seeking – which can be manifested in vivid dreams, auditory hallucinations, "sightings" of the deceased, all in a constant search to find what has been lost. During this vulnerable period of separation distress, it is also common for the bereaved to have thoughts of rejoining the deceased, without suicidal ideation, such as increased thoughts that death may one day bring them reunification with their deceased loved one. *In working with a bereaved client, it is important to explore these thoughts, normalizing and validating them while screening and assessing for potential suicidality – both passive and active.*

We see this separation distress and proximity-seeking behavior in *Deadpool 2* as Wade has dream-like conversations with Vanessa. However, his proximity-seeking manifests in strong suicidality, with multiple attempts, in what he believes is the only way to rejoin her. *It is important to note that a critical teaching point is to ask about a previous history of suicide attempts, which is known to be one of the biggest risk factors for suicide. Also, observe Wade's increasing lethality of death methods.* Vanessa, on the other hand, believes he should not end his life because his "heart is not in the right place" (Kinberg et al., 2018, 0:21:25) and directs him toward a sense of meaningful attachment and purpose in life. *Another observed lesson is the importance of exploring protective factors, such as those meaningful attachments that may anchor the bereaved to life.*

A fundamental risk factor for Wade is his portrayed history of childhood attachments, which influences his adult attachment styles. These styles contain distinct strategies to alleviate distress after a significant loss by death and hyperactivate our natural attachment response to find what is lost – our deceased loved one, sometimes with intense repetition, distress, and protest. Our attachment style aids, impairs, or destroys us in the crucial and necessary attachment reorganization after loss. The four identified attachment styles are secure and three types of insecure attachment style (avoidant/dismissive, anxious/preoccupied, and disorganized/fearful). Those with a secure style are more likely to work through the distress of separation and lean on the secure internalized relationship with the deceased as they integrate their grief and identify love as enduring beyond death. Those with an anxious style are more likely to have difficulty deactivating painful thoughts, memories, or feelings related to the deceased. Those with an avoidant style tend to suppress them, and those with disorganized/fearful style may literally become emotionally and behaviorally disorganized after a loss – triggering feelings related to unresolved losses, including trauma and abuse. *Important take-home messages are that individuals with different attachment styles will grieve and express themselves in different ways after a significant death loss. However, research indicates that those with insecure styles experience less posttraumatic growth and are more prone to complicated grief* (Cohen & Katz, 2015).

We know from Wade that his dark and sarcastic sense of humor hints toward an abusive childhood, as when he refers to his family as an "F-Word" (Kinberg et al., 2018, 0:10:25). Wade was also dishonorably discharged from the military, potentially contributing to a perceived sense of rejection, abandonment, and thwarted belongingness. With an approach-avoidance orientation toward relationships, Wade exhibits features of all insecure attachment styles, developed most likely from abusive and unreliable caregivers. When faced with the separation distress of losing a safe and secure attachment (Vanessa), something he had never experienced and now cherished, the trauma of this profound and violent loss triggers overwhelming anxiety, disorganization, and pain avoidance – contributing to a suicidal mind. *Separation distress is a vulnerable period for the newly bereaved, and the potential for suicide should be monitored and competently explored.* However, Wade possesses significant preexisting factors in his attachment history, as noted, that increase his risk of suicidality during this time of separation distress.

## 23.3 Additional Bereavement Risk Factors

***Sudden, Violent Death Loss.*** Research shows us that when a loss is the result of violence (i.e., suicide, homicide, fatal accident), bereavement is often associated with poorer mental health outcomes, including posttraumatic stress disorder, depression, substance abuse, and complicated grief (CG) (Nakajima, Ito, Shirai, & Konishi, 2012). Loss by traumatic means can lead to more intrusive symptoms and greater functional impairment.

***Complicated Grief (CG)*** is a form of bereavement marked by elevated and persistent separation distress (i.e., searching for the deceased, loneliness, and preoccupation with thoughts of the deceased) and symptoms of traumatic distress (i.e., feelings of disbelief, mistrust, anger, shock, detachment from others). There is a derailment in the ability to integrate and adapt to loss. Rynearson (2006) also contends that violent death comprises three V's that complicate grief – violence, violation, and volition – and severely interfere with sense-making (Currier, Holland, & Neimeyer, 2006) as well as acceptance of the death by the bereaved. Research supports that CG significantly heightens the risk of suicidality in the bereaved (Latham & Prigerson, 2004).

***Relationship to the Deceased (Widowed Persons).*** Worden (2018) draws attention to kinship to the deceased as one of the best predictors of grief outcomes. This is further influenced by the strength and emotional security of attachment to this person (Worden, 2018). As portrayed in the *Deadpool* films, Wade and Vanessa have a strong attachment – finding a sense of security, meaning, purpose, and love in their relationship. They are each other's new "F-Word" (Kinberg et al., 2018, 0:10:25), which equals love and security through the toughest of times.

The death of a loved spouse/partner is consistently ranked at the top of stressful life events (Utz, Caserta, & Lund, 2012). Widowed persons are a high-risk group, with males having a three times greater risk of suicide in the first week after the loss of their spouse/partner (Ajdacic-Gross et al., 2008). Within the first year after the loss, widowed persons remain a higher risk group, especially young widowed persons and older male widowers (Ajdacic-Gross et al., 2008).

***Additional Risk Factors.*** Wade has all these additional bereavement risk factors. However, it is also important to note that Wade is a former Special Forces operative with a dishonorable discharge, a researched risk factor for suicide in military veterans (Barr, Kintzle, Alday, & Castro, 2018). His military experience also involves exposure to combat and military training that may cause habituation to the fear of painful experiences, such as suicide (Selby et al., 2010). Certainly, in Deadpool's case, he is unafraid of physical pain; however, the psychological pain brought forth by Vanessa's death creates a psychache (Shneidman, 1993) that Deadpool believes he is unable to endure.

## 23.4 Joiner's Theories

The Interpersonal-Psychological Theory of Suicidal Behavior (Joiner, 2005) offers insight into the development of suicide risk in *Deadpool 2*. Joiner's theory contends that an individual will not die by suicide unless that person has both the desire to die and the ability to do so (Joiner, 2009). The theory hypothesizes that three components must be in place for an individual to die by suicide: (1) the acquired capability to enact lethal self-injury; (2) the sense that one is a burden on loved ones or society (burdensomeness); and (3) the sense that one does not belong or feel connected with a valued group or relationship (thwarted belongingness) (Joiner, 2009). When these three components exist together, risk is considered high and should be assessed.

In *Deadpool 2*, Deadpool repeatedly exposes himself to danger and physical pain in many situations and attempts to end his life. He presents with a fearlessness that should be taken into serious consideration when assessing risk. This fearlessness may have evolved over time but is most likely highly correlated to Deadpool's military service, training, and habituation to pain as a result of childhood abuse. Service members are trained to push through pain and tolerate it at very high levels. Quotes such as "pain is weakness leaving the body" is a common chant to encourage troops to ignore pain and push on. Over time, service members can become desensitized to pain and death, leading to what Joiner would call an "acquired ability to enact lethal self-injury" (Joiner, 2009, para 8). Deadpool's lack of fear of pain or death and his access to lethal means – as a superhero who has bottomless options – elevates his risk and makes him vulnerable to self-harm and suicide.

So, what about Joiner's (2005) two other essential components, burdensomeness and thwarted belongingness? We see these core beliefs emerge throughout the movie as Deadpool aimlessly tries to navigate his grief, trauma, and inability to trust and connect with others. Deadpool desperately wants to take care of Russell but struggles with how to do this without hurting him or developing an attachment that may cause Deadpool fear and anxiety. At times we witness his self-loathing as he tells Russell to "make friends with someone. Anyone but me" (Kinberg et al., 2018, 0:41:34). In assessing suicide risk statements, such as these, they could possibly reflect feelings of burdensomeness and thwarted belongingness; therefore, they should be explored and examined to better understand the client's view of the world, themselves, and what *intentions* are connected with the thoughts.

In cases such as Deadpool, self-directed anger can be directed at others, increasing risk not only for suicide but also murder. Murder-suicides are rare (Arensman & McCarthy, 2017), but nonetheless are horrific events that can develop out of suicidal intentions filled with rage and what Joiner (2014) calls a "perversion of virtue" (p. 5). According to Joiner (2014), murder-suicide always involves the misguided invocation of one of four interpersonal values – mercy, justice, duty, and glory and "involve the gross misconception of when and how these four virtues should be applied" (p. 8). Deadpool illustrates this repeatedly, as he violently approaches the world with a misguided ideal of justice and duty. It is important to note that individuals presenting with these misconceptions and rage should be screened for homicidal ideation, plan, and intent.

## 23.5 Healing Factors

So, what helps to heal Deadpool and essentially save his regenerative life? What we learn from Deadpool is that he has healing factors from shattering, fatal physical dismemberment, but the greatest lessons of loss learned through this film are the healing factors that save his life after catastrophic emotional loss. Healing after devastating loss can happen, but one of the most important lessons of *Deadpool 2* is that *in order for real healing to happen, it is necessary to face grief and actively deal with the pain so it can be transformative instead of destructive.* The film also teaches us that oftentimes this journey cannot be made alone; it requires connection and help from supportive others. This is especially necessary following the sudden, traumatic death of a close, loved person, when suicide risk is likely to increase. Professional help, peer support, and trauma-informed bereavement approaches can decrease risk, help integrate grief, and promote growth.

The Tragedy Assistance Program for Survivors (TAPS) Suicide Postvention Model lays out a road map for decreasing risk, finding a health-promoting grief rhythm, and ultimately finding meaning and growth as a result of traumatic loss. In this three-phase model, the first phase, stabilization, is the most important when there are concerns regarding safety and risk. During this phase, the program assesses risk, mental health, and exposure to trauma as well as connects the bereaved to the appropriate professional care for treatment and/or to build coping skills. Additionally, in this phase, the program looks at specific issues directly related to the death, which, if not addressed, could interfere with an integrative grief journey and increase suicide risk. The importance of this phase is highlighted in Deadpool's constant recall of Vanessa's death in which he blames himself for her death and thinks he should have been able to save her. This core, unilateral belief of self-blame contributes to his view of himself as a bad person who doesn't deserve to live and may lead to dangerous self-talk such as "everyone would be better off without me" and "I am a burden". During this phase, identifying risk factors and warning cues, such as high self-blame and getting the appropriate help is vital for safety and stabilization.

Phase two of the Model is grief integration. There is much misconception about grief, which leaves those who are suffering to try to navigate it alone. Deadpool spends much of his time following Vanessa's death trying to numb his pain with alcohol/drugs, self-destructive behavior, and pushing away anyone who tries to support him. At one point in the movie he exclaims, "I am not ready to be touched again" (Kinberg et al., 2018, 0:23:11), which seems to be a metaphor for not wanting to be vulnerable with his grief and an expression of his fear of attachment following so much abandonment and loss. Avoidance and numbing following a traumatic loss can lead to additional complicating factors such as substance abuse and reclusiveness, all of which can develop into a sense of thwarted belongingness. The Model approaches grief in a direct, proactive way by identifying grief as "love" and encouraging mourners to embrace it, feel it, express it, and then rest. This approach decreases anxiety in trying to avoid "grief bursts" and gives the survivors a sense of control over their emotions. Recognizing these grief bursts as love and moving toward them also works to repair ruptured attachment issues related to the death. Using this model, survivors can reconnect with their loved one in a new way and build a new kind of relationship with the deceased to take forward: a secure attachment in which love is an enduring bond across time and space, transcending even death. We see this happen in the scene where Deadpool sees Vanessa again in the afterlife. He cannot reach her in the typical way that he was accustomed to in life, but he does communicate with her, receiving lessons about how to go forward and find growth from her loss. Vanessa tells him that he is not ready to be with her because "your heart's not in the right place" (Kinberg et al., 2018, 0:21:25) – meaning he had to heal his broken heart first before their time would come. This could not be accomplished as long as he viewed their love as a poison that was fueling his bitterness, rage, and self-hate after her death. She helps him to relocate his heart in the right place, because of her love, not her loss, and to save him through confronting his pain, by connecting to something that gives him meaning and purpose (helping abused children) while learning to build trusting relationships with others. She helps him, in other words, to realize that – because she was no longer alive, he must find his new "F-Word" (Kinberg et al., 2018, 0:10:25), the X-Force to give him a sense of belonging and purpose.

The third phase of the TAPS Suicide Postvention Model is posttraumatic growth (PTG), a concept defined as an experience of positive change that happens as a result of the struggle with a distressing life experience (Tedeschi & Calhoun, 2004). It is what Vanessa hopes for Deadpool when she gives him guidance while living, telling him, "Kids, they give us a chance to be better than we are" (Kinberg et al., 2018, 0:11:16) and then again in the afterlife. The program sees thousands of loss survivors who guide their journey with this model. Through the TAPS Suicide Postvention Model, there is evidence that not only is PTG possible following traumatic loss, but also this population is uniquely poised to achieve growth (Moore, Palmer, & Cerel, 2018). Many survivors who have lost a loved one in a traumatic way struggle to understand and make meaning out of a death that is violent, unexpected, and seemingly unfair. This struggle can lead to a desperate search to find something positive and life-affirming in an otherwise horrific event. If seen as an opportunity instead of an obstacle, survivors can actively pursue meaning-making in a great variety of ways.

We first encounter an introduction to PTG early in the movie when Deadpool is visiting with Blind Al and is deep within his pain and grief. She encourages him to "listen to the pain. It's both history teacher and fortune teller. Pain teaches us who we are, Wade. Sometimes, it's so bad we feel like dying" (Kinberg et al., 2018, 0:19:50). Blind Al then responds with the age-old wisdom, "We can't really live 'til we've died a little" (Kinberg et al., 2018, 0:23:24). This statement is poignant in that it highlights that good can come of bad, that true depth of character comes from all experiences, not just those that are positive and easily navigated. When Deadpool first hears this statement, he doesn't seem to understand the meaning and forges ahead in pursuit of self-destruction. However, when he meets a young boy, Russell, who he accurately surmises is being emotionally and physically abused in an orphanage for mutants, he begins to see a reflection of himself – bullied, rejected, angry, and pushing people away. He instinctually moves toward helping Russell instead of hurting him. He uses what he has learned in his own painful journey to help save him. The sense of purpose he develops in trying to save Russell shows up in his new ambivalence about whether he really wants to die and his desire to build a team of rogue peer mutants with whom he can forge connection and, most importantly, trust.

The movie ends with a powerful example of how one can move through tremendous loss and trauma to find new meaning as well as purpose through trust and connection. In this last scene, Deadpool is dying not because of the desire to be out of the pain of his grief, but in a loving and selfless effort to save Russell. Because of this, his heart is now in the right place. This affords him a healing afterlife visit with Vanessa, who embraces him then pushes him back toward life, which he welcomes because, through the process of transforming his grief and connecting it to her love, Deadpool has slowly, somehow, accepted that his life after her loss was will somehow be "okay". We see Deadpool's ambivalence about suicide change through a healed heart, secure and safe relationships, and a new sense of belonging. We learn this powerful lesson from Deadpool himself, in the last scene of the movie, where he walks side by side proudly with his new X-Force team, who he refers to as his family, to the song "We Belong" (Lowen & Navarro, 1984, track 2) as he tells us "if there is anything you take away today … it's that we all need to belong to someone" (Kinberg et al., 2018, 1:49:22–1:49:27).

## 23.6 Conclusions

Suicide after bereavement is a serious yet overlooked problem. Bereavement, in and of itself, can increase suicidal thinking (Jordan & McGann, 2017) and the risk of suicide attempts and completions (Latham & Prigerson, 2004). Other risk factors, such as sudden, traumatic death; exposure to trauma related to the death; preexisting mental health and developmental issues; exposure to suicide and history of suicide attempts; as well as the nature of the relationship to the deceased can converge during the agony of separation distress, making grief seem so unbearable and unrelenting that suicide may be sought as the ultimate form of psychic pain relief (Parkes, 1982).

In working with the bereaved, especially the newly bereaved or at-risk, it is vitally important to screen for active and passive suicidal thinking (Jordan & McGann, 2017). Passive suicidal ideation is described as "a diminution of the wish to live/or in the psychological investment in staying alive" (Jordan & McGann, 2017, p. 660). For example, expressions such as "I could care less whether I live or die" are indicators of passive suicidality. Active suicidal ideation is when a client has lost their will to live and is actively contemplating ending their life. Parkes (1982) urges practitioners to "never be afraid to ask" (p. 4) direct questions because research indicates that asking about suicide does not increase risk (Sommers-Flanagan & Shaw, 2017).

In addition, practitioners should listen for cues that indicate a risk for suicide, such as talking about being a burden to others, feelings of hopelessness or being trapped ("I am drowning"), feelings of self-loathing, preoccupation with death, and/or talking about suicide ("I'd be better off dead"). They should also look at behavioral cues as well, such as withdrawing from others, self-destructive behaviors, unusual visits, seeking or access to lethal means. It is important to also notice positive or negative affective changes; an example can be a sudden surge in positive, hopeful feelings, which need to be further explored, as they may indicate relief over having a plan to end the pain. It is also critical to note changes in body language and tone. Pay attention to cues that are increasing in intensity (e.g., agitation or sleep disturbance), as well as to accumulating risk factors that can paint a fuller picture over time. *Deadpool 2* is a powerful and insightful movie that teaches many lessons about the issue of suicide after bereavement. This chapter has attempted to highlight just some of the major lessons to be garnered. Free, confidential, and always available: **National Suicide Prevention Lifeline 1-800-273-8255.**

## References

Ajdacic-Gross, V., Ring, M., Gadola, E., Lauber, C., Bopp, M., Gutzwiller, F., & Rössler, W. (2008). Suicide after bereavement: An overlooked problem. *Psychological Medicine*, 38(5), 673–676. https://doi.org/10.1017/S0033291708002754

Arensman, E., & McCarthy, S. (2017). *Emerging survivor populations: Support after suicide clusters and murder-suicide events*. In K. Andriessen, K. Krysinska, & O. T. Grad (Eds.), *Postvention in action: The international handbook of suicide bereavement support* (p. 225–236). Boston, MA: Hogrefe Publishing.

Barr, N., Kintzle, S., Alday, E., & Castro, C. (2018). How does discharge status impact suicide risk in military veterans? *Social Work in Mental Health*. Advance online publication. https://doi.org/10.1080/15332985.2018.1503214

Bowlby, J. (1958). The nature of the child's tie to his mother. *The International Journal of Psycho-analysis*, 39(5), 350–373.

Cohen, O., & Katz, M. (2015). Grief and growth of bereaved siblings as related to attachment style and flexibility. *Death Studies*, 39(1–5), 158–164. https://doi.org/10.1080/07481187.2014.923069

Currier, J.M., Holland, J.M., & Neimeyer, R.A. (2006). Sense-making, grief, and the experience of violent loss: Toward a mediational model. *Death Studies*, 30(5), 403–428. https://doi.org/10.1080/07481180600614351

Deadpool (2020, June 3). Retrieved from https://www.marvel.com/characters/deadpool-wade-wilson/in-comics/profile

Joiner, T.E. (2005). *Why people die by suicide*. Cambridge, MA: Harvard University Press.

Joiner, T.E. (2009). The Interpersonal-psychological theory of suicidal behavior: Current empirical status. *American Psychological Association Science Briefs*. Retrieved from https://www.apa.org/science/about/psa/2009/06/sci-brief

Joiner, T.E. (2014). *The perversion of virtue*. New York, NY: Oxford University Press.

Jordan, J.R., & McGann, V. (2017). Clinical work with suicide loss survivors: Implications of the U.S. postvention guidelines. *Death Studies*, 41(10), 659–672. DOI: 10.1080/07481187.2017.1335553

Kinberg, S., Reynolds, R., & Donner, L.S. (Producers), & Leitch, D. (Director). (2018). *Deadpool 2* [Motion picture]. United States: Twentieth Century Fox.

Kinberg, S., Reynolds, R., & Donner, L. S. (Producers), & Miller, T. (Director). (2016). *Deadpool* [Motion picture]. United States: Twentieth Century Fox.

Kosminsky, P.S., & Jordan, J.R. (2016). *Attachment-informed grief therapy: The clinician's guide to foundations and applications*. New York, NY: Routledge.

Latham, A. E., & Prigerson, H. G. (2004). Suicidality and bereavement: Complicated grief as psychiatric disorder presenting greatest risk for suicidality. *Suicide & life-threatening behavior*, 34(4), 350–362. https://doi.org/10.1521/suli.34.4.350.53737

Lowen, D.E., & Navarro, D. (1984). We belong. [Recorded by P. Benatar]. On *Tropico* [Record]. Glendale, CA: MCA Whitney Studios.

Moore, M., Palmer, J., & Cerel, J. (October, 2018). *Growth and hope after loss: How TAPS facilitates posttraumatic growth in those grieving military deaths*. [Conference Session]. *Presented at the National Military Suicide Seminar of the Tragedy Assistance Program for Survivors*, Tampa, Florida.

Nakajima, S., Ito, M., Shirai, A., & Konishi, T. (2012). Complicated grief in those bereaved by violent death: The effects of posttraumatic stress disorder on complicated grief. *Dialogues in Clinical Neuroscience*, 14(2), 210–214.

Parkes, C.M. (1982). The risk of suicide after bereavement. *Bereavement Care*, 1(1), 4–5, DOI: 10.1080/02682628208657044

Rubin, S.S., Malkinson, R., & Witztum, E. (2016). *The multiple faces of loss and bereavement: Theory and therapy*. Haifa: University of Haifa/Pardess Press.

Russel, G., & Davis, C. (1979). All out of love. On *Lost in love* [record]. Sydney, Australia: Trafalgar Studios, Paradise Studios and EMI Studios 301; San Clemente, CA: Allen Zentz Recording.

Rynearson, E.K. (2006). Restorative retelling after violent dying. In E.K. Rynearson (Ed.), *Violent death: Resilience and intervention beyond the crisis* (195–216). New York, NY: Routledge.

Selby, E.A., Anestis, M.D., Bender, T.W., Ribeiro, J.D., Nock, M.K., Rudd, M.D., Bryan, C.J., Lim, I.C., Baker, M.T., Gutierrez, P.M., & Joiner, T.E., Jr (2010). Overcoming the fear of lethal injury: Evaluating suicidal behavior in the military through the lens of the Interpersonal-Psychological Theory of Suicide. *Clinical Psychology Review*, 30(3), 298–307. https://doi.org/10.1016/j.cpr.2009.12.004

Shneidman E.S. (1993). Suicide as psychache. *The Journal of Nervous and Mental Disease*, 181(3), 145–147. https://doi.org/10.1097/00005053-199303000-00001

Sommers-Flanagan, J., & Shaw, S.L. (2017). Suicide risk assessment: What psychologists should know. *Professional Psychology: Research and Practice*, 48(2), 98–106. https://doi.org/10.1037/pro0000106

Tedeschi, R.G., & Calhoun, L.G. (2004). Posttraumatic growth: Conceptual foundations and empirical evidence, *Psychological Inquiry*, 15:1, 1–18. DOI: 10.1207/s15327965pli1501_01

Utz, R.L., Caserta, M., & Lund, D. (2012). Grief, depressive symptoms, and physical health among recently bereaved spouses. *The Gerontologist*, 52(4), 460–471. https://doi.org/10.1093/geront/gnr110

Worden, J.W. (2018). *Grief counseling and grief therapy* (4th ed.). New York, NY: Springer Publishing.

# 24 Complicated Grief, Bruce Wayne, and Batman

## A Conversation with M. Katherine Shear

*M. Katherine Shear and Jill A. Harrington*

[**New York City** – As the elevator doors open to the Center for Complicated Grief at Columbia University School of Social Work, I feel like Dick Grayson in *The Lego Batman Movie*, when he was "accidentally" let into the Batcave by Alfred and recognizes where he is. The scene plays through my head, and it is hard to contain my professional demeanor, hearing his super excited voice as he is about to meet one of his superheroes, "Oh my gosh, oh my gosh, oh my gosh, oh my gosh, oh, my gosh ..." (Allegra, Ashton, & McKay, 2017, 0:37:58). I am about to meet one in the field of thanatology, Dr. M. Katherine Shear, Marion E. Kentworthy Professor of Psychiatry and Director of the Center for Complicated Grief. And here in Gotham, oops, New York City! She shakes my hand, giving me a better reception then Batman did with Dick, and I sit across from her desk, staring at the beautiful skyline of the Upper West Side of Manhattan through her office windows. Much brighter and warmer than a cave but symbolically, a place where, much like Batman, Dr. Shear and her staff work to investigate complicated grief and to train professionals and educate the bereaved. I open my pad, click my pen, and begin ...]

JH: Dr. Shear, comic book fans, writers, critics, and psychologists have long been exploring Batman, aka Bruce Wayne, from a psychological perspective. I mean, he is a grown man who dresses up like a bat and hunts down criminals in Gotham City. There has been so much speculation about the nature of Bruce's reactions to his parents' loss (including "maladaptive" thoughts, persistent and intense anger at criminals, and social isolation) that complicated grief is one of the top ten "diagnoses" given to Batman. Given your expertise in the research and treatment of complicated grief, what are your thoughts on the idea that Bruce Wayne might be experiencing complicated grief (CG)?

KS: Well, Jill, I would like to start off with a caveat.

JH: (Curious, slightly hesitant and questioning.) Sure?

KS: As compelling as I find Batman, you know that Bruce Wayne, aka Batman, is a fictitious character (while looking me in the eyes, pause), right?

JH: (There is a long, awkward pause by me as I ponder this. I think about it, then a joining of the eyes and a wave of the hand in agreement.) Of course, I do (I question myself silently). (Pause) But, if he was real …

KS: (Without hesitation, firm, but gentle.) But he's not … and that means that we are doing two things that many of us are hesitant to do.

JH: (Pause, okay, a meeting of the minds. Tone a little defeated.) Point taken. (Long pause as I think of how we can join in this conversation.) I might be able to guess – but what do you have in mind?

KS: You are asking us to attempt to diagnose someone without ever talking to them – something you and I know is always inadvisable, and to make matters worse, this individual is a creation of someone's imagination.

JH: So, why do you think there is so much interest in the fictitious character, Bruce Wayne, and pop culture "diagnosing" him with complicated grief?

KS: (She looks up from her desk.) Probably because people can be uncomfortable with behavior that is outside of the norm and want to be able to name it in a way that can either fix the behavior to be normative or give them a reason to think of this person as not belonging. I'm sure there are other, perhaps more playful reasons as well. Perhaps, too, people are interested in the idea of complicated grief.

JH: (Shaking my head in agreement.) Good point. To help them better understand, can you help explain – what is complicated grief?

KS: Complicated grief (now being called Prolonged Grief Disorder in ICD11) is a recently recognized condition that occurs in about 7% of bereaved people overall, and at least twice that proportion after death by violent means, as Bruce was imagined to "experience". It's the condition that occurs when something stalls or halts the natural process of adapting to an important loss. The result is a persistent impairing form of grief that can be very debilitating. When I talk about it, I always start by defining terms because people mean different things when they use the word *grief.* In fact, people mean different things by "complicated grief". I'll get back to that in a minute. So, here's how we use common terms. Bereavement is the experience of having lost someone close by death. Grief is the response to loss. The definition is simple, but the experience is messy – it's complex and multifaceted. Grief includes thoughts, feelings, behaviors, and physiological changes that vary in pattern and intensity over time. Considering that death is forever, so too is our response to the death of a loved one. We never stop feeling sad that our loved ones are gone or stop missing them. However, grief usually evolves from an acute, all-encompassing response to becoming integrated into our life. We say grief emerges naturally and finds a place in our lives. Acute grief is usually characterized by intense yearning and unrelenting sorrow, along with thoughts, memories, and images of the person who died. You can think of this as a mix of separation and traumatic distress. Gradually, over time we adapt to the loss and all the changes it brings. We assimilate information about the finality and consequences of the loss into memory systems and restore a capacity for joy and satisfaction. Grief is integrated into our lives as we adapt to the loss. That said, it can still surge up on some calendar days or at the time of an important life event.

JH: What factors influence grief in the context of bereavement?

KS: The unique way we each grieve depends upon who we are as a person, things like our prior experiences, including prior losses, our personal coping style, the nature of our relationship with the person who died, their age and circumstances of their death, the social and environmental context of our lives and theirs, and the consequences of the loss, including all the changes it brings. In general, the death of a child or a spouse are associated with the most difficulty adapting to the loss. Any death of a young person or a death by violent means also comprise risk for more difficulty adapting. Interestingly, though, we have found that the framework of grief is similar across different circumstances of death. The more difficult the death, the more persistent obstacles may be, but the process of adaptation is similar. The character, Bruce Wayne, was created as having witnessed the murders of his parents in front of a theater in Gotham City when he was eight years old. We don't know much about the long-term risk of prolonged grief disorder in children who lose parents at a young age, but a study by Nadine Melhem and colleagues suggests that about 10% of children who lose their parents can be diagnosed with prolonged grief disorder about three years later (Melhem et al., 2011). It's hard to know if those children would still be suffering from PGD well into adulthood. Notably, too, only a small proportion of these children had persistent grief.

JH: What do you mean by the process of adaptation?

KS: The process of adapting to a loss includes accepting the reality and restoring well-being. However, remember, Jill, the way we do this is unique for each griever because we are unique, and the relationships we have with loved ones are also unique. As my students helped me see, grief is the form love takes when someone we love dies. Love, too, is unique to each person and each relationship. Like grief, it's a natural instinctive response and an experience shared by virtually all humanity. We all love, and we all die, so we all grieve, so it makes sense that adaptation to loss is also a natural process. You can think of it as a survival instinct. With that said, the trajectories of adaptation are as varied as the relationships that were lost and the people who are bereaved. There is no one way to adapt. In fact, there is tremendous variability in what it is that a person must adapt to and how they adapt. Adaptation to any loss can progress by a number of distinct paths and progress at varying rates. We know that most bereaved people make their way along the path of grief, notwithstanding obstacles they must often confront.

JH: So, if I understand you correctly, through the rough road and obstacles, people find a way to adapt to loss, and grief finds a place in their life as they do this. How is complicated grief different?

KS: (She smiles.) Good question. Complicated grief results when something derails the process of adapting to the loss. When this occurs, intense grief is not transformed, so the symptoms of acute grief are prolonged, sometimes indefinitely.

JH: What does that look like? What are the signs or symptoms of CG?

KS: Another good question. We now know a fair amount about this. But before I tell you these symptoms, I want to straighten out the terminology again. The term complicated grief was first introduced by Mardi Horowitz in the late 1990s. He was the first to notice that there was a form of grief that grabbed people by the heels and wouldn't let go. He called this persistent impairing grief "complicated grief". The next person to study this was Holly Prigerson, who was a postdoctoral fellow with Charles Reynolds. She developed a questionnaire called the Inventory of Complicated Grief that is the most widely used way that researchers around the world have identified this condition. Holly got me involved in this work because her questionnaire was identifying people who were not responding to treatment for depression, even when it had a grief focus. Our group went on to develop a highly efficacious short-term treatment called Complicated Grief Treatment that turned out to be pretty effective. Three studies funded by the National Institute of Mental Health showed an overall 70% response rate. This was significantly greater than really good treatment for depression – which was the control treatment. In the meantime, Holly conducted a community-based study of complicated grief and, working with others in the field, decided to change the name to prolonged grief disorder. The World Health Organization and the DSM5.1 committees have now combined the findings from Holly's work and our clinical findings, along with a large body of other research, to create a new condition called Prolonged Grief Disorder (PGD) in the ICD11, which has been approved as official by member countries of the World Health Organization. We can use the ICD 11 guideline to identify people with complicated grief, aka prolonged grief disorder. This is the way we now define complicated grief. The hallmark of PGD is persistent, intense yearning, longing, or preoccupation with thoughts and memories of the deceased. In addition, there is evidence of emotional pain. This may be manifest as unrelenting sorrow, other strong grief-related feelings (e.g., anger, guilt, anxiety) difficulty comprehending the reality of the death, identity confusion, emotional numbness, loss of a sense of purpose or meaning in life, profound emotional loneliness, feeling unable or unmotivated to plan for the future, trying to ignore, avoid, or rewrite the actuality of the death (e.g., frequent thoughts of self-blame or blaming others, protesting the death as wrong or unfair, counterfactual "if only" thoughts, difficulty managing emotional pain, excessive avoidance of reminders of the death or excessive proximity seeking in attempt to keep deceased close). These symptoms last well beyond six months. Those with PGD find themselves in a repetitive loop, kind of like what The Flash character does to gain speed, of intense yearning and longing that becomes the major focus of their lives, accompanied by persistent, overwhelming sadness, frustration, and anxiety. They stay in that continual loop and often perceive their grief as frightening, shameful, and strange. They think that their life is over and that the extreme persistent pain will never cease. This is one reason those with CG have an elevated risk of suicide. At the same time, they often do not want the grief to end, as they feel that it is the only way for them to stay close to their deceased loved one. They think that by letting grief go, they are letting the relationship go. With effective treatment, they learn to accept grief into their life and let it find a place where it is not disrupting their ability to restore a sense of purpose and meaning with possibilities for happiness. Often people with PGD struggle with survivor guilt, meaning they feel that it is somehow wrong or not right to live their own life fully – to enjoy their life because their loved one cannot do so. Preoccupation with the deceased may include frequent daydreams, spending an excessive amount of time at the cemetery or place of interment, or prolonged avoidance of dealing with personal effects or rearranging, and assimilating belongings. It is as if time stood still. Simultaneously, those with PGD may avoid activities and situations that remind them that the loved one is gone, along with the good times, they spent with the deceased. They also commonly feel a sense of disconnection from others, including people that used to be close.

JH: So, is this why psychologists, pop psychologists, and pop culture are so interested in the association between Bruce Wayne, Batman, and complicated grief? Do they think he fits this description?

KS: Maybe, but we can't know whether the character of Bruce is experiencing these symptoms. Partly, that's because we get little access to Bruce's inner life. People with PGD often walk around the world – as they put it – "wearing a mask", so perhaps that's what we are supposed to think of Bruce. However, without knowing his private thoughts and feelings, it's impossible to know whether and how he might be struggling. Bruce does not appear to be experiencing persistent, intense yearning and longing for his parents. He does not appear to be preoccupied with thoughts and memories of his parents. Nor does he seem to have clear evidence of other ongoing prominent grief-related emotional pain. It appears that Bruce Wayne goes to galas, experiences other emotions doing other daily acts of living. He visits the thoughts of his parents when he wants to connect with them. He does appear to have carried on in a new and meaningful life. Of course, he might have other psychological problems. If he does, it is very possible that there is some connection with the deaths of his parents. It is not uncommon for survivors of violent death to develop psychological problems as a consequence of this experience. However, not all problems that stem from bereavement are manifestations of prolonged grief disorder.

JH: Hmm?

KS: From the story arcs, we don't see evidence that he is still experiencing a strong sense of disbelief that his parents died, a common experience with PGD. Although there are times when he is dealing with anger and bitterness about his parents' deaths, he also has tender moments with Alfred and other emotions of joy and meaningful activities. Moreover, who among us would be able to think about the murders of our parents without lasting anger or bitterness? And remember, a person with PGD struggles with frequent intense emotional pain so the anger and bitterness would be constant and very strong. Another relevant observation is that Bruce does not appear to avoid the painful loss; he takes it head-on with a new meaning and purpose in life as Batman. Many who have been afflicted by violent death transform their loss by finding occupations to help prevent crime or advocate for new laws. One could argue that the Batman identity and work is maladaptive because it is overinvolvement, or it could be highly adaptive if he has found new purpose in life. Like the childhood cancer survivor who becomes a clinical-research oncologist and spends a lifetime waging war against the enemy of cancer, and I know a lot of people who would like to have Batman powers. Bruce seems to honor his continued bond with his parents as he visits their grave and pictures when he needs to connect with them. If the majority of his time was spent at the cemetery, then he couldn't be off catching criminals. Of course, he has rebuilt his house to include a cave. Now, we have to give him a break, because most billionaires with family estates typically keep some historic preservation to the house, especially with family pictures and heirlooms. At least that is what I hear. He has taken on his father's position at Wayne Enterprises and feels grief because he also remembers the good times. Joy and grief dwell together. Also indicative of his ability to restore his capacity for well-being, he seems to have pretty close relationships with Alfred, Robin, Batgirl, Commissioner Gordon, Catwoman, and he even fights in partnership with The Justice League. Hmm?

JH: Wow, it seems like we can learn a lot about grief from Batman. What do you think grief therapists can learn from the meaning of the Batman superhero narrative?

KS: That comic strip characters and maybe also people (including ourselves) are complex, with strengths and vulnerabilities. This is what it means to be human and/or an interesting fictional character. There are many ways to grieve and many ways to adapt to loss. As we work with the bereaved, we want to share the pain and honor the range of ways people grieve and adapt. We also want to watch for ways people can get derailed and assess for PGD. The bereaved do not have to live in intractable suffering, like the Bat-Signal, there is hope.

JH: (I smile and think to myself, I am writing about one of my favorite superheroes, but right now I am listening to one of my own. And then, just then, curiosity got the cat, "Meow" [Catwoman reference]. I had to ask it.) So, Dr. Shear, do you think Bruce Wayne, aka Batman, has complicated grief?

KS: (She leans across her desk, looks me in the eyes, with a slightly stern look on her face, sunlight bouncing off the buildings through the window behind from her window. Her look is quite intense. There is a long pause.)

JH: (Oh boy, I did it now, curiosity killed the cat.)

KS: Well, Jill (she then smiles, playfully), if I were a CBT Therapist, aka Comic Book Therapist, Bruce Wayne would always be welcome to walk, fly, or drive into to the Center for Complicated Grief here in Gotham, aka New York City (she winks at me), and have an assessment. But because I am a CGT therapist, aka Complicated Grief Therapist, if he did have PGD, I would probably be able to help him.

KS AND JH: (We join in a smile. Grief Mentor to Mentee. Like Batman to Robin [Nightwing].)

For more information: https://complicatedgrief.columbia.edu

## References

Allegra, W., & Ashton, M. (Producers), & McKay, C. (Director) (2017). *The Lego Batman movie* [Motion picture]. USA: Fox Studios

Melhem, N.M., Porta, G., Shamseddeen, W., Walker Payne, M., & Brent, D.A. (2011). Grief in children and .adolescents bereaved by sudden parental death. *Archives of General Psychiatry*, 68(9), 911–919. doi:10.1001/archgenpsychiatry.2011.101

# 25 Traumatic Loss and How the Flash Could Benefit from Restorative Retelling

*Sharon Strouse*

The Flash was created by writer Gardner Fox and artist Harry Lampert in January 1940, during the Golden Age of Comics. DC Comics revived the series in 1956, after its postwar decline in popularity and again in 2008. Barry Allen, "the fastest man alive", is genuine and honest with "actions guided by sacrifice, caring and compassion" (Rogers, 2017, p. 20). He adheres to the "superhero code, never kill and protect and defend the weak" (Rogers, 2017, p. 15), a quality that is imbued by his personal history of loss. Barry Allen is a testament to the enduring quality of this genre, which experienced resurgence in the aftermath of 9/11. The Flash is currently a popular staple in the DC Comic Universe films and an award-winning TV series.

The hero, as defined by Joseph Campbell, is "someone who has given himself or his life to something bigger than himself" (Campbell & Moyers, 1988, p. 151). He steps out of the ordinary world and into a special world – challenged by trials and tribulation. During that adventure he undergoes a transformation. As an art therapist, working in the field of grief and bereavement, I am privileged to walk beside clients who are real-life heroes in the midst of a traumatic loss. I bear witness to arduous journeys of self-discovery in creative spaces where imaginative modalities (Strouse, 2013) are explored in service to meaning reconstruction, "the establishment of a coherent self-narrative that integrates the loss, while permitting (a personal) story to move forward along new lines" (Neimeyer, Burke, Mackay, & van Dyke Stringer, 2009, p. 73). Most people are surprisingly resilient and successfully navigate the territory of loss and transition, or the hero's descent and return from the underworld. They find their way, with support, to healthy levels of functioning within a few months of the death. "However for a notable minority of about 10% of the bereaved, grief becomes complicated" (Shear, Boelen, & Neimeyer, 2011, p. 139), "more painful, preoccupying, and prolonged" (Neimeyer, 2019, p. 80). "Sudden and violent deaths by (homicide, suicide and fatal accident) carries with it greater risk of a complicated bereavement trajectory as mourners react to the horrific nature of the dying process itself" (Jordan & McIntosh, 2011, p. 227). For those bereaved by homicide, the incidence of complicated grief may approach 50% (McDevitt-Murphy, Neimeyer, Burke, Williams, & Lawson, 2012). These deaths involve "violence, violation and volition, all ingredients of a human act that transform the dying into something abhorrent" (Rynearson, 2001, p. 21), and set it aside from other types of losses. Those who suffer severe and disabling responses experience an "inability to accept the loss, preoccupation with the deceased, confusion about one's role in life and loss of a purpose and hope for the future" (Lichtenthal et al., 2004). They often need professional help.

## 25.1 What the Flash Can't Outrun

I enter the world of *Superhero Grief* with this in mind and discover the arch of this fictional character's story hinges on the fact that Barry is a homicide loss survivor, a childhood witness to his mother's murder. The premature, traumatic death of his mother is more than a death, it disrupts Barry's life story in ways that are profound and pervasive. He says, "I cannot figure out why some people come into your life and others go … what lasts is the pain when that person is gone" (Berlanti, Kreisberg, & Johns, 2014, Ep. 5, 00:38:50). His inability to process the homicide launches him into an anguished search for meaning that includes "retaliation, retribution and punishment" (Rynearson, 2001, p. 21). After the violent, sudden, and seemingly meaningless death of his mother, Barry's world is dangerous, unpredictable, and unjust (Janoff-Bulman, & Berger, 2000). This makes Barry's transformation into a crime-fighting superhero impressive, given the fact that he is possessed by traumatic memories and repeatedly returns to the event story of his mother's death. His childhood flashbacks include memories of being bullied. They are intrusive, vivid reminders; he ran from his aggressors and was a powerless observer of his mother's murder. "The compulsive retelling of the violent dying of a family member often eclipses the retelling of their living" (Rynearson, 2001, p. ix). He says, "I am stuck in Central City. Fear has kept me in the living room (site of his mother's murder) for 14 years" (Berlanti et al., 2014, Ep. 9, 00:38:24). No matter how fast The Flash runs, he is trapped in the self-destructing forces of remembering and retelling, which cannot be undone and has no resolution. He says, "My past is stalking me, as fast as I am … it's almost caught up to me" (Berlanti et al., 2014, Ep. 19, 00:01:26). Ultimately, his super-speed heroism is not enough. Inner demons get the better of him, and fatal errors in judgment upend his superhero world. He says, "We are all running to and from. Some things you cannot outrun" (Berlanti et al., 2014, Ep. 3, 00:01:12).

Those in the field of grief and bereavement, recognize that Barry could benefit from professional guidance in his search for coherence amidst the ongoing chaos and confusion of his mother's murder. Restorative Retelling (RR), which is "the narrative reframing of a violent dying story to include the teller as a participant, rather than a horrified witness, and to reconnect the teller with the living memories of the deceased" (Rynearson, 2001, p. ix), is an evidence-based therapy to help the bereaved.

In the first episode, a flashback invites us into Barry's earliest memories. A victimized little boy dressed in red runs from a gang of bullies. They eventually catch him. He cowers to protect himself. This slow-motion scene fades, but reappears, a fixed, repetitive and intrusive memory that plays an important part of the first two seasons, or 46 episodes, of Barry's life as The Flash. In episode six, The Flash comes face-to-face with one of his former bullies, now a powerful iron-fisted meta-human, who says, "Looks like you were born to take a beating" (Berlanti et al., 2014, Ep. 6, 00:01:12). Afterwards Barry laments, "There is nowhere to run. I was tormented then and am tormented now. I could not stop him, I am powerless" (Berlanti et al., 2014, Ep. 6, 00:22:49). This wounding gives shape to Barry's developing personality and is relived during his mother's traumatic murder. He cannot save her and runs from the murder scene, consumed with guilt and shame. These unresolved experiences influence the rest of his life as a speedster. His determination to honor his mom's life, find her murderer, and secure justice derive from psychological wounds. The themes of reversal and restoration are played out in his role as The Flash, who saves the world's helpless victims from meta-human supervillains. Barry's transformation into a superhero opens the door of possibility, an opportunity to go back in time, which ultimately spells disaster.

He becomes The Flash when a containment system fails. This explosion destroys all known life in Central City and mirrors the destruction of Barry's life as witness to his mother's murder. The explosion sets up a powerful chain reaction; he is struck by lightning and doused with chemicals. He wakes up with superspeed powers, after nine months in a coma, a gestational parallel that announces Barry's superhero initiation and rebirth. He is an ordinary citizen, unless called upon to save the city from meta-human villains, at which time he transforms into a costumed crime-fighting hero. He is masked and dressed in a red jumpsuit, emboldened with a yellow lightning bolt. The juxtaposition between the little boy in red, running away from his attackers, and The Flash, dressed in red running toward danger, links past and present. Each episode includes two intertwined story lines, the first is grounded in the present supervillain drama and the second weaves in his traumatic past, with flashbacks of childhood bullying and the murder of his mother. As The Flash, Barry attempts to right the wrongs in his personal life, he seeks purpose and meaning for a life marred by the failure of his own psychological "containment system" and the missed opportunity of RR.

At the end of season one, The Flash makes use of his superpowers and enters the speed force in order to go back in time. He returns to the night of his mother's murder determined to save her. He witnesses her murder and makes the decision not to intervene because it will alter the time line. He will lose the life he has and the people he loves. He tells his mom he loves her, she forgives him, they say goodbye, she dies, and he cries over her body. During this revisiting, forgiveness sets him free but at a terrible cost, for the time line is altered in his unhealthy revisiting, and his world is upended. Barry realizes, in traveling back, he lost his way, "one decision impacts everything … things happen the way they do, we may not understand but there is always a reason" (Berlanti et al., 2014, Ep. 23, 00:05:40–00:08:40).

## 25.2 The Power of Restorative Retelling

I imagine the impact of RR on Barry's superhero adventure and step into this world with him. Rynearson's (2001) protocol for RR, offered by trained mental health professionals, guides Barry "toward a harbor of refuge" (Rynearson, 2001, p. X), where conditions of high safety yet low avoidance of traumatic details (Rynearson, 2001) set the stage for Barry's retelling. Before exposure to the slow unpacking of his story, great effort is made to ground Barry in restorative experiences. He shares comforting memories about his mother and their relationship, which realign him to living memories and a reengagement with the world. Barry embraces the support of family, friends, and coworkers and listens to wise advice. "Everyone loses someone; it's what you do about it that matters, what you do once they are gone.... You are who you are because of it, a true hero" (Berlanti et al., 2014, Ep. 23, 00:09:40).

Over the course of several sessions Barry shares the traumatic story of his mother's murder in detail. This experience helps him locate himself as participant rather than victim and moves him toward a more meaningful narrative. RR helps Barry disengage from irrational and meaningless questions, such as: "How could this have happened? How could I have kept this from happening? How can I find retribution for this dying? And, how can I prevent this from happening again?" (Rynearson, 2001, p. xv). Bracing, pacing, and facing (Neimeyer, 2019) is implemented throughout the process. Bracing offers Barry support in regulating upsurges of strong emotion. Pacing eases Barry's retelling and allows him to stay present with feelings and difficult details, as new insights emerge. Facing leads to mastery of the trauma story as Barry confronts and moves toward the story rather than running and avoiding it. RR reorientates Barry and empowers him. He redefines who he was before his mother's murder, a loving, devoted son and blameless little boy rather than a coward. He embraces who he is now as a result of his loss, a crime-fighting superhero. Treatment releases him from the unrealistic burden of "saving the world", which will never change the fact of his mother's murder. Barry integrates the event story of his mother's death into the narrative of his life as a crime-fighting superhero, free to do his job, unencumbered by his past.

## 25.3 Clinical Considerations

The Flash offers me a unique opportunity as an art therapist working in the field of grief and bereavement. Its lessons come through an art form rather than words, through television, one frame at a time. Children, adolescents, and adults easily relate to this superhero genre. This storytelling art form harnesses the imagination, for "in an imaginary world, thoughts and feelings and behaviors are unfettered by logic or barriers of time and space. Everything is possible and nothing is improbable. Imagination mixes and merges living and death" (Rynearson, 2001, p. 56).

I add The Flash to my art therapy treatment toolbox and recommend it to bereaved individuals and families. I advise them to sit, watch, connect, and find

*Figure 25.1* Drawing by Alex, bereaved teen.

inspiration. I am grateful to Barry Allen, who takes us on a hero's journey into heartbreaking lessons learned, for in the end he is both human and hero.

## 25.4 Intervention Strategies

Collage is a powerful art therapy modality used in the treatment of traumatic loss and fits with Rynearson's (2001) RR process and Neimeyer's (2019) tenets of bracing, pacing and facing. Collage is a composition made of cut up materials, images from magazines and ephemera that are glued onto a surface (Chilton & Scotti, 2014). The processes and product support the safe exploration of lost relationships and fragmented trauma stories (Strouse, 2014, 2019). Unconscious content emerges when associations are made to images. Details are filled in and glued down that enhance RR (Figure 25.1). "Artful retelling of violent dying shifts the telling perspective from witness to participant and finally, to a survivor changed by the retelling" (Rynearson, 2001, p. 140). The finished products address separation distress and trauma distress and serve as tangible reminders of transformation, like that of Barry Allen – The Flash.

Additional expressive therapies techniques may be of interest when offering RR: *The Chapters of Our Lives* (Neimeyer, 2014) and *Performance Retelling* (Smigelsky & Neimeyer, 2018).

## References

Berlanti, G., Kreisberg, A., & Johns, G. (Developers) (2014). *The Flash* [Television]. Bonanza Productions and Warner Bros. Television.

Campbell, J., & Moyers, B. (1988). The hero's adventure. In S.B. Flowers (Ed.), *The power of myth* (p. 151). New York: Anchor Books.

Chilton, G., & Scotti, V., (2014). Snipping, gluing, writing: The properties of collage as an arts-based research practice in art therapy. *The Art Therapy Journal of the American Art Therapy Association*, 31(4), 163–171.

Janoff-Bulman, R., & Berger, A.R. (2000). The other side of trauma. In J. H. Harvey & E. D. Miller (Eds.), *Loss and trauma*. Philadelphia, PA: Brunner Mazel.

Jordan, J.R., & McIntosh, J.L. (2011). Is suicide bereavement different? Perspectives from research and practice. In R.A. Neimeyer, D.L. Harris, H.R. Winokuer, & G.F. Thornton (Eds.), *Grief and bereavement in contemporary society bridging research and practice*. New York, NY: Routledge.

Lichtenthal, W.G., Cruess, D.G., & Prigerson, H.G. (2004). A case for establishing complicated grief as a distinct mental disorder in the DSM-V. *Clinical Psychology Review*, 24 (6), 637–662.

McDevitt-Murphy, M.E., Neimeyer, R.A., Burke, L.A., Williams, J.L., & Lawson, K. (2012). Assessing the toll of traumatic loss: Psychological symptoms in African Americans bereaved by homicide. *Psychological Trauma*, 4(3), 303–311.

Neimeyer, R.A. (2019). Meaning reconstruction in bereavement: Development of a research program. *Death Studies*, 43(2), 79–91.

Neimeyer, R.A., Burke, L.A., Mackay, M.M., & van Dyke Stringer, J.G. (2009). Grief therapy and the reconstruction of meaning: From principles to practice. *Journal of Contemporary Psychotherapy*, 40(2), 73–83.

Rogers, K. (2017). *Heroes, villains, and healing: A guide for male survivors of child sexual abuse using D.C. comic superheroes and villains*. USA: Strategic Book Publishing and Rights Co., LLC.

Rynearson, E.K. (2001). *Retelling violent death*. Philadelphia, PA: Brunner-Routledge.

Shear, M.K., Boelen, P.A., & Neimeyer, R.A., (2011). Treating complicated grief converging approaches. In R.A. Neimeyer, D.L. Harris, H.R. Winokuer, & G.F. Thornton (Eds.), *Grief and bereavement in contemporary society: Bridging research and practice* (pp. 139–162). New York, NY: Routledge.

Smigelsky, M.A., & Neimeyer, R.A. (2018). Performance retelling: Healing community stories of loss through Playback Theatre. *Death Studies*, 1–9. DOI: 10.1080/07481187.2017.1370414

Strouse, S. (2013). *Artful grief: A diary of healing*. Bloomington, IN: Balboa Press.

Strouse, S. (2014). Collage: Integrating the torn pieces. In B.E. Thompson & R.A. Neimeyer, (Eds.), *Grief and the expressive arts: Practices for creating meaning* (pp. 187–197). New York, NY: Routledge.

Strouse, S. (2019). Art therapy and dreamscaping. In N. Gershman & B.E. Thompson (Eds.), *Prescriptive memory in grief and loss: The art of dreamscaping*. New York, NY: Routledge.

# Part VII

# Posttraumatic Growth, Superheroes, and Personal Stories Addressing the Five Factors

# 26 Posttraumatic Growth, Superheroes, and the Bereaved

*Melinda M. Moore*

Stories of personal growth in the aftermath of traumatic loss are ubiquitous. Standing in the bitter winter night looking up at the sky from the courtyard of a concentration camp, Viktor Frankl pondered the value of his own life, not knowing if his parents and wife, who were in concentration camps, were alive or dead. Ultimately, it did not matter. The very concept of his family was enough to keep him alive. "Nothing could touch the strength of my love, my thoughts, and the image of my beloved" (Frankl, 2006, p. 50). Abraham Lincoln, despairing over his own suicidal thoughts and feelings as a young lawyer, found promise and hope in the possibility of doing something great with his life (Shenk, 2005). The idea of pain shapeshifting through personal changes into joy or hope is common in the Bible. The characters of Joseph, Job, and Moses are a few of the many biblical "superheroes" who triumphed in the wake of tremendous adversity, tragedy, and loss.

While these stories are everywhere, even in superhero tales and comic books, and have been around for thousands of years, the creation and scientific investigation of this concept, called Posttraumatic Growth (PTG), has only been around since the mid-1990s. Tedeschi and Calhoun (2004) describe Posttraumatic Growth as a construct of positive psychological change that occurs as the result of one's struggle with highly challenging, stressful, and traumatic event(s). It is a cognitive process whereby an individual experiences a traumatic event and, as they begin to manage the emotional distress of the event, they reflect upon the traumatic experience. This reflective thought process allows the individual the opportunity to build a new philosophy of their life, their place in the world, and their relationships with others. It is from these internal personal changes that dimensions of growth are developed.

Defined by Tedeschi and Calhoun (2004), the presence of PTG can manifest itself in several domains: **Relating to Others, New Possibilities, Personal Strength, Spiritual Change,** and **Appreciation for Life**. **Relating to Others** is a dimension that allows for new relationships or a special kind of compassion for people who have experienced what you have experienced or, perhaps, developing stronger relationships with those who are already in your life.

**New Possibilities** is the potential for new vocations or new missions in your life, created by a desire to do something meaningful with your experience – it is a sense of hope. **Personal Strength** signals a new kind of internal strength, which does not necessarily ensure being "bullet proof", but rather an awareness that you have been through the worst possible experience of your life and you can probably sustain almost anything else that comes your way. **Spiritual Change** may mean becoming more spiritual, although it does not necessarily mean that you are more religious. However, some individuals do become more religious. Last, **Appreciation for Life** suggests that you understand the fragility of life and are more mindful of the beauty and gift of every day.

Superhero tales are full of backstories where enormous traumatic personal loss propels the superhero forward into a choice in their grief. Do they choose a life of service to others or that of personal revenge? The greater good is that which we see creates changes within them, a growth for humanity and not for personal gain. We see this phenomenon in some of the greatest superheroes, including Batman, Superman, and Spider-Man, all of whom lost their biological parents early in their life due to traumatic, violent death. While they all do honorable things with their lives, these superheroes are rarely very far emotionally from the memories of these tragedies. The irony of Posttraumatic Growth is that it occurs within the context of distress and ongoing symptoms of trauma and loss. Superheroes are powerful characters not just because of their strength, skills, smarts, and the service they provide, but because of their continued wrestling with a roller coaster of painful, often conflicting, emotions and their own frailty in order to do it.

## 26.1 Batman

Many superhero fans consider Batman the greatest example of Posttraumatic Growth in the comic book literature. Of the three superheroes who experience parental loss early in their life, including Superman and Spider-Man, Batman may be the most grim and tragic story of them all. However, trauma as a precursor to growth was not well established early on in Batman's biography. For the first six months of his creation, Batman's origins were unknown (Langley, 2012). It was not until November 1939 and *Detective Comics #33* that Batman's creators, Bob Kane and Bill Finger, decided to give him a backstory that explained his desire to fight crime and solve mysteries while cloaked in a costume that masked his identity. *The Legend of the Batman – Who He Is and How He Came to Be*! (DC Comics, 1940a) described Bruce Wayne's early adolescent traumatic experience of witnessing the murders of both of his parents, Dr. Thomas and Martha Wayne, who were shot by Joe Chill, a thief after Mrs. Wayne's pearl necklace. The creators conjectured that there was "nothing more traumatic than having your parents murdered before your very eyes" (Daniels, 1999, p. 31). According to the story, several days after his parents' deaths, the young Bruce Wayne knelt by his bed, clasping his hands in prayer, vowing to avenge his parents by spending the rest of his life fighting criminals.

Like other figures who demonstrate Posttraumatic Growth, this personal transformation occurs close in time to the traumatic event rather than farther away (Calhoun & Tedeschi, 2006). It is the adolescent Bruce Wayne who commits himself to learning detective skills, training in the martial arts, and diligently schooling himself to learn how to fight crime. He becomes passionate about making Gotham City a better place to live, safe from criminals like the one who murdered his own parents. His mission in life has changed, and he appears to have developed the PTG dimension of **New Possibilities** for his life.

Another dimension, **Personal Strength**, also surfaces for the adolescent Bruce Wayne. His relationships are forever altered in the wake of his parents' deaths. While he becomes very close with surrogate father and butler, Alfred Pennyworth, he has distant relationships with others in his life. Bruce seems to have raised himself (Langley, 2012). This **Personal Strength** dimension does not reduce the traumatizing and distressing memories of his loss throughout his life. We know that Bruce Wayne visits "Crime Alley", the site of his parents' murders on the anniversary of their death every year. As Batman, he is portrayed as experiencing recurrent thoughts of his parents' murders. In *Detective Comics #457*, a graphic representation of Batman's profile with images of his childhood kneeling before his parents' lifeless bodies are drawn inside the profile, as if to suggest they were always on his mind.

Other manifestations of this transformation appear as told through the cartoon stories of Batman. The creators symbolized the physical conversion from civilian Bruce Wayne to superhero Batman, as he accesses the Batcave by a secret passageway behind a grandfather clock. In order to access the passageway, he must physically move the clock's hands to the very hour of his parents' murders, thus allowing Bruce to transform himself into the crime-fighting superhero by literally moving through the hour of his parents' deaths and the traumatizing memory of their loss (Langley, 2012).

The portrayal of Bruce Wayne's early traumatic loss experience and his ability to use that for the good of his community by fighting crime is foreshadowed on the television show *Gotham*. On the premier episode of *Gotham*, Detective James Gordon is called to the scene of a double homicide, which turns out to be Bruce Wayne's parents, Dr. Thomas and Martha Wayne. We see Bruce as a boy, shivering, crying, in shock, and unable to speak. Gordon asks the young man his name, but he remains silent and then utters that his name is Bruce. Detective Gordon sits down beside him and tells Bruce that he was sitting beside his father in the car as a boy, when a drunk driver hit his father's car and killed him. Detective Gordon survived it and provides comfort to Bruce, as only one who has lived the experience can, "No matter how dark and scary the world might be right now, there will be light, Bruce" (White, Cutter, & Cannon, 2014, 00:07:14).

## 26.2 Robin

The creation of Batman's sidekick, Robin, was also one born of loss and trauma. The youthful character Dick Grayson was a boy whose trapeze artist parents died when their ropes broke after they were tampered with by gangsters attempting to intimidate the circus owner. The Flying Graysons were killed in front of Dick and in front of horrified audience members, including Bruce Wayne. In *Detective Comics #38* (DC Comics, 1940b), we see a grief-stricken Dick Grayson vowing to go to the police, but Batman reminds him that a mobster boss runs the town and that Dick's life is in jeopardy. Batman agrees to hide Dick and make him his sidekick, as Batman reveals to Robin, "My parents too were killed by a criminal. That's why I've devoted my life to exterminate them". Dick responds, "Then I want to also! Take me with you – please!" (DC Comics, 1940b). Robin, who was named by Batman creators for "Robin Hood", begins to train to fight crime with Batman and soon avenges the deaths of his parents by putting the mobster boss in jail. Robin develops **New Possibilities** in his early career as a crime fighter and finds solace in **Relating to Others**, such as Batman, on this path.

## 26.3 Catwoman

Selina Kyle first appeared as "the Cat" in *Batman* #1 (Spring, 1940). Catwoman is a Gotham City burglar and jewel thief, who dons a cat suit and represents the ultimate femme fatale. She was originally written as a supervillain and adversary of Batman, but later becomes his crime-fighting companion in *Batman #65* (June 1951) and *#69* (February 1952) – she is an antihero. Although she returns to a life of crime in *Detective Comics #203* (January 1954), she prevents thugs from murdering Batman and, instead, takes him hostage and saves his life. She is frequently portrayed as a foil to Batman, doing all the wrong things for the right reasons.

In the *Gotham* television series, the observer views an adolescent Selina Kyle slinking in catlike movements behind unsuspecting residents, stealing milk from their grocery bags to give to the feral cats who live in the alleyways of Gotham City (White, Cutter, & Cannon, 2014). She appears at the scene of Bruce Wayne's parents' murders and observes him from above sympathetically, as if she is connecting with him emotionally over his loss. In a modern DC Comic retelling of Selina Kyle's backstory in the graphic novel *Under the Moon: A Catwoman Tale* (2019), we find out more detail of Catwoman's origins. Selina is abused and exposed to violence as a child. She runs away from home and is hungry, cold, and lonely, but being on the streets by herself is better than being in the environment of her chaotic home. She spends the rest of her early life connecting with others, especially other homeless, abandoned teenagers, **Relating to Others** differently over their shared losses and developing a new purpose or **New Possibilities** in the wake of her childhood trauma.

## 26.4 Daredevil

Matt Murdock, better known as Daredevil, is another Marvel Comics superhero who first appeared in *Daredevil #1* (April 1964) and had special gifts conferred through early trauma and injury. Matt is a youth growing up in Hell's Kitchen, a crime-ridden part of New York City, when he saves a blind man's life from an out-of-control truck barreling toward him. Matt is blinded by a radioactive substance that falls from the truck. While he can no longer see, he develops a "radar sense" that allows his senses to be heightened beyond normal human ability. His devoted single parent, Jack, helps Matt to recover. However, Matt experiences another tragedy when his father, an aging boxer, refuses to throw a fight and is killed by gangsters. Jack has instilled in Matt the importance of education and nonviolence with the aim of his son becoming a better man than himself. In the wake of his injury and his father's murder, Matt commits himself to a life of service toward the innocent. He demonstrates the Posttraumatic Growth dimensions of **New Possibilities** and **Personal Strength**, becomes a lawyer, graduating from Columbia University Law School with settlement money he received from the accident. He and his best friend and roommate, Franklin "Foggy" Nelson, are both examples of a new path or **New Possibilities** in their legal careers. Having promised his father not to use violence to deal with his problems, Matt gets around that by adopting a superhero identity who can use physical force and is initially in a yellow and black costume made from his father's boxing robes – a continuing bond. Matt Murdock takes this a step further as he dons a dark red costume and vows revenge against his father's killers. He fights for justice as a lawyer and fights crime as a superhero. The memory of his father's death is never far from his mind and frequently intrudes upon his consciousness. In the ultimate act of transcendence, Daredevil confronts his father's killer and unintentionally causes the man to have a fatal heart attack. He does not defy his father's wishes, but justice is served, nonetheless.

## 26.5 Posttraumatic Growth among the Bereaved

Posttraumatic Growth has been investigated in broad range of traumatically bereaved survivors, including suicide-bereaved parents (Moore, Cerel, & Jobes, 2015) and in families of military service members who have experienced a variety of sudden and violent deaths (Moore, Palmer, & Cerel, 2018). The potential for growth in the aftermath of traumatic experiences is not guaranteed, but strategies for healing and growth through service to others is a theme that is being captured in the current scientific literature around Posttraumatic Growth. Real-life examples of these themes of growth are present everywhere and a testament to the ability of "even a helpless victim of a hopeless situation, facing a fate he cannot change, may rise above himself, may grow beyond himself, and by so doing change himself. He may turn a personal tragedy into a triumph" (Frankl, 2006, p. 146).

Like Victor Frankl, let us hear from some real-life superheroes, the bereaved, and how they have found growth through profound traumatic loss, as they share their personal stories.

## References

Calhoun, L.G., & Tedeschi, R.G. (2006). *Handbook of posttraumatic growth: Research and practice*. New York, NY: Erlbaum.

Daniels, L. (1999). *Batman: The complete history*. New York, NY: DC Comics.

DC Comics. (1940a). *The legend of the Batman: Who he is and how he came to be*. New York, NY: DC Comics.

DC Comics. (1940b). *Detective Comics #38*. New York, NY: DC Comics.

Frankl, V.E. (2006). *Man's search for meaning*. Boston, MA: Beacon Press.

Langley, T. (2012). *Batman and psychology*. Hoboken, NJ: Wiley.

Moore, M., Cerel, J., & Jobes, D. (2015, July). Fruits of trauma? Posttraumatic growth among suicide-bereaved parents. *Crisis: The Journal of Crisis Intervention and Suicide Prevention*, 36(4), 241–248. doi: 10.1027/0227-5910/a000318

Moore, M., Palmer, J., & Cerel, J. (2018, October). *Growth and hope after loss: How TAPS facilitates posttraumatic growth in those grieving military deaths*. [Conference Session]. Presented at the *National Military Suicide Seminar of the Tragedy Assistance Program for Survivors*, Tampa, Florida.

Shenk, J.W. (2005). *Lincoln's melancholy: How depression challenged a president and fueled his greatness*. New York, NY: Mariner Press.

Tedeschi, R.G., & Calhoun, L.G. (2004). The foundations of posttraumatic growth: New considerations. *Psychological Inquiry*, 15, 93–102. doi.org/10.1207/s15327965pli1501_03

White, S., & Cutter, R.P. (Producers), & Cannon, D. (Director). (2014). *Gotham* [Television Series]. United States: Warner Brothers Television.

# 27 Relating to Others

## In the Aftermath of Loss, I am STORM

*Toya Clebourn-Jacobs*

Nothing prepared us for the day we lost "our hero". It felt like a normal day, I rushed off to work and my son to school. We said our "goodbyes", like any other day, not knowing they would be our last. Just like all of those whose lives are forever altered by a split moment in time, it seemed as "normal" a day as any. On December 21, 2011, "Dad", my husband and best friend, went into a coma after suddenly suffering a hemorrhagic stroke and never woke up again. He died on February 2, 2012.

Finding the words to describe the feelings of this experience has been difficult. The sudden, unexpected, traumatizing loss of losing our hero was devastating. Heroes are invincible, so how could we lose ours? He was more than a husband, father, and son. He was the friend everyone relied on and the friend you wish you had. How could our hero leave us? How do we survive without Dad? He was gone, and memories were all we had left. Our son was 11 years old and our daughter was only 2. Life as we knew it changed forever.

*Ororo Munroe, aka "Storm", is a fictional superhero whose life was changed when she suffered the tragic loss of her parents. They were killed when a plane crashed into their house. Though Storm survived, she would develop claustrophobia due to her time trapped in the rubble of her home. The traumatic event surrounding her parents' deaths left a psychological impact on Storm throughout her life (*"Ororo Munroe", n.d.).

The physical and emotional reactions we faced following our tragic loss began immediately, from insomnia to loss of concentration, anger, and through the pain of protest, to acceptance. As we worked through the reactions to our loss and grief, it was during this time I realized how my children were observing my actions and emotions as I went through the days of profound loneliness and internal turmoil. I could feel my son was quietly witnessing how I responded to every single emotion that he also shared with me. We were both grieving, simultaneously, in different ways and at different times, but nonetheless, we intimately shared almost the same emotional reactions. He was watching me as his sole caregiver now. What do I do? How do I parent my children who are grieving while I am grieving? Everyone tells you, "You need to be strong". I felt the need to remain strong, but what is strength? Putting on a façade? To show the world you are not "strong enough" to manage the natural pain of tears? I felt pressured to uphold the idea of the "strong black woman" in different aspects of my life, but can I uphold this idea even during grief? These were the implicit and explicit messages about grief I thought I had to abide by, but why? It was a self-imposed pressure I was putting on myself because to be anything less than strong was weakness I couldn't allow myself to succumb to, and if I did, I'd crumble. Therefore, I chose to cry in silence when my children were not looking but soon realized, sometimes my silence became a falsehood that my son could see through. Like Storm, I too had become claustrophobic – in my grief. It came to a point I could no longer hide behind the pain. So, I made a decision to cry in front of my son, so he could see the pain and accompany me in my process of working through my suffering. The times he saw me cry were when we were discussing a story about his father, and I might cry due to missing him but instead of turning away and waiting to cope with the pain, I allowed the tears to flow. As we continued our conversations, I explained, "Mommy still misses daddy, and it still hurts that he is gone, so sometimes I cry". I expressed that I could not change what happened, and although life does not always feel fair, how we now navigate through this journey, we decide "how" the journey of grief is traveled. I wanted him to know it was okay to express how he was feeling, and whatever type of emotions he was feeling were okay. There is no right way or wrong way to grieve, and it is a natural emotion we feel in life when we face the loss of people we love. How he chose to individually process his feelings was okay. As his mother, I tried to demonstrate although the pain of losing his father may have felt like a storm crashing over us (Samuel, 2017), after the storm, the sea subsides, and even though the landscape of the land may have changed, there comes a peace that allows you to rebuild. With the storm of all the crying, my tears, our tears eventually calmed, and the pain slowly subsided. The acute, raging storm of grief does not last forever. Riding it out required bracing and embracing, in order to survive the storm. Samuel (2017) explains coping with the pain requires work on many different levels physically and psychologically, and I wanted my son to know he was supported and did not have to do the work on his own. Love from others is key to helping to survive the loss of a loved one. With my support, my son could endeavor to find a way of bearing the pain and going on without his father, moving forward, learning to trust in life again (Samuel, 2017).

Sharing with my son how I work through my grief became a part of our regular routine. We grew closer in our relationship simply by conversing during our car rides to his soccer practice or after picking him up from boy scouts on the way home. Our car conversations were in-depth, strength-based dialogues on everything from school to how to handle his friendships. Listening to his daily challenges and sometimes new adventures brought us closer together. We connected in a different way. He knew whenever he needed help or just a listening ear, I was there for him, ready to help him navigate through his new life without dad – I had "his back". The ability to connect with people who are able to provide this level of assistance and support through active, attentive, and compassionate listening can lead to not only to grief adaptation but can also foster posttraumatic growth. This may include a therapist, close friend, family member, spiritual leader, and/or mentor ("Post-traumatic Growth", n.d.).

*Losing her parents so young forced Storm into an early life of scavenging and isolation, thus making the friends she is connected to as an adult all the more significant. X-Men founder, Charles Xavier, was a mentor and surrogate father-figure for Storm and the main inspiration for her becoming a mentor to other younger pupils* ("Ororo Munroe", n.d.).

Similar to Charles Xavier's relationship with Storm, my children looked to me for strength. I was their teacher, and as their mother, I had to guide them through this time of painful emotions. Throughout this experience, the relationship with my children continued to grow as I took measures to be more of an example of strength. The will to keep myself strong in the wake of heartache and pain was a struggle, but knowing two young children were depending on me to be their mother, their strength, made coping a necessary challenge. What is essential to keep in mind is that posttraumatic growth is not a direct result of trauma but rather related to how the individual copes with struggles as a result of the trauma (Tedeschi & Calhoun, 2004). There are a number of things that people who have experienced trauma and subsequent growth identify that were significant to their struggle. These include having relationships where they felt "nurtured, liberated, or validated" in addition to experiencing "genuine acceptance from others" (Woodward & Joseph, 2003).

During this time as I struggled, my son was also struggling to cope with his father's death. I discovered he skipped school within the first couple of months after his father died. When I asked "why", he stated everything was foggy, and he could not concentrate while attending school. This led to further conversations about how he should begin to communicate his feelings. He faced the consequences of his actions by boundaries being put in place to monitor his school attendance, but we began the process of discussing how he was "truly" feeling. By doing so, I realized he was still in shock and disbelief over the death of his father and how alone he felt because none of his friends had experienced the loss of a parent.

Unaware of his feelings of loneliness and profound grief, I shared how I was starting to cope by journaling. I bought my son a journal and we began discussing how he could use the journal to process his experience and write about the stories he remembered about his father. We had many conversations or storytelling sessions about his father, laughing about the good times we shared as a family. We discussed journaling these stories for his sister for when she was older, she could read about her father – to know about him through memories. The more we discussed his father, we bonded, and my son seemed to be working through his process and be a little more at peace. Rather than harboring the pain that caused fogginess and loss of concentration, he had another outlet. I believed he was beginning to feel a sense of a continuing bond with his father, which gave him a connection, a sense of normalcy again, and a feeling of becoming emotionally stronger.

*Throughout the X-Men movies and comics, we see Storm transition from an orphan who tragically lost her parents and was left to wander the streets, picking pockets and stealing to survive. She joined the X-Men and would later become the Queen of Wakanda. However, Storm is best known for joining, and in many cases leading, groups like the X-Men, the Morlocks, and the New Mutants, which provided Storm with many close friends and allies* ("Ororo Munroe", n.d.).

These close relationships and bonds demonstrate the importance of family and friendships and how they play a critical role in the integration and adaptation to life after the loss of a loved one. Storm is considered a powerful Mutant because she can control the weather; however, she also exerts another power that I felt in myself and my son as we began our journey of healing. The power to cope and grow through a tragic loss, by transforming into a positive role model through providing the emotional strength to others, building improved relationships, and creating a new normal. My family suffered the loss of our Superhero, and at times we still feel the pain of that loss, but the deeper understanding of ourselves and the close bonds we have gained have in time have felt like growth (Samuel, 2017, p. 20). There is a saying that "life's roughest storms prove the strength of our anchors". My children's Dad was a lost hero, but I found the courage and strength within me, just as he would have expected, and love was our anchor. I AM STORM.

## References

Ororo Munroe: Storm. (n.d.). Retrieved from https://www.marvel.com/characters/storm/in-comics

Post-traumatic growth. (n.d.). Retrieved from https://trauma-recovery.ca/resiliency/post-traumatic-growth/

Samuel, J. (2017). *Grief works: Stories of life, death, and surviving*. New York, NY: Scribner.

Tedeschi, R.G., & Calhoun, L.G. (2004). Manitoba Trauma Information and Education Centre. Trauma recovery. Retrieved from https://trauma-recovery.ca/resiliency/post-traumatic-growth/

Woodward, C., & Joseph, S. (2003). Manitoba Trauma Information and Education Centre. Trauma recovery. Retrieved from https://trauma-recovery.ca/resiliency/post-traumatic-growth/

# 28 New Possibilities in Life

## Superman and Finding Hope after Loss

*Gloria Horsley*

I have always loved the idea of superheroes, and I believe the world needs heroes, both real and imagined. Daring deeds in the service of others create a world based on hope, faith, friendship, and resilience. Superman and other superheroes gave me that secure feeling as a child that there were adults around me who could and would fight for good. In his role as Clark Kent, I loved Superman's friendships with Lois Lane and Jimmy Olsen, the young photojournalist working for the Daily Planet. I was thrilled with the Superman mantra: "Faster than a speeding bullet! More powerful than a locomotive! Able to leap tall buildings at a single bound!" ("Superman on Radio", n.d., para 7). The infant of Krypton was now the Man of Steel – Superman!

I thought it didn't get any better until I saw the film *Man of Steel* (Roven, Nolan, Thomas, Snyder, & Snyder, 2013), where Lois Lane asks Superman what the "S" stood for. Superman responded, "It is not an S. In my world, it means hope" (Roven et al., 2013; 1:11:20). I love it because hope in the face of adversity has played a significant role in my personal as well as my professional life.

### 28.1 Preparing for the Journey

Growing up in the 1940s and 1950s, surrounded by the Marvel and DC comic books, I was enthralled by the feats of those who took on the evilest villains, defeating them with their superpowers. Superman was my favorite. In my dreams, I could picture myself flying above the hands of the villains my dad and uncles fought in World War II. I listened to the adventures of Superman on the radio and watched the Superman serials in the small-town movie theater owned by my grandfather. My favorite was *Atom Man vs. Superman* (Katzman & Bennet, 1950). I was enthralled by Superman's resilience, determination, messages of hope, and superhuman feats like flying over tall buildings. The powerful image of Superman showed me I could rise up above adversity and fly away from problems and troubles, including frequent night terrors. Later, with the death of my 17-year-old son Scott in a fiery car crash, I was again called on to exhibit superhuman powers; not to fly, but to survive. As was often the case with Clark Kent, I was called to action by a strange set of circumstances.

## 28.2 The Call

It was one o'clock in the morning when the call came.

"Your son and his cousin have been in an automobile accident".

"Are they okay?"

"No, they are both dead".

It has been over thirty years since I received that call from hell, the one I felt I would never survive. In the same way that Clark Kent is always Superman at his core, I was still Gloria Horsley at my core – the kid who, like Superman, could fly and conquer adversity – but I was a broken mother. And I didn't have Lois Lane or Jimmy Olsen to comfort me. I felt that my life had been shattered and that there was no hope. Who would have thought that the story and kindness of a total stranger would enable me to again don the "S" cape and put me back on the journey toward hope?

## 28.3 The Journey Begins

Scott had been dead for eight months, and although I felt broken, I somehow managed to return to work and resume my duties at the University of Rochester Medical Center, continuing in my role as the clinical nurse specialist to the surgical service. Christmas was approaching, filling me with bittersweet memories as I realized Scott wouldn't be there to put up the tree and help hang the ornaments. I wasn't sure how I would get through another day, let alone a whole festive season. As luck would have it, a superhero woman named Floe changed everything for me.

## 28.4 A Stranger Enters My Life

It was a cold dark night, and I was getting ready to log out for the evening when the pager I was wearing started to vibrate. I was called to the surgical service to visit a woman who had been in an automobile accident and had a badly fractured leg. The staff felt she needed some psychological support. My shift was finished, and I considered not answering the call, but I reminded myself of my professional advice to other bereaved clients, "sometimes you have to fake it until you can make it". I took a deep breath, gulped some water, and trudged off to the medical unit.

Entering the patient's room, I was surprised to find a relaxed middle-aged woman propped up on her hospital bed. Her left leg was in a stretcher held high by straps fastened to large pins running through her leg. She looked uncomfortable, but showed no emotion other than an inquiring look that said,

"What now?" and "Who the hell are you?" I explained that the nurses were concerned and had asked me to look in. She said she had been in a great deal of pain until they finally medicated her. Because the nurses had asked me to make an assessment, I asked if I could sit down for a few minutes and talk with her. She agreed, and we discussed what bad luck it was that she had been injured in an automobile accident. The timing was lousy as the holidays were approaching.

I don't remember how it came up, but I told her, with tears running down my face, about my son's death in April. Rather than giving me the usual sad and shocked response, she gave me a long look. She then paused and said, "Ten years ago, I lost seven children in a house fire, and I made it through. So will you. It will not be easy, but trust me. You can and will make it".

I will never forget that moment of hope. As I left Floe's room, I knew with certainty that I would not only get through the holidays but would make something meaningful from my loss. For the rest of the season, I carried Floe's message of hope with me and relied on her promise that I would make it through. It was the greatest Christmas gift I had ever received.

## 28.5 Choosing Hope over Despair

With each passing year, my hope got stronger. With the help of my family, friends, God, and the stories of superheroes, I eventually donned the "S" cape of hope and began to help others. We started a family foundation with the mission of helping people find hope after loss. We named it *Open to Hope*, as we wanted others who had lost a loved one to join us on the path of hope and healing. Our family mission has been very satisfying, as we have helped millions of people while paying tribute to Scott.

This is not to say that life does not come back to bite me and that I don't have the occasional painful reminder, but over time, my feelings of despair have decreased markedly, and it is easier to enjoy the beautiful life I have been given. Recently I had one of those "trigger" days. I was shopping with my 17-year-old, football-playing grandson for school clothes when he came out of the dressing room looking very strong and handsome. He asked me if I thought the shirt he was trying on was too tight in the shoulders. As I touched his muscular arms, I had a flashback to the last day I spent with Scott. I had taken him shopping for school clothes, and he was fun and delightful. Only six hours later, he was dead. When the triggers occurred, I pulled my "S" cape around me and chose hope over fear and despair, feeling a sense of gratitude that life had blessed me with not one but two beautiful boys.

## 28.6 Time to Fly

I invite those who are stuck in their grief to join me by putting on a superhero cape, choosing to stay open to hope. If they do, I promise that – like Superman – hope will carry them through, and they will succeed far beyond their expectations. Hope has helped me believe in the ability not only to survive but also to thrive. What our superheroes really bring into the world is hope that even after profound loss we can rise again and possibly even fly.

"Faster than a speeding bullet! More powerful than a locomotive! Able to leap tall buildings at a single bound!" ("Superman on Radio", n.d., para 7). Isn't it time we don the Superman cape and embrace the "S" as the Kryptonian symbol for hope? Our hope, our life, and our purpose. Don the cape!

*Thanks to the creators of Superman and other superheroes and blessings on all of you who give the gift of hope to others, and remember if you have lost hope, please visit us online at Open to Hope* (www.opentohope.com), *where we invite all to "lean on our hope until you find your own".*

## References

Katzman, S. (Producer), & Bennet, S.G. (Director). (1950). *Atom Man vs. Superman* [Motion Picture]. United States: Sam Katzman Productions.

Roven, C., Nolan, C., Thomas, E., & Snyder, D. (Producers), & Snyder, Z. (Director). (2013). *Man of steel* [Motion Picture]. United States: Warner Bros. Pictures.

Superman on Radio. (n.d.). The adventures of superman. Retrieved from https://www.supermanhomepage.com/radio/radio.php?topic=r-radio

# 29 Personal Strength

## Combat Death, Love, Loss, and the Emergence of the Wonder Woman Within

*Malia Fry*

My husband, Gunnery Sergeant John David Fry, was killed in action on March 8, 2006, near Habbaniyah, Iraq. To tell you the truth, part of me was surprised to be asked to write a chapter on strength after loss 14 years after his death. Many times, I still feel like I'm back at the very beginning when I first lost John. But as I look back and see how far I've come, I realize I've grown into a woman I don't even recognize.

When I think back to the first days of my grief, I recall one day vividly. One day that set my journey in motion. It was just days after the dreaded knock on my front door when a Marine in full dress blues told me that my whole life, as I knew it, was over. As I sat in my kitchen listening to the Marines all around me, I feared that my John would be forgotten. The thought that his life would simply be one of the thousands terrified me.

I remember wanting to make his death mean something, wanting this all to mean something, never realizing that my journey was just beginning and that this gut-wrenching pain would somehow make the Wonder Woman within me blossom and grow – that she would end up changing the lives of so many and at some point, I would have posttraumatic growth. I couldn't imagine I would rise from what I felt were the ashes of my life to become a much stronger woman. All I knew at this time was that I could not breathe without pain. I didn't believe I would live. My heart, soul, and mind felt broken beyond repair. My soul mate, the love of my life, the father of my children, was gone. I had loved this man since I was 15 years old. All I ever wanted was to be his wife and to be the mother of his children. Who was I now? How could I move forward? How could I breathe without him in this world? He was my first everything, and I truly believed I was going to stop breathing. I was lost, tumbling through the days. The days blurred together. I was simply existing, going through the motions of life without truly feeling anything.

I lived in that fog for six months. Then my world was rocked again with the second knock on the door and another Marine in dress blues. Once again, I was facing a Marine telling me, "We're sorry, ma'am". I knew why he was there. My husband was in Explosive Ordnance Demolition (EOD), which was the bomb squad for the U.S. military. John had prepared me that secondary remains were something I would likely face. No matter how much I thought

I was prepared, I was still knocked to my knees. I was going to have to bury him all over again. However, this was no normal secondary remains case. There had been a mistake, and I was determined to find out the truth.

Like Wonder Woman with the lasso of truth, I wanted to know what happened, why it happened. What I found changed me forever. Half of my amazing husband's body had been accidentally frozen at the military mortuary. A clerical mistake had taken six months to fix. Then I was told that the military would not supply a second flag for his remains as he flew home. I felt rage growing inside me. Suddenly, I had power growing within me to ensure that John was not just one of the thousands who died. The emotional roller coaster and the truth of what had happened to my husband had me putting on Wonder Woman armor. I needed to pull myself together and fight. I felt that John's service had been dishonored, and I had to right this. This was my first step in my posttraumatic growth journey. I knew I needed to do something to honor John's life and service, but did not have the direction to put my newly discovered power to use.

Asking my children what they would want – the school or post office – named after their dad was at first a joke. But I could not stop thinking about how I had to do something. My first action was to have the post office in our town dedicated in his name. This was a two-year process that meant opening my life up for scrutiny. When the actual dedication day came, I met Congressman Chet Edwards face-to-face for the first time. He did what every other politician had done before. He asked me, that same question, "What can I do to help?" By this point, I was angry. I had put my armor on, and I was ready to fight. Like Wonder Woman with her lasso of truth, I decided I would let him know the truth.

I laid my heart out. How was I going to pay for my three kids to go to college? I was so scared of not being able to give them the very best. I told him about several other widows I had met who had the same fear. Congressman Chet Edwards said, "Let's try and fix it". Most times, I would have said thank you and moved on, but not this time. Instead, I said, "Yeah, right. I've heard that before", which surprised him and even me. Maybe I was becoming more comfortable with this Wonder Woman within me, so I proceeded to tell him I was tired of the pleasantries and platitudes.

Congressmen Edwards promised he meant what he was saying. Three months later, I received an invitation to meet with the Congressman. He wanted to show me what he had put together. The bill Congressmen Edwards had written was for each child of a fallen military member to receive a Veteran's Administration (V.A.) benefit equal to a fully paid state college tuition as well as a monthly stipend for living expenses. I had a few changes I wanted him to make. At first, he had the classification for qualification as "killed in action", but I explained this would eliminate anyone whose loved one had made it off the battlefield and to the hospital before dying, as well as to all those who have died in many differing ways in service to our nation. I also had to fight for the children to keep their benefit if they were married; I had married my John at 18, so I wanted a longer period for the children to be able to use this benefit after high school. I told him that our children have been through so much, they might need extra time before they were ready for college.

The biggest thing Chet Edwards needed from me was to be the face and voice of this bill. I would need to be ready for interviews and phone calls to other members of congress. I didn't know until the bill passed that it was named in my husband's honor, the Marine Gunnery Sergeant John D. Fry Scholarship.

In the years since the Fry Scholarship became law, I've had many opportunities to speak not just about my husband but on behalf of all the families of the fallen, even though one of my greatest fears was public speaking. In my everyday life, I'm just Malia, an average person who is just a mom. However, when it's time to speak when I'm getting ready to continue the fight that started so many years ago, I become the Gunny's widow. I become the Wonder Woman within. Pulling on my personal strength and the armor of John's love, I feel I can conquer anything.

I know I have honored my husband and his military service. I know I have reached the goal that he will be remembered. But now that I've let the Wonder Woman within emerge, I'm not done fighting. I don't know if I'll ever be done fighting. Since the Fry scholarship has become law, it has been extended to include spouses of the fallen. I have also worked on the state level to get a property exemption for the families of the fallen. My heart has opened to the families of other men and women who have died while serving. I find myself answering phone calls and emails, calling colleges and other congressmen to make certain that these children who gave so much get everything they deserve. In Wonder Woman's words, "I stay, I fight, and I give" (Roven, Snyder, Snyder, Suckle, & Jenkins, 2017, 2:10:00). I believe that!

It would have been so easy to lie down in my grief – never moving forward, never growing – and let the pain overcome me. My memories of my husband and the love we shared propel me forward. His love let me release the pain and do good. If it were not for the personal strength I found through loss, I would never have accomplished anything. The belief I had in my husband's love and my love for him made it possible for the Wonder Woman within me to emerge. With loss, one can start to believe that loss is all you deserve, but as Wonder Woman says, "It's not about deserve, it's about what you believe, and I believe in love" (Roven et al., 2017, 2:05:05). I live my life with this knowledge propelling me forward – just like Wonder Woman.

## References

Roven, C., Snyder, D., Snyder, Z., Suckle, R., & Jenkins, P. (Producers), & Jenkins, P. (Director). (2017). *Wonder woman* [Motion Picture]. United States: Warner Bros. Pictures.

# 30 Spiritual Growth After Loss

## Dr. Strange and My Spiritual Journey Amidst Profound Loss

*Brendan Prout*

When people think of comic book characters who personify wrestling through the throes of grief, they don't immediately think of Doctor Strange. Perhaps because the initial story centers on the mystical, the supernatural, and the magical, the casual observer might dismiss the important contributions that Strange makes in illuminating some of the pervasive challenges of grief.

In many ways, Strange's story is about personal and spiritual growth, which can be triggered by a traumatic event. For Stephen Strange, it was a car accident (admittedly his own fault) that led to the loss of the use of his hands, which led in turn to a series of cascading events: the loss of his surgical profession, the loss of relationships, and the loss of self-respect and identity. He hit rock bottom in a third-world alley after an exhaustive search for physical restoration, not even realizing his dire need for emotional and spiritual restoration. His rescue came in the form of a new spiritual path that required a completely new approach to life. He resisted at first, in the midst of his grief-fueled angst. Fortunately, the one who came to Strange's rescue recognized his condition and told the hapless doctor, "I once stood in your place" (Feige & Derrickson, 2016, 00:24:12).

I, too, have experienced the biting pangs of unexpected loss. I was set on that pathway on May 17, 1995, when my father – a two-star admiral in the U.S. Navy – was killed in an F/A-18 crash. I was just out of my teens and was living on my own. My family had recently moved back into the town where I lived, so we'd been able to enjoy renewed contact. The night before Dad was killed, I went to their home for dinner. I was vaguely aware that he was flying across the country the next day, and my last words to him were, "I love you. See you when you get back".

The next day at work, I got a phone call. My father's plane was missing. It would be 24 hours before we knew what happened; the plane was simply "missing" until its wreckage was found strewn across a three-mile debris field on a snow-covered mountain. That next morning, when my mother collapsed in uncontrollable sobbing, I knew without being told ... and my world was forever changed. Much like Dr. Strange, I found myself at the end of my ability to cope. As I walked into my family's living room, my strength to stand simply wasn't there anymore. It wasn't a feeling of sinking or growing faint; I simply found myself on the ground. My legs just didn't work in those moments. Not much did, other than my body's crying response. My heart seemed to melt and pour out in liquid form through my eyes.

In the case of Dr. Strange, his physical injuries amplified the negative cognitive and emotional states, propelling him into a downward spiral until he exhausted the resources of his own creation, forcing him to consider alternative solutions. In the same way, those walking the path of grief resort first to familiar ways of coping, with varying degrees of success. If they experience negative outcomes, they may branch out to weigh options that formerly would have been out of their personal bounds for rational consideration.

In my case, my car had the nerve to blow its transmission about a mile from our family's house the next day. I pushed it there, mad as hell. The crowd of people with our family in our time of loss didn't really notice ... until I grabbed a baseball bat and beat the living snot out of the car, smashing every possible part that I could. I beat on that thing until I was completely spent. But I slept better that night.

When he reached the end of his abilities, Dr. Strange discovered a spiritual community that introduced him to magic and mysticism. Grieving people can also discover the strong link between spirituality and healing. Strange's storyline serves as a unique model among the comic book world of superheroes in that it focuses more on the spiritual dimension, rather than on external characteristics such as strength and agility. The powers manifested by characters in his narrative have little to do with physical stature or prowess, making more of a statement regarding the equity of accessibility any person has to the potential of spiritual growth.

Prior to my father's death, I'd been on a spiritual path, but I found that the experience of sudden, violent loss was not easily soothed by my young faith. If anything, I reacted against my faith, angry at God. After a year of self-nullifying behavior accompanied by feelings of spiritual bankruptcy, I re-engaged with my beliefs and sought to reconcile my grief journey with my faith journey, assisted by others walking similar paths. Twenty years later, I'm still walking that path and can help others on their journey of grief and healing.

A significant theme inherent to the storyline of Dr. Strange is his change from narcissism to altruism. Strange is first introduced as an arrogant neurosurgeon of worldwide renown. His ambition is demonstrated by flamboyant displays of disrespect toward other doctors and the callous way he evaluates medical cases, pondering how they could further his career. By the close of the film version, Strange puts more value on others than on himself. This change of heart reveals a monumental moral lesson that can only be learned in the kiln of intense personal challenge: life is not about me.

Following intense loss, our most painful moments often revolve around our insistence that the world stop and recognize our pain, tend to our needs, bind up our wounds. Grief forces us inward, making us narcissistic. It's a completely normal response, it's completely understandable, and for most people close to us, it's completely forgivable. For about a year after my father's death, I acted out in a great many ways in an extended temper tantrum. But such anger and self-centeredness can't become a persistent state of being. Like Strange, we have to grow from that narcissistic place toward an others-centered place where altruism helps us to heal. When we make life about others – finding fulfillment in the joy of others – we find that our own joy comes along. We find there is a radical balance achieved; we help ourselves through helping others.

Another strong theme is that "Sometimes you must break the rules for the greater good" (Feige et al., 2016, 01:25:16). Strange acts in defiance of the rules of the spiritual order – finding creative ways to circumvent entirely or just plain ignore them – because he sees a benefit that outweighs the purpose of the restriction. When it comes to grief after loss, many rules are placed on the grieving by popular culture and conventional thought. Don't cry in public. Don't cry in front of your kids. Don't cry after X amount of time has passed. Do see a counselor, but not too often and not for too long. Do stop talking about it. But grief follows no rules, and our journey toward healing cannot be expected to follow a neatly defined pathway.

Some troubling issues are delved into through the story of Doctor Strange. But it is often the uncomfortable scenarios – which are usually ignored to the emotional and spiritual detriment of all involved – that need to be discussed the most. One such issue comes after discovering that the person who died wasn't completely what others thought they were. Learning negative details can leave the mourning parties in greater pain. One lesson learned from Dr. Strange is that while we may not have any say in the choices our loved ones made, we do have choices regarding what others find out about us after we've died. Such choices are entirely within our own power, and no one else can take responsibility for them.

A further significant theme from Strange's storyline is found in the change in approach from drawing power from pain to drawing power from life. This is illustrated allegorically by the revelation that the powers manifested by the wizards are being drawn from a place called "the dark dimension", an unseen source of death and suffering in the story world. Strange comes to the realization that more power is to be found in life than from death. This paints a poetic picture that mirrors our reality: early in the grief journey, our focus is on the death event, the circumstances surrounding it, and on processing the pain we experience. As we experience growth through the grief journey, we find power by focusing on the life, the love, and the legacy of the person we miss. By directing our energies toward reflecting on the positive aspects of that person's life, we are able to honor and remember them with passionate intent.

Ironically, in the story of Doctor Strange, though he sets out with the goal of restoring his hands so that he can return to his former life, he never achieves that goal. His goals are changed by his journey, and he eventually accepts his condition, following the wisdom of his spiritual mentor: "We never defeat our demons; we only learn to live above them" (Feige et al., 2016, 00:32:46). The events of Strange's life story alter the story itself, and his choices take him in a wildly different direction than he'd originally intended. So, it is with grief and loss. Spiritually, emotionally, mentally, and physically, we are put on a pathway that we did not choose.

Among the strongest messages delivered by Strange is his statement: "Death is what gives life meaning, to know that every moment is meaningful and fleeting" (Feige et al., 2016, 01:25:48). Strange counters the negative effect of death by applying the knowledge that a life well lived has a ripple effect, influencing countless others. Those left behind to mourn are ultimately confronted with the choice of how to respond to death, with one of the better choices being to continue their loved one's legacy and, in doing so, memorialize and honor that person and the values they stood for. Having the choices set before us of how to respond, we can certainly take a few lessons from the character of Dr. Stephen Strange.

## References

Feige, K. (Producer), & Derrickson, S. (Director) (2016). *Doctor Strange* [Motion picture]. USA: Marvel Studios.

# 31 Appreciation for Life

## We Rise Like the Dark Knight

*Ashlynne Haycock and Weston Haycock*

In the aftermath of a loss, it is common for the newly bereaved to seek refuge from their feelings, to find ways to avoid confronting the grief that looms over their lives. The death of a parent completely alters the dynamic of a family; it changes the role people have to take in their own homes. When one loses their father, oftentimes, the children feel a need to step in as the "man of the house". When a mother is lost, the family might wonder who will hold everyone together. In the immediate loss of both parents, the very fabric of the family is torn apart. There is less of a question of "How can we make things seem like the way they were?" and more of a question of "Can anything ever be the same?"

Bruce Wayne, also known as Batman when he dons his crime-fighting attire, lost his parents suddenly to a double homicide. Understandably, he was left devastated by his traumatic loss and suddenly altered life. Bruce took many years to work through and learn to control his feelings of grief. Initially, he did this in unhealthy ways, seeking out danger, and using his loss to justify his unfavorable actions. But with time, Bruce found his true calling for making amends with the feelings of emptiness his loss made him feel. He acquired a new identity, one where he was not a victim but a visage of hope – a new persona, one where he was defined by the lawfulness he inspired, not by the lawlessness that stripped him of his family.

At a young age, we lost our parents suddenly – our father to sudden illness and then, a few years later, our mother to suicide. During these precarious times of our lives, we too masked our grief; it was a means to survive as we were trying to find new identities. In this quest that loss thrusts upon you, a suddenly altered identity, one that is scary and unknown, especially at first, and with feelings of pain that plague every moment of your day, sometimes you try to hide from your grief. For Weston, it involved moving across the country and pretending his previous life hadn't really happened. For Ashlynne, it was attempting to thrive in a college environment where everyone knew the "old Ashlynne" and trying to pretend that person still existed.

While the nature of our losses may not be identical with Bruce Wayne's, our feelings of loss could be described as similar in nature. We were not billionaires; our story was not etched in the newspapers across the world following our parents' deaths. But our feelings of confusion, fear, and anger were etched into our lives at the time. Both of us spent some time soul searching and trying to find ways to move forward as new people. The thing about that was that grief doesn't work that way. One cannot simply move on, and the whole loss no longer affects them. Living with grief is an everyday event, one you have to consciously choose to battle and learn to manage in order for it not to consume you. Feelings of anger and pain fester if left alone. Look at what happened to Bruce; he almost let his feelings of anger drive him to kill a man, something his parents would have found reprehensible.

We see the identity transformation in Bruce as Batman by his self-realization through years of a painful grief journey, "It's not who I am underneath, but what I do that defines me" (Roven, Thomas, Franco, & Nolan, 2005, 01:57:40). Just like Batman, we could have let our grief define us. We could have let it be the defining event in our lives in a very negative way. We could have let it consume us. In *Batman Begins* (Roven et al., 2005), everyone believes that about Bruce Wayne. They believe he is living off of his parent's money, and that's all he is. His life is simply an extension of the event that tragically cut his parents' lives short. Many people in our lives thought our loss would prove to define our futures, that our lives would be irreparably damaged by the loss of our parents. And because we were both in our teens when our mother died, people expected very little of us. Instead of letting it consume us, though, we let it empower us. We both graduated from college and pursued careers in service. Weston is a staffer in the legislature, and Ashlynne does policy and legislation for a military nonprofit called Tragedy Assistance Program for Survivors (TAPS). An organization that helps grieving surviving military families – our surviving community became our Justice League.

Batman started the Justice League for two main reasons, to connect with those like himself and to pursue a greater good. He sought out other people who shared his desire for the greater good and could understand the burden of his loss. Superman was the last of his entire planet. The Flash felt isolated by the world and put himself into his work to close out his feelings of loneliness. The members of the Justice League became Batman's family (Roven, Snyder, Berg, Johns, & Snyder, 2017). Which is exactly what our military surviving community became to us. We got involved with TAPS after our dad died in 2002 when we were 10 and 6 years old. TAPS gave us the ability to connect with other bereaved military children, like ourselves, kids who were grieving the loss of a parent(s) and gave us a community. A community of people who embraced us. A community that encouraged us to do more than we ever thought we could. TAPS created opportunities for us to be a part of the greater good too. It reiterated the sense of service to one's country that the military had taught us. That we could be more and do more than we believed in. It empowered us and everyone involved!

Through the years, as we became adults, we transformed our grief. We grew to have a deeper appreciation for the lives we had, the relationships we made, and our connections with other military surviving families – our community.

We grew deeper in our bond as siblings and learned to not sweat the small stuff. For us, we wanted to give back to bereaved military children, maybe some of whom were also orphans like us. Our mentors from the TAPS Good Grief Camp were our heroes. They were there through thick and thin when both our parents died. Our peer mentors were trusted allies, advocates, and caring role models. They gave of their time, but they also gave of their hearts – to help heal our broken ones and let us know we were not alone. Through this, we learned a deep appreciation of selfless service to others. Much like Batman, who through his life, dedicated himself to a life of service for the greater good, we too rise like the Dark Knight, in service to other bereaved military children now as their adult peer mentors, who themselves were transformed and grew through the loss of their parents. We take up the charge for them and for our eternal gratitude for our peer mentors – some of our life's true superheroes – we now wear the cape!

## References

Roven, C., Thomas, E., & Franco, L. (Producers), & Nolan, C. (Director) (2005). *Batman begins* [Motion picture]. United States: Warner Bros. Studios.

Roven, C., Snyder, D., Berg, J., & Johns, G. (Producers), & Snyder, Z. (Director). (2017). *Justice league* [Motion Picture]. United States: Warner Bros. Studios.

# Part VIII

# Superheroes, Grief Leadership, Social Justice, and Advocacy

# 32 Grief Leadership

## Examples from the Life and Service of Captain America

*James A. Martin, David F. Carey and Stephen J. Cozza*

Human loss, whether in a military or first responder unit, a civilian neighborhood (e.g., a school or business), or larger settings such as a community, a geographic region, or the nation may result in acute grief that involves intense emotional pain, distress, and disorganization and stunned disbelief, especially for those closest to the deceased. We understand grief to be a personal experience that leaves the bereaved with an overwhelming sense of sadness, loss, and disorganization, as well as a profound yearning for the deceased person. Grief is equally social in nature. Grief is experienced within our families, our workplaces, schools, or units (e.g., military, police/fire, healthcare, and rescue services), as well as across broader neighborhoods, communities, and countries (Faust, 2008). Whether traumatic death involves the loss of an individual or many people, communal mourning, whether in a small group or across an entire nation, affects the well-being of those involved, potentially belying a previously clear sense of meaning and purpose and often undermining the ability to effectively function and move forward with the demands of daily life and professional responsibilities.

The death of a military or first-responder unit member is likely to affect morale and readiness, as well as diminish a unit's ability to successfully perform required functions. Similarly, lives lost due to natural or man-made disaster, a pandemic, or acts of terrorism disrupt community functioning and typically result in local, regional, and even national mourning. For example, the September 11, 2001, terrorist attacks undermined America's sense of safety and led to great uncertainty about our way forward as a nation. In these circumstances, it is the responsibility of leaders at every level to step forward to assist community members in making sense of the loss, to help members mourn and memorialize those who have died, and to communicate a sense of purpose and clear expectations for the restoration of individual and collective health and well-being. In certain circumstances, for example, a pandemic, recognition of individual and group grief may have to be acknowledged in the moment with collective morning deferred until safe conditions are achieved.

These and similar functions that bolster the well-being of bereaved communities define *grief leadership*. This chapter explores the principles and practice of grief leadership by examining the life and service of Captain America, a superhero from the Marvel Universe, as well as by offering historical and personal examples of what real world leaders need to know and do in the face of traumatic grief.

## 32.1 Grief Leadership as Seen in the Life and Service of Captain America

Who was Steve Rogers, aka Captain America? Captain America, "Cap" to his friends, was many things: he was a smallish, scrawny, sickly young man from Brooklyn, who, over time, evolved as a volunteer soldier, a loyal friend, committed to and always doing the right thing. Steve Rogers became Cap, a military leader, a war hero, and a national symbol. In his service as a superhero, Cap was exposed to repeated combat-related trauma. Steve Rogers was born in Brooklyn in the early twentieth century between the World Wars, and his personality was forged as an orphan during the depression era. Rejected time and again for military service because of disqualifying medical conditions, his perseverance was observed and rewarded by a government scientist, Dr. Abraham Erskine, who saw unique leadership qualities in Cap (Feige & Johnston, 2011).

As a military leader in the prolonged struggle against global evil, Cap exemplified the core principles and practices of grief leadership. For example, Cap understood how individuals vary in their reactions to traumatic losses, and he was able to integrate that knowledge in his responses to the grief experienced by his friends and military team members. By effectively communicating both empathy and hope, Cap helped community members adjust to the losses they experienced while continuing to promote individual and collective resilience, even while continuously being challenged by the forces of evil (Feige & Johnston, 2011). Cap helped team members recognize their individual and collective importance to the ongoing Avengers' mission. He inspired team members to honor their lost comrades by linking those losses to the team's abiding shared values in order to face the daunting tasks required to achieve their shared goal of overcoming evil and offering a hopeful future for America and the world (Feige & Whedon, 2015; Feige, Russo, & Russo, 2016). His penultimate response occurring after the snap, or global pandemic, that affected the entire world (Feige, Russo, & Russo, 2019). Cap recognized that in order to be effective in the face of such challenges, leaders must attend to their own personal grief through self-care, seeking the assistance of interpersonal support and wise advisors.

**Table 32.1** highlights Bartone's (2019) Principles of Grief Leadership and incorporates various principles and practices from the Uniformed Services University (USU) Center for the Study of Traumatic Stress (CSTS) *Grief Leadership Fact Sheet*, juxtaposed against examples from Captain America and Avenger movies.

*Table 32.1* Grief leadership highlighted in the life and service of Captain America

**Grief Leadership Principles & Practices with** *Examples from Captain America*

**1. Provide public acknowledgment of the profound nature of the group's loss, as well as the validity of the associated pain and suffering experienced by group members.**

Throughout the Avenger series, as an American and world symbol, Cap's presence at the forefront of tragedies calms and steadies both his teammates and the public. Cap's public willingness to be court-martialed after disobeying orders to save SGT Bucky Barnes and the rest of the unit in *Captain America: First Avenger* gives reassurance to the group that their losses will be worth it.

**2. Provide group members with the necessary information to comprehend what has occurred, as well as a perspective that helps the group understand the loss and its significance.**

Cap gives the Avengers a perspective that unifies them as a team after the loss of Agent Colston in *Avengers.* During *Captain America: Civil War*, Cap consoles Wanda by giving her a different perspective about the blast that killed the Wakandan delegation, while at the end of the movie, Cap gives Tony Stark the information he needs to comprehend his loss. During *Avengers: End Game*, Cap again provides the Avengers the perspective necessary to continue the mission when Black Widow is killed.

**3. Lead members in a public mourning process that allows memorialization of the victim(s) in a way that is culturally sensitive to the group's beliefs, norms, and developmental status.**

During both Peggy Carter's (*Civil War)* and Tony Stark's (*End Game*) funerals, Cap is front and center during the public morning process.

**4. Connect the loss to the group's shared values; noting the useful lessons that may emanate from the loss experience.**

During the losses of Bucky (*The First Avenger*), Quicksilver (*Age of Ultron),* the loss of half the population in the snap or ultimate pandemic (*Infinity War),* and in Black Widow (*End Game*), Cap connects the losses to the group's shared values and builds on the lessons to move the team forward.

**5. Offer a vision for the pathway forward, a vision that includes a sense of purpose associated with the group's shared values and beliefs.**

During the losses of Bucky (*The First Avenger*), Quicksilver (*Age of Ultron*), half the population in the snap or ultimate pandemic (*Infinity War*), and Black Widow (*End Game)* Cap articulates the pathway forward to include the next steps in the mission while sharing the values and beliefs of the team.

**6. Identify critical tasks that the group needs to pursue, even during the immediate grief process, tasks critical for achieving shared goals for the future.**

During the *First Avenger* while the unit was reeling and shutting down from the loss of Bucky and the Unit, Cap identified the tasks, assembled a team, and moved through the immediate grief to accomplish the mission. During *Civil War,* as the Avengers were reeling from the loss of the Wakandian delegation, Cap maintained the core values to identify the critical tasks necessary to continue the mission.

(*Continued*)

*Table 32.1* (Continued)

| |
|---|
| **7. Present a sense of hope even in the presence of seemingly overwhelming grief; hope that reflects the group's ability to move forward in an enduring process that promotes individual and collective resiliency.** |
| While presented as part of Cap's core values, throughout the various movies Cap is steadfast – "I can do this all day" (Feige & Johnston, 2011, 010:14), he never gives up even in the face of overwhelming odds or grief. Cap's resiliency after the "snap" in *End Game* showcases how to enable a group to move forward through overwhelming grief. |
| **8. Ensure that the leader's own behaviors convey the importance of self-care and the value of interpersonal connections to the group/community/nation.** |
| During *Civil War* Cap frees his team from prison, coming back to convey the importance of taking care of the team. During *End Game,* Cap forms self-help groups and mentors Black Widow to convey the importance of self-care and the connections formed. Cap demonstrated his own commitment to self-care at the end of *End Game* by staying to live life with Peggy Carter. |
| **9. Set the stage for an effective leadership transition once the initial grief/ bereavement process has been navigated.** |
| Cap mentors both Black Widow and later Falcon to take over primary leadership of the Avengers. By doing this throughout the movies, and then specifically in *End Game*, Cap ensures that the Avengers will continue with leadership in the event of his departure. |
| **10. Revisit the group at a future point in time to help memorialize the loss and to acknowledge that grief is an ongoing process uniquely experienced across time by each person, group, and community.** |
| Cap returns to the team (Falcon, Bucky, and Hulk) with a new shield at the end of *End Game* to validate and help memorialize the transition of leadership from the Captain America/Iron Man era to the new era of Avengers while enabling them to find peace with his own decisions to live an alternative life with Peggy. |

*Captain America: First Avenger* (Feige & Johnston, 2011); *Avengers* (Feige & Whedon, 2012); *Avengers: Age of Ultron* (Feige & Whedon, 2015); *Captain America: Civil War* (Feige, Russo, & Russo, 2016); *Avengers: Infinity Wars* (Feige, Russo, & Russo, 2018); *Avengers: End Game* (Feige, Russo, & Russo, 2019).

## 32.2 Grief Leadership in Real-World Practice

Although these examples are from the fictional world of Captain America, leaders in the real world, at all levels of society, need to be prepared to step forward to practice grief leadership in response to overwhelming loss. This is true whether losses result from a natural disaster like a hurricane that involves multiple injuries and deaths across a wide region, a pandemic like the COVID-19 crisis where there is a prolonged spread of disease and death across wide geographic areas, a commercial aircraft crash in which all passengers and crew perish, a local school shooting where both adults and children die, or line-of-duty deaths that involve law enforcement, first responders, or military service members. Whether the bereaved group is large or small, effective grief leadership requires timely actions that address and support the group's grief responses and promote individual, as well as collective, recovery and resilience.

There are excellent examples of grief leadership by elected and appointed leaders at different organizational levels and representing a range of scenarios. We present two vignettes that showcase real-world grief leadership. The first is President Ronald Reagan's response to the loss of the Challenger, and the second is a more personal account by one of the authors, reflecting on his 2005 experiences as a company commander during combat operations in Iraq.

President Reagan's response to the loss of the Challenger spacecraft and crew, including Christa McAuliffe, a 37-year-old schoolteacher and first ever "civilian astronaut", is a noteworthy example of how grief leadership can heal after a national tragedy. Thousands of American schoolchildren were watching from their classroom desks as the seven American astronauts lifted off in the shuttle Challenger. Almost immediately, and on national television, Challenger was consumed in a fireball, and all on board perished. The nation was shocked and heartbroken by the tragedy. Just a few hours later, President Reagan took to the airwaves, honoring these pioneers and offering comfort and assurance, especially to America's children. To quote the president:

> *And I want to say something to the school children of America who were watching the live coverage of the shuttle's takeoff. I know it's hard to understand, but sometimes painful things like this happen. It's all part of the process of exploration and discovery. It's all part of taking a chance and expanding man's horizons. The future doesn't belong to the faint-hearted. It belongs to the brave. The Challenger crew was pulling us into the future, and we'll continue to follow them.*
>
> (Note: for a more detailed account of this event and President Reagan's remarks, see: https://www.upi.com/Archives/1986/01/28/Full-text-of-President-Reagans-speech-after-Challenger-disaster/2641507272400/)

By framing the Challenger disaster in such a direct and compassionate way, in particular the loss of a teacher Christa McAuliffe, President Reagan provided schoolchildren and their teachers a way to collectively mourn this profound loss while still identifying the importance of continuing to dream the seemingly impossible – America's exploration of space – as a representation of our individual and shared capacity to move forward even when confronted by such a powerful tragedy. President Reagan offered America's schoolchildren a sense of hope and a vision for their future.

Although most remembered after national disasters, exceptional grief leadership is equally compelling in support of smaller groups, and it is fundamental to sustaining military readiness and helping units function effectively after the death of one of their own service members. Our second vignette is most effectively told by one of our authors in his own voice:

> *In May 2005, one of my unit's rising superstars was killed during a combat patrol in Iraq. I will always remember our unit's memorial service for him. Our Division Commander, a Major General, attended the memorial (he actually attended every memorial service in the division) and provided public acknowledgement of the loss at the level of senior leadership, mourning alongside unit members of all ranks. One purpose of the Division Commander's presence was to ensure that a set of established rules surrounding memorial services was followed without deviation. While this might appear draconian and micro-managing, squashing our unit's ability to define how we mourned, I quickly realized that the imposed framework focused and facilitated our ability to grieve in the moment. Three time-limited speeches were allowed at the memorial service – one by a squad mate, one by our battalion commander, and my own speech as the company commander. Imposed restrictions did not squelch our unit's ability to mourn. In fact, the structure highlighted our shared military values and our capacity to continue our combat mission despite our immediate and profound grief. It was the Division Commander's understanding and implementation of grief leadership that helped heal our unit and fostered our resilient return to the mission.*
>
> *~ David F. Carey, LTC U.S. Army (Retired), Combat Veteran, (OIF I, OIF III, & OEF 2013)*

Uniformity is an important part of the military regimen. Even in death, rites and rituals are conducted in very specific and purposeful ways. As a result, every military memorial service is personal, but uniform, and therefore no memorial service is greater or lesser than another, something of great importance in wartime situations when many deaths are likely to occur. Structured military honors allow military units to grieve in a manner that honors their fallen Soldiers in a meaningful and uniform way, while supporting their rapid return to the combat mission – effectively promoting individual and unit resilience.

Many examples of effective grief leadership exist in the responses of local leaders after community tragedies and in the words and actions of leaders in military, police, fire department, and other first responder organizations after tragic loss of unit members performing their duties. During the COVID-19 crisis, at regional and national levels, many elected officials, as well as institutional and civic leaders, have provided effective grief leadership during the pandemic, even while struggling with a virus that creates great ambiguity and changing circumstances.

The coronavirus 2019 (COVID-19) pandemic provides an additional example of the daunting challenges leaders can face and how grief leadership must be woven into crisis leadership principles and practices. With the mounting loss of life, employment, and opportunity, all in the face of future uncertainty, leaders during the COVID-19 pandemic were called upon to act decisively, basing their actions on goals and values that address the well-being of all those they serve while specifically showing compassion to those most affected. During the crisis, leaders must recognize and thoughtfully respond to a diversity of opinion and perspective and pay attention to the unspoken voices of those, who, because of their station and/or status in society, typically go unheard. They must provide timely, clear, and specific information on planned responses to the crisis as they show receptiveness to knowledge and wisdom from experts regarding the issues that have to be addressed. Leaders need to message those they serve in a language and tone that conveys confidence, provides clarity, reflects a sense of selflessness, demonstrates empathy, and models compassion for those affected. They must make it clear to everyone that we are in this crisis, and will get through this crisis, together. While providing necessary reassurance, crisis leaders must back up their words with deeds – recognizable measures, quickly and confidently put into place to both prevent the situation from getting worse and once under control, providing clear guidance on how the crisis will be resolved. Effective leaders help people see beyond the immediate moment toward a longer perspective and a positive outcome – they offer realistic hope. Integrating grief leadership practices, skilled leaders acknowledge and honor present sacrifice, and at an appropriate later time, they will memorialize the deeds and self-sacrifice of those who have and are continuing to meet the requirements of society – heroes big and small. A crucial and complex responsibility, grief leadership is not a job for the fainthearted.

As noted by Bartone (2019), there are many examples throughout history, and across the spectrum of leadership levels, where those in positions of authority and responsibility have failed to effectively address the grief of the nation, the community, or the unit. A common denominator in these failures is a lack of compassion for those overwhelmed by loss. These failures, especially the absence of demonstrated compassion, often prolonged the suffering and promoted discouragement and even despair among survivors.

As demonstrated in the life and service of Captain America, as well as in these real-world examples, grief leadership ensures continued safety for all, acknowledges and values the profound loss that occurred, and offers hope, providing a vision for moving forward. Leaders who acknowledge their own need for self-care and appropriately transfer the mantle of leadership also support the organization's mission by ensuring continuity of leadership, and in turn encourage individual and group resilience. For groups as well as individuals, acute grief is emotionally distressing as well as disorganizing. Effective leaders have the capacity to show compassion and comfort those who are bereaved, reduce their distress, restore their functioning, and offer hope and a vision for moving forward. This is the essence of effective grief leadership – an essence portrayed by the world's first Avenger, Captain America.

## References

Bartone, P.T. (2019). Grief leadership: Leader influences on resilience and recovery following community disaster. In S. Rawat (Ed.), *Cadet diary 2.0: Psychology of warrior ethos and cadet leader development*. New Delhi: Rawat Publications.

Faust, D.G. (2008). *This republic of suffering: Death and the American Civil War*. New York, NY: Knopf.

Feige, K. (Producer), & Johnston, J. (Director). (2011). *Captain America: The first avenger* [Motion Picture]. United States: Marvel Studios

Feige, K. (Producer), & Russo, A., & Russo, J. (Directors). (2014). *Captain America: The winter soldier* [Motion Picture]. United States: Marvel Studios

Feige, K. (Producer), & Russo, A., & Russo, J. (Directors). (2016). *Captain America: Civil war* [Motion Picture]. United States: Marvel Studios

Feige, K. (Producer), & Russo, A., & Russo, J. (Directors). (2018). *Avengers: Infinity war* [Motion Picture]. United States: Marvel Studios

Feige, K. (Producer), Russo, A., & Russo, J. (Directors). (2019). *Avengers: End game* [Motion Picture]. United States: Marvel Studios

Feige, K. (Producer), & Whedon, J. (Director). (2012). *The avengers* [Motion Picture]. United States: Marvel Studios

Feige, K. (Producer), & Whedon, J. (Director). (2015). *Avengers: Age of Ultron* [Motion Picture]. United States: Marvel Studios

Grief leadership. (n.d.). Leadership in the wake of tragedy. Retrieved from www.cstsonline.org/resources/resource-master-list/grief-leadership-leadership-in-the-wake-of-tragedy

# 33 Parental Grief and Activism

## On Becoming Your Friendly Neighborhood Spider-Man

*Joyal Mulheron*

### 33.1 The Radioactive Bite

No other relationship conjures more emotion and identity than one between a parent and their child. Like a spider, we spin a web, one that is protective, to nurture them, invest in their future, and tend to skinned knees and broken hearts, unconditionally. We help our children strive toward their dreams, many of us abandoning our own hopes in the process. But when our children die, something deep within our soul alters and irrevocably changes our outlook on life and purpose. Like a spider, we dangle from a painfully broken web, and in our grief, look to where we can begin to mend the web of our lives.

The death of a child at any age and from any cause is a unique hardship resulting in a radioactive fallout for all of those whom the child touched. My own exposure began when our unborn child suffered from a "condition not compatible with life" and propagated as she lived on borrowed time. Watching our infant daughter die slowly and painfully induced prolonged radiation sickness. Over time, a paranormal transformation took place where doing nothing for future bereaved families was not an option. I started to feel new senses and strengths transform within me, much like young Peter Parker, after being bit by a radioactive spider.

Soon, I saw an invisible crisis pervading many American doorsteps. It was hiding in plain sight among our national media headlines: *Hadiya Pendleton (murdered, age 15), Hot Shots firefighting brigade (19 killed, ages 21–33), Sandy Hook Massacre (26 murdered, ages 6–56), Joplin tornadoes (158 fatalities in 38 minutes)*, an uptick in Chicago homicides, Iraq and Afghanistan wars, not to mention the millions of American families whose losses to overdoses, suicide, or disease that garner no acclaim. Each of these deaths was *someone's* child. With each story, my sense of urgency and anxiety grew.

As a bystander and knowing the devastation families were experiencing, waves of nausea struck, and my spidey-sense matured. Each of these deaths send shockwaves throughout families exposing parents, siblings, grandparents, and communities to potentially toxic doses of radiation. Knowing this reality all too well, I became compelled to do something – anything. My "sense" turned into a conviction that our nation can, and should, do more to help bereaved families in an effective and holistic manner.

Much like Peter Parker (aka Spider-Man), I wanted to look out for my community – bereaved parents and families. Transforming and honing my radioactive exposure, it was with this newfound sense that I wanted to use my strengths and gifts to help protect and advocate for my bereaved community. With this conviction, I could relate to Peter's response to Tony Stark's offer to initially join the Avengers, "I'm good … I'd rather just stay on the ground for a little while. Friendly Neighborhood Spider-Man" (Feige, Pascal, & Watts, 2017, 2:00:15–2:00:25). Determined, I left my career and began building a national public health platform to address the implications of child death on American families. As Peter said to Tony, "Somebody's got to look out for the little guy, right?" (Feige et al., 2017, 2:00:26). And my community of bereaved American families, I found, is one that is marginalized. Similar to Spider-Man, I felt it was my calling to help, protect, and defend my "neighborhood".

## 33.2 The Neighborhood: Child Death and Bereaved Families

The death of a child at any age and from any cause is an invisible public health crisis in the United States. It is an injurious event that causes a cascade of health, social, and economic ramifications for all family members leading to household instability, decreased well-being, and decreased solvency. These hardships pervade nearly every aspect of life, making functional coping and adaptive processing a significant challenge, if not insurmountable for some. Unlike many public health priorities, child death transcends race, socioeconomic status, religion, and geography, leaving anyone and everyone at risk. Ask parents what their greatest nightmare is, and many will say it is the death of a child, and for good reason.

According to the Institute of Medicine, "While bereavement is stressful whenever it occurs, studies continue to provide evidence that the greatest stress, and often the most enduring one, occurs for parents who experience the death of a child" (Institute of Medicine et al., 2003, p. 1693). Scientific evidence demonstrates that bereaved parents are more likely to suffer cardiac events (Li, Hansen, Mortensen, & Olsen, 2002), immune dysfunction (Spratt & Denney, 1991), depressive symptoms, poorer well-being, less purpose in life, more health complications, marital disruption (Rogers et al., 2008), psychiatric hospitalization (Li, Laursen, Precht, Olsen, & Mortensen, 2005), and even premature death for both mothers and fathers as early as age 40 (Li, Precht, Mortensen, & Olsen, 2003). Surviving siblings face significant risks, too, including a 71% all-cause mortality risk following the death of a sibling during adolescence (Yu et al., 2017).

Despite the toll, the issue remains invisible because the Centers for Disease Control and Prevention collects death events, but not who survives them. In

2017, from stillbirth to age 54 (when one surviving family member is conceivable), 400,000 children died (Hoyert & Gregory, 2016; Murphy, Xu, Kochanek, & Arias, 2018). Thereby, if one parent survived each death, a half million parents were impacted, if two parents survived, nearly one million Americans are impacted, and if both parents and a sibling are impacted, then upwards of 1.5 million Americans were directly exposed to this toxic radiation annually.

Not all communities or survivors are equally impacted, however. Black families experience exponential prevalence rates of child death when compared to whites. By age 20, black Americans are more than twice as likely as whites to experience the death of a child; by age 30, they are 2.7 times more likely, and by age 80, they are 4.2 times more likely to experience the death of a child when compared to whites (Umberson, 2017). Given the unequal burden, black communities experience increased parental bereavement and prevalence of grief and are at heightened risk for associated poor health outcomes.

## 33.3 Advocating for Webs of Support

We know that when a child dies, how we respond to a family's needs can make all the difference. Professional education does not construct "webbing" to catch families from experiencing this specific form of trauma. As such, there is no subspecialty among therapists to differentiate how the cause and manner of death impacts a parent's ability to cope. Losing a child to murder is different than suicide or stillbirth, disease, or overdose; thus the webs of support should also be modified.

Family programs should recognize and address varied life experiences, cultural values, religious doctrines, geographies, and the circumstances pertaining to the child's death. Programing in an inner-city community center focused on violent death, for example, should be different than one located in frontier America, or within the halls of the Department of Defense or among labor and delivery wards.

To make a compelling case for action, a national research agenda outlining key facts and figures, demographics, and trends by race, geography, cause, and age of death is required. Interrelationships between death statistics, family income, health, causes of death, and community support systems should be explored to provide a clear understanding of the problem and opportunities for interventions.

Further, the death of a child is not a qualifying event for Family Medical Leave Act job protection (Department of Labor Wage and Hour Division, 1993). If your child dies, there are no legal employment protections to prevent parents from being fired. While 88% of American employers offer some form of paid bereavement leave (Society for Human Resource Management, 2018), most report only four days of paid leave. That number drops to two days for a stillbirth or miscarriage (Society for Human Resource Management, 2016).

## 33.4 Protecting the Community, Preserving a Nation

As a nation, we have made significant and worthy investments in the prevention of death, but we cannot stop there. Death, and thus bereavement, remain a part of everyday life experience, and we should acknowledge and invest in strategies accordingly. Restoring a family's ability to work, learn, and play not only directly impacts our ability to compete in the global economy, but it also expedites the prosperity and stability of American households.

The death of a child at any age and from any cause is a seminal event sending shockwaves throughout survivors, rendering them at risk for their own health events, psychological, spiritual, and occupational struggles. With the great power of this knowledge, "comes great responsibility" (Ziskin, Bryce, & Raimi, 2002, 0:35:46). We can, and must, do better. Like Spider-Man, I know I must.

## References

Department of Labor Wage and Hour Division. (1993, February 5). *The Family and Medical Leave Act of 1993, as amended.* Retrieved from https://www.dol.gov/whd/fmla/fmlaamended.htm#SEC_102_LEAVE_REQUIREMENT)

Feige, K., & Pascal, A. (Producers), & Watts, J. (Director). (2017). *Spider-Man: Homecoming* [Motion Picture]. United States: Marvel Studios.

Hoyert, D.L., & Gregory, E.C.W. (2016). Cause of fetal death: Data from the Fetal Death Report, 2014. *National Vital Statistics Reports*, 65(7). Hyattsville, MD: National Center for Health Statistics.

Institute of Medicine (US) Committee on Palliative and End-of-Life Care for Children and Their Families, Field, M.J., & Behrman, R.E. (Eds.). (2003). *When children die: Improving palliative and end-of-life care for children and their families*. Washington, DC: National Academies Press.

Li, J., Hansen, D., Mortensen, P.B., & Olsen, J. (2002). Myocardial infarction in parents who lost a child: A nationwide prospective cohort study in Denmark. *Circulation*, 106(13), 1634–1639.

Li, J., Laursen, T.M., Precht, D.H., Olsen, J., & Mortensen, P.B. (2005). Hospitalization for mental illness among parents after the death of a child. *New England Journal of Medicine*, 352(12):1190–1196.

Li, J., Precht, D.H., Mortensen, P.B., & Olsen, J. (2003). Mortality in parents after death of a child in Denmark: A nationwide follow-up study. *Lancet*, 361(9355), 363–367.

Murphy, S.L., Xu, J.Q., Kochanek, K.D., & Arias, E. (2018). Mortality in the United States (2017). NCHS Data Brief, no 328. Hyattsville, MD: National Center for Health Statistics.

Rogers, C., & Floyd, F.J., et al. (2008). Long-term effects of the death of a child on parents' adjustment in midlife. *Journal of Family Psychology*, 22(2), 203–211.

Society for Human Resource Management. (2016, October 6). SHRM survey findings: Paid leave in the workplace. Retrieved from https://www.shrm.org/hr-today/trends-and-forecasting/research-and-surveys/Documents/2016-Paid-Leave-in-the-Workplace.pdf

Society for Human Resource Management. (2018). 2018 Employee benefits: The evolution of benefits. Retrieved from https://www.shrm.org/hr-today/trends-and-forecasting/research-and-surveys/Documents/2018%20Employee%20Benefits%20 Report.pdf

Spratt, M.L., & Denney, D.R. (1991). Immune variables, depression, and plasma cortisol over time in suddenly bereaved parents. *Journal of Neuropsychiatry*, 3(3), 299–306.

Umberson, D. (2017). Black deaths matter: Race, relationship loss, and effects of survivors. *Journal of Health and Social Behavior*, 58(4), 405–420. doi: 10.1177/0022146517739317

Yu, Y., Liew, Z., Cnattingius, S., et al. (2017). Association of mortality with the death of a sibling in childhood. *JAMA Pediatrics*, 171(6), 538–545. doi:10.1001/ jamapediatrics.2017.0197.

Ziskin, L., & Bryce, I. (Producers), & Raimi, S. (Director). (2002). *Spider-Man* [Motion Picture]. United States: Columbia Pictures, Marvel Enterprises, Laura Ziskin Productions.

# 34 X-Men

## What They Teach Us About Oppression and Marginalization of the Bereaved

*Erica Goldblatt Hyatt*

## 34.1 The Issue at Hand

Roberta clenches a wad of shredded tissues. She refuses to meet my gaze, and her head is bent over two slumped shoulders. The energy in the room is still and static, and in the air, I can feel Roberta's sense of shame swirling. Her son, Marcus, died three years ago. Roberta came to me, a grief therapist, just a few weeks ago. Her head hurts, she is always exhausted, and she cries at the smallest of reminders of Marcus. She whispers, "I don't know what's wrong with me". Tears fall slowly down her cheeks. "I should be feeling better by now".

Roberta's concerns are common. Whether days, months, or years after loss, my clients fear that their inability to "heal" promptly means that they are mentally ill. However, their problem lies within our death-denying society. While approximately 7% of grievers experience complicated grief (Shear, 2012), the overwhelming majority of bereaved individuals find pathways to adapt to loss and integrate grief into their lives. However, for some, this does not come without challenges that make the road forward extremely difficult. One of these challenges is Western norms and values about grief – which can be in direct opposition to compassion and understanding. Almost universally, they teach disenfranchisement, medicalization, and suppression.

## 34.2 Grief, Norms, and X-Men

This chapter introduces the concept of oppression and marginalization of the bereaved, as illustrated by X-Men. X-Men chronicles the adventures of humans with superhuman genetic mutations resulting in abilities that range from accelerated healing powers to telekinesis, teleportation, and more. The undercurrent of the original *X-Men* film (Donner, Winter, & Singer, 2000) focused on the stigmatization of mutants by humankind, just as grievers face judgment from society at large.

In our fast-paced Western world, little time is permitted to mourn. Values of individualism and a capitalistic emphasis on production, consumption, and consumerism govern the norms around "who, when, where, how, how long, and for whom people should grieve" (Doka, 1989, p. 4). The rules of grief are created to engender social conformity and focus on the abilities of the living: reminders of sickness, aging, and death are shuttered away in the interests of serving the dominant groups in power (Harris, 2009), which, in the case of the West, are usually governed by individuals of wealthy, heteronormative, patriarchal heritage (Bonds & Inwood, 2016). The bereaved are briefly reprieved from work, condolences are provided, and then, life moves on. If grievers can't catch up, the problem is theirs. They may begin to feel ignored, isolated, useless, and ashamed. This trend is so common that it can be illustrated by the plight of the X-Men.

**Disenfranchisement.** According to Doka (1989), not all losses may be viewed equally from society's perspective. Rather, some losses are not worthy of public acknowledgment. For example, death by suicide is commonly stigmatized and followed by shame in grievers, who may feel judged by religious or social groups. Grief over a pet may be deemed ridiculous. Men who express grief by crying instead of "being strong" may be avoided. Disenfranchised grievers come to believe that they are not permitted to mourn. In *X-Men*, a human senator attempts to pass a bill that would require all mutants to publicly self-identify, essentially exposing mutants as undeserving of the same privileges and rights as regular humans. Mutants, like grievers, are not socially validated. Mourning that appears "wrong" or "different", or deaths that do not fit the norm, are categorized as different and unworthy of support. As a result, disenfranchised grievers, like mutants, may feel forced to hide among the "normal", feigning healing while suffering inside.

**Medicalization.** In Western society, symptoms of grief that interfere with production, consumption, and other capitalistic pursuits can be labeled as a psychological condition that must be treated, as these interfere with the "right to happiness" (Granek, 2014). This medicalization of grief, whereby certain behaviors require monitoring, treatment, and even prescription of pharmaceuticals (Bandini, 2015), not only serves a capitalistic agenda by transforming grief into a profitable commodity but also invalidates and turns the individual experience of grief into a disease to be medically managed. The plot of *X-Men: The Last Stand* (Donner, Winter, Arad, & Ratner, 2006) exemplifies this. In the film, the capitalist Warren Worthington is the father of Angel, who is a mutant himself and can grow giant wings. Worthington's development of the vaccine is an attempt to "cure" his son of his mutation. While Angel initially feared his mutation, he eventually rejects the idea of a cure. This is a metaphor for the power of grief to both cause the bereaved to stand out, but also to transform into something magnificent. Like Angel, grievers can reject the medicalization of their symptoms, learn to grow into their experiences of loss, and be changed by it in enduring ways.

**Suppression.** Perhaps the largest example of how society marginalizes and oppresses the bereaved is found in the example of suppression. Grievers internalize gender-biased messages: women should express themselves by crying, and men should be strong, avoiding emotion. Both genders should not express symptoms for too long, as this is abnormal. Of course, this perspective reflects a gender-biased, binary, and overly simplistic expectation of the expression of grief. Grief is as unique as the individual griever and the relationship they are mourning. However, in the West, grief that interferes with Western norms of vitality, health, and success must be suppressed. We should not be reminded of grief, face grief for too long, or think of our own deaths, lest they impact our productivity and falsely perceived sense of immortality. Multiple examples are featured across *X-Men.* The character of Wolverine (aka Logan), whose story is depicted in *X-Men Origins: Wolverine* (Donner, Winter, Jackman, Palermo, & Hood, 2009) is compelling. As a boy, Logan witnesses the murder of the man he believed to be his father, only to kill his true birth father. As a response, Logan flees his home. Affected by a mutation that provides him the ability to heal from injury, Logan pursues a career of violence, fighting in multiple wars across the 20th century, until he settles down with his girlfriend, Kayla, who is then murdered by Logan's brother. Desiring revenge, Logan is transformed into the Wolverine, and his memory is erased. A viewer might understand Logan's journey as a continual suppression of grief, wherein Logan's symptoms of loss are suppressed and channeled toward more appropriate "male" bereavement responses such as anger and violence.

The case of Jean Grey (aka Dark Phoenix) provides a feminine example of suppression. The film *Dark Phoenix* (Kinberg, Parker, Donner, & Hallowell, 2019) begins with the tragic car accident that kills Jean Grey's parents, leaving her as the sole survivor. She is rescued by Charles Xavier, who is aware of her powers of telekinesis and telepathy. Xavier alters her mind to protect her from the trauma of the loss – in essence, suppressing Jean's grief. As she grows, Jean begins to remember the accident and realizes that she was the cause. This fills her with pain and rage, resulting in her inadvertently killing another X-Man, and injuring another. Jean embarks on a journey to suppress her powers. During this process, she learns that if her powers are removed, she will die. At the end of the film, instead of dying, Jean transforms into a phoenix. In this way, one message from *Dark Phoenix* is that grief cannot be suppressed but must be felt and endured and will result in our own transformation.

## 34.3 Clinical Considerations

While *the X-Men* series illustrates themes of oppression and marginalization of the bereaved, it is imperative for bourgeoning clinicians to recognize those especially at risk of disenfranchisement, medicalization, and suppression. Clinicians should be aware of ambiguous loss, a form of grief in which a death occurs without verification, or a person is lost in some way, including physically or mentally, and may not recover (Boss, 2000). Among this group are women who have experienced miscarriage, stillbirth, or ended a wanted pregnancy due to fetal anomaly. These women may struggle with a lack of acknowledgment that they are grieving mothers who require special care. Other mourners experiencing ambiguous loss are found at the other end of the lifespan: the loved ones of individuals with dementia who experience the loss of their loved one as they once knew them. It is important to validate that while a person has not yet died, they will also never return to the familiar person they were. Finally, while not necessarily suffering from ambiguous loss, both child and adult siblings of those who have died tend to be particularly forgotten or marginalized, as the focus of bereavement support usually falls upon spouses or parents.

## 34.4 Intervention Strategies

First and foremost, work with the bereaved involves immediately acknowledging the loss, as well as validating and normalizing the griever's experience. Grief appears in unique and sometimes unexpected ways across individuals, and while difficult to endure, it is important for clients to know that grief in itself is not harmful. Clients often internalize societal expectations and feel as though "I should be moving on" or "Everyone else has moved on" and can become hyperfocused on their grief, as well as overly judgmental of themselves. It can be helpful to explore the unrealistic assumptions clients have about themselves through cognitive-behavioral methods (Beck, 1979), which focus on substituting unhealthy, irrational thoughts with more realistic and nuanced expectations. For example, a useful substitute thought might be "I am grieving as strongly as I have loved" or "My relationship with my loved one lasted X amount of years; I can't expect to feel better in X amount of days". It is also useful to link clients to peer support with grievers who have endured similar losses so that they can create some kinship and recognition that they are not isolated, alone, or unusual in their responses to grief. While everybody grieves differently, usually peer support groups are helpful as peers find that they do share similar experiences of feeling that they should be suppressing grief or worries about grief being abnormal.

Additionally, while clients may feel compelled to run away from their symptoms of grief, it is important to face them instead. Exposure to sadness, pain, and anger is difficult, but suppressing these will only cause the feelings to increasingly emerge. Creating a sense of mindfulness and observing symptoms, for example, "I notice my heart feels hot, and my breathing is shallow. My skin feels irritated, and it's hard to concentrate", can help slow down racing thoughts or the urge to react to feelings and responses to grief that can seem unbearable, creating a space for grief to exist and explore.

Creative expression through art, poetry, dance, or other endeavors can also channel grief and, at times, the inability to express grief and disenfranchisement in words. I often encourage my clients to narrate their stories of loss and include metaphor. One recently described grief as a sleek, stealthy panther, always waiting for a moment of weakness and to pounce unexpectedly. We carried this metaphor forward, both exploring how she might create compassion for the panther, but also how to not feed it.

Above all else, a therapeutic relationship where the experience of grief is valued and explored can be healing. Our openness to clients who feel like "mutants" in the face of a society urging them not to grieve too hard and too long can create a lasting and meaningful experience that honors grief, the griever, and the person or relationship they lost.

## References


Bandini, J. (2015). The medicalization of bereavement: (Ab)normal grief in the DSM-5. *Death Studies*, 39(6), 347–352.

Beck, A.T. (1979). *Cognitive therapy and the emotional disorders.* New York NY: Penguin.

Bonds, A., & Inwood, J. (2016). Beyond white privilege: Geographies of white supremacy and settler colonialism. *Progress in Human Geography*, 40(6), 715–733.

Boss, P. (2000). *Ambiguous loss: Learning to live with unresolved grief.* Cambridge, MA: Harvard University Press.

Doka, K.J. (1989). *Disenfranchised grief: Recognizing hidden sorrow.* Lexington, MA: Lexington Books.

Donner, L.S., Winter, R., & Arad, A. (Producers), & Ratner, B. (Director) (2006). *X-Men: The last stand* [Motion picture]. United States: Twentieth Century Fox.

Donner, L.S., Winter, R., Jackman, H., & Palermo, J. (Producers), & Hood, G. (Director) (2009). *X-Men origins: Wolverine* [Motion picture]. United States: Twentieth Century Fox.

Donner, L.S., & Winter, R. (Producers), & Singer, B. (Director). (2000). *X-Men* [Motion picture]. United States: Twentieth Century Fox.

Granek, L. (2014). Mourning sickness: The politicizations of grief. *Review of General Psychology*, 18(2), 61–88.

Harris, D. (2009). Oppression of the bereaved: A critical analysis of grief in Western society. *OMEGA – Journal of Death and Dying*, 60(3), 241–253.

Kinberg, S., Parker, H., Donner, L.S., & Hallowell, T. (Producers), & Kinberg, S. (Director). (2019). *Dark phoenix* [Motion picture]. United States: Twentieth Century Fox.

Shear, M.K. (2012). Grief and mourning gone awry: Pathway and course of complicated grief. *Dialogues in Clinical Neuroscience*, 14(2), 119–128.

# Part IX

# Superhero-Based Strategies of Care: Interventions and Creative Approaches

# 35 Avengers Endgame

## What It Can Teach Us About Individuals and Families Facing the End-of-Life

*Lisa Holland Downs*

Superheroes and their stories are rich with symbolism. When thinking about superheroes like Superman, Captain America, Spider-Man, Wonder Woman, and Iron Man, one automatically thinks about strength, power, fighting the enemy, and never giving up. The less obvious symbols include hope, integrity, strength, and rebellion. Superheroes are used in many forms in everyday life. They are used in apparel, home goods, tattoos, toys, and even cars. The use of these heroes and what they represent even extends into medical treatment of illness, such as cancer (Easterling, 2018). The use of these symbols can give hope, comfort, and even coping to children as well as adults (Shortland, 2015). Therefore, this chapter will explore the use of superheroes with individuals and families with life-threatening and life-limiting illnesses.

### 35.1 Background

Superheroes have been used most often by children who are fighting illness, and the most commonly thought of is childhood cancer. Therefore, cancer is the ultimate villain in symbolic terms. It is unbeatable; it targets good people and wreaks havoc on the lives of the innocent. It is an easy association for one to think of caregivers as superheroes who become saviors from this "villain". The direct use of cancer in the world of the superhero is actually not well known, but in the comics, it does exist. In fact, Superman dies of cancer (Mythologist, 2018) as well as Thor's love, Jane (Peters, 2014). Superman's archenemy, Lex Luther, finds a way to expose him to the radioactive rays of the sun, giving him cancer. Once he is diagnosed, he chooses to use his life to do as much good as he can, for Lois Lane, and for the city of Kandor (Nierstedt, 2016). He is an inspiration despite his terminal disease. These superheroes want to live their lives despite the struggles they now face daily. These stories create a feeling of empathy and compassion for those who have the illness. They need a purpose or to fight for the greater good. It makes them more human; in fact, Langley (2018) wrote that the superhero's humanity is a critical part of their character. It also shows us the people we wish we could be. It shows purpose in the life of the sick despite the shortness of that life.

## 35.2 Symbolic Themes as seen in *Avengers: Endgame*

These symbols can translate into everyday heroes as well. The caregivers of people with cancer can often be seen as a superhero to a person who is in a battle for their lives. The caregiver takes a journey with the person who is ill and joins in the fight. Caregivers of ill and terminal patients include family, medical and psychosocial staff, friends, community, and members of faith groups.

Many illnesses are considered life-limiting, chronic, and terminal. These can alter one's ability to cope, live a "normal" life, and to be able to plan for the future while dealing with today. Individuals and families undergo many anticipatory and ambiguous losses. People experience the gamut of emotions as they search for coping with these illnesses.

Doka (2014) discusses life-threatening illness as phases. This includes the prediagnostic phase, where anxiety can build; the diagnosis phase, when there is almost relief knowing what you are dealing with; the chronic phase, where anxiety can go through many cycles over time; and the terminal phase, where initially anxiety climbs but eventually declines with acceptance and one's ability to make peace with the reality of their decline. He defines many tasks a person faces throughout the illness, which in my experience as an oncology and palliative care nurse are often felt by the majority of people, although often to differing degrees. I have also found many people can get stuck in a phase of their illness and, along with family, find it difficult to cope. Along the journey of one's illness, they often find inspiration in different ways. They can define a single source of comfort and strength, or many. They may define their "superhero" in different ways. This may include their caregivers, be it their doctor, nurse, family, spouse, or sometimes an actual superhero (dressed in costume by an individual) can become a source of comfort, inspiration, or strength.

Hope is central to all people who face illness, dying, and death. Hope will often change over the course of an illness. This hope can become hope for less pain, or hope for a good day, rather than hope for survival. In a study done by Eliott and Olver (2009), they found that "rather than death-denying, patients' hope appeared life-affirming, functioning to value patients, their lives, and connections with others" (p. 609). It can be the unwitting job of the caregivers to walk the patient through this journey. Because of this, the caregiver often becomes that symbolic superhero.

In the film *Avengers: End Game* (Feige, Russo, & Russo, 2019), the death of Iron Man took center stage. The movie begins following the failure of the Avengers to save the world from Thanos. In an article written by Tyler Daswick, he states, "the mission of *Endgame*, then ends up reflecting the mission of its title characters. It's about people who give themselves over to a cause and see it through whether it means impossible victory or a second horrible, traumatic failure" (Daswick, 2019, para. 10). Just like the entire care team for someone with an illness, from the physician, nurses, aides, social workers, family, and friends can all see the meaning of this is the same as the care for the ill person. Over the course of several movies, you can also see there were battles fought, some lost, and others won. This is often the case with someone who has a life-limiting illness. There may be periods of remission, and times of active disease, times of decline and times of stability.

Several of the characters took traumatic changes in the world around them as a personal failure (Feige et al., 2019) and having survived a traumatic event, appear to have survivor's guilt. Thor began drinking and gave up on being a superhero. Hawkeye became an assassin and killed "bad guys". Iron Man, who thought of himself as one of the leaders of the group, placed much of the blame on himself. Despite the fact that he had found a new life with a family, he could not let go of the possibility of changing what had happened – this is very common for those who suffer from survivor's guilt. Black Widow sacrificed herself in order to save the world (Biro et al., 2019). Through this lens, you can draw comparisons between the reactions of these superheroes and the caregivers of people with life-limiting illnesses. In real life, these may also be the struggle of bereaved caregivers and family members.

Caregivers often will feel responsible for the outcome, like Iron Man. They may struggle to make decisions at the end of life of the patient. Often, in the end, they do their best under the most difficult of circumstances, but getting to this decision can be an excruciating and painful process. Caregivers may fantasize about if they could just change one thing, it would make all the difference, which was actually the theme of the movie and the purpose of the Avengers. They may elevate their mistakes, become hypervigilant about their caregiving, and have difficulty with self-care and taking time for themselves. This is a comparison to the unrelenting and exhausting sacrifices of Black Widow. They may give up their responsibilities like Thor, isolate themselves, and push people away. There are times when caring for the sick takes a personal toll on caregivers. This can cause some people to retreat (Flores, 2019).

Captain America, another leader in the Avengers, was the eternal optimist. During the care of someone with an illness, this can be positive or negative. At the beginning of *Avengers: End Game* (Feige et al., 2019), you can watch as the members of the team talk about the plan, some dismissing it as impossible, and others remaining optimistic and little by little they convince each other the fight is worth it.

Initially, after diagnosis, there is often a period of fight; this is true of most people with cancer, ALS, Parkinson's, and other life-threatening illnesses, such as we have seen with the COVID-19 pandemic. This reaction is common by both the patients and the care team. For example, in a newly diagnosed leukemia patient, they will start by getting treatment and hoping for a cure. The physician, nurses, and medical team help them in this fight. Some are cured, and for some, when that cure does not happen, they often look to science in the hopes of a continued pursuit of a cure. This is a time of action and fight, where they lean into optimism. They are full of hope, like Captain America. Unfortunately for some, when their disease does not respond to treatment and turns to terminal illness, this is where a transition in goals of care should take place. However, for some, this can be a struggle for acceptance, by both the one fighting the illness and the caregivers.

For example, the scene between Black Widow and Hawkeye is one where they are both fighting to try to save the other (Feige et al., 2019). In order to get the soul stone, they must make a sacrifice of love. They therefore fight each other, ironically, because they love each other. Black Widow only ends up "winning" and sacrifices herself by begging Hawkeye to let her go (Biro, Barry, Williams, & Immel, 2019). This is a parallel to a family who may be caring for a dying loved one. The one who must die often wants the caregiver to let them go. This is time and again a struggle and many times does not happen until the loved one dies. Dealing with some of these things in the heat of the battle often results in complex grief issues for the bereaved family member(s). It would be a perfect world if everyone dealt with these types of things in real time at the right time, but no perfect world exists. Eventually, Black Widow took the matter in her own hands and pushed herself to her own death. You can see how some patients give up before the loved one is ready for this to happen. This may leave the family with unresolved issues they may need to work through in their own time.

At the end of the final epic battle in *Avengers: End Game*, Pepper, now Iron Man's wife says to him, "Tony, look at me. We're going to be OK. You can rest now" (Feige et al., 2019, 2:33:31). This was her giving him permission to die, to rest. Something Tony Stark had never done – he was always the problem solver, saving the world from annihilation, taking care of his personal and superhero family. Giving a dying loved one permission to go is the most difficult, yet utterly most selfless and loving of all human acts. We see Pepper lean on an incredible amount of strength and love, putting aside her own fear to do what is best for her dying husband – to release him from his fear that he is abandoning his responsibility to his family (Feige et al., 2019). The dying also have fears that their loved ones may not be able to find a way forward. They fear that their death will forever change the course of the future for the ones they love. Although this is, of course, true no matter what, they may need that permission to allow them to die. They may need to know that their loved ones will somehow carry on (MacLeod, 2013).

## 35.3 Conclusions

In Palliative Care and Hospice, we often speak about a "good death". This is obviously in the eye of the beholder, but in general, it has to do with a way of dying with diminished pain, comfort, preservation of control, dignity, and, if possible, surrounded by loved ones. In essence, Tony Stark/Iron Man, had a good death. In one aspect, Thanos was correct; death is inevitable, even with the best of outcomes, there is no altered reality that we live infinitely (Feige et al., 2019). We often talk about the power in working with families in deciding it is time and that it is okay for them to die – to be free of the battle of unrelenting suffering and to help the dying and their families find some control in the uncontrollable. In this author's observation, this is often the exception, not the rule. There are more times than not when a family is just not ready for this to happen, and they often fight it any way they can. This is a natural human response; we don't want to lose so much of what we love. This is often steeped in fear and uncertainty, as well as loss and grief (MacLeod, 2013). This is when inspiration and guidance are needed, when the larger care team of professionals, friends, and family can become those superheroes, much like those surrounding Tony Stark, in the support and assistance of the dying and their families.

## References

Biro, C., Barry, S., Williams, C., & Immel, E. (2019, May 3). "Avengers: Endgame" – From heartbreak to hope. Retrieved from https://thejesuitpost.org/2019/05/avengers-endgame-from-heartbreak-to-hope/

Daswick, T. (2019, April 25). Review: "Avengers: Endgame" might give you hope for this broken world. Retrieved from https://relevantmagazine.com/culture/film/review-avengers-endgame-might-give-you-hope-for-this-broken-world/

Doka, K.J. (2014). *Counseling individuals with life-threatening illness* (2nd ed.). New York, NY: Springer.

Easterling, M. (2018, January 21). Superhero created to battle cancer cells in sick kids | City of Hope Breakthroughs. Retrieved from https://www.cityofhope.org/superhero-created-to-battle-cancer-cells-in-sick-kids/

Eliott, J.A., & Olver, I.N. (2009). Hope, life, and death: A qualitative analysis of dying cancer patients' talk about hope. *Death Studies*, 33(7), 609–638.

Feige, K. (Producer), & Russo A., & Russo J. (Directors). (2019). *Avengers: End game* [Motion picture]. USA: Marvel Studios.

Flores, G. (2019, September 10). A caregiving superhero shares the rewards of caring. Retrieved from http://www.shieldhealthcare.com/community/caregivers/2013/01/18/a-caregiving-superhero-shares-the-rewards-of-caring-for-his-mom-with-multiple-sclerosis/

Langley, T. (2018, July 1). Symbolic power among Marvels [Blog Post]. Retrieved from https://www.psychologytoday.com/us/blog/beyond-heroes-and-villains/201807/symbolic-power-among-marvels

MacLeod, B. (Ed.). (2013). Advanced illness: Holding on and letting go. Retrieved from https://www.caregiver.org/advanced-illness-holding-on-letting-go

Mythologist, T. (2018, November 28). 10 comic book superheroes who battled cancer. Retrieved from https://www.popmythology.com/superheroes-who-battled-cancer/

Nierstedt, E. (2016, November 2). Superhero sickness: Why disease in comics is important. Retrieved from https://comicsverse.com/superhero-sickness-why-it-matters/

Peters, M. (2014, September 22). Comic book characters who fought cancer. Retrieved from https://www.salon.com/2014/09/21/comic_book_characters_who_fought_cancer/

Shortland, G. (2015, April 03). Superhero therapy. Retrieved from https://fridaymagazine.ae/life-culture/people-profiles/superhero-therapy-1.1483159

# 36 Childhood Grief and the Healing Power of Superheroes

*Donna Gaffney*

Superheroes capture the imaginations of young and old, on paper and on screens large and small. Their appeal transcends physical powers and strength. The superhero genre is central to the human belief in the fight between good and evil, balancing the scales of justice, and pursuing the impartiality of the law to right the wrongs levied upon them (Bell, 2014). However, there is another superpower shared by all superheroes – the power of healing. Superheroes face adversity, trauma, and loss. They strive to heal and overcome these life-changing obstacles (Cohen-Manor, 2019).

Perhaps there is no greater injustice in the eyes of a child than the death of a parent. The very person who will protect and nurture them is gone, leaving the child to navigate the challenges of an unjust world. How else could a child survive to adulthood unless they have superhuman qualities?

The body of literature emerging on childhood grief is persuasive. After death, grief is a natural, expected, nonlinear, and multidimensional experience that continually changes over time (Gaffney et al., 2016). Grief is not only influenced by a child's development, but also by parental separation, the impact on their day-to-day existence and identity, and the circumstances of the death (Kaplow et al., 2013). Adjustment after loss can be affected by social support, communication, sociocultural environments, the prior relationship with the deceased, and exposure to reminders of loss and trauma (Kaplow & Layne, 2014). Parenting is the overarching and vital experience incorporating many of the above-named influences.

Children, their caregivers, and clinicians can learn from the superheroes that live on pages of comic books, and on the screens of film and television. In some ways, they are no different from their human counterparts – at least before they come into their superpowers.

## 36.1 Circumstances of Death and the Origin Story

Death is not an isolated moment, it is framed by time, place, cause, and people who come together to create a story; a narrative that children carry with them for the rest of their lives. In fact, when children talk about the death of a parent, they refer to it as "my story" (personal communication, August 22, 2019).

The story can be incomplete or riddled with misconceptions. How and what children are told influences the way they integrate the loss. As children mature, their story is revised or expanded, the bereaved child at 5 will come to new understandings at 10 and 15. Superheroes also have stories that capture the beginnings of their heroic journey – the origin story, i.e., how Bruce Wayne became Batman. One could say that bereaved children have their own "origin story". Like superheroes, bereaved children have the potential to develop abilities and survival skills uncommon for other children their age. They also have the opportunity to model skills they see in caregiving adults and develop their own "powers" of adaptation.

## 36.2 Batman

Like many young children his age, nine-year-old Bruce Wayne engages in games of competition with his peers. A scene in *Batman Begins* (Roven, Thomas, Franco, & Nolan, 2005) shows Bruce and his friend Rachel frantically chasing each other over possession of an ancient arrowhead. Rachel grabs it from Bruce and simply exclaims to him, "Finders Keepers!" (Roven et al., 2005, 0:01:03). A dejected Bruce makes one last attempt to get the arrowhead from Rachel but slips and falls into a well. Tumbling through the darkness, bats soar and flutter around Bruce, terrorizing him. When his father pulls Bruce out of the well, his father rhetorically asks Bruce while carrying him, "And why do we fall, Bruce?" His father answers, without anger or judgment, "So, we can learn to pick ourselves up" (Roven et al., 2005, 0:10:40–0:10:44). Thomas Wayne's teaching and words of support will become a defining thread in young Bruce's life, words that will be spoken to him, reminding him of the continuing bond with his father by his trusted Alfred.

The origin story of Batman is perhaps one of the best known and most revisited in film and comic books. A young Bruce Wayne, the only child of Thomas and Martha Wayne, accompanies his parents to the opera in Gotham, a once vibrant but now crime-infested city. Bruce tries to watch the opera, but black costumes and fluttering movements on stage remind him of the terrifying bats in the cave. Overcome with anxiety, he asks to leave. The family exits the theater, a mugger confronts them and kills both parents in front of Bruce. As Bruce bends close to them, his father whispers, "Don't be afraid" (Roven et al., 2005, 0:14:18). Within minutes of seeing his parents tragically killed, a police officer announces to Bruce, "Good news. We got him, son" (Roven et al., 2005, 0:15:30). How does a child process the absurdity of the officer's good news with the painful emotions of the worst day of his life?

At his parents' funeral, Bruce is overcome with guilt. People tell him he is in excellent hands, but Bruce can only think back to the night his parents were killed. If only he hadn't asked to leave the theater. Bruce tells Alfred that he misses his parents. Alfred responds, "So do I" (Roven et al., 2005, 0:16:53), and embraces him.

Bruce's childhood friend Rachel had always supported him, but while Bruce was in Asia studying martial arts, they lost touch. When Bruce returns home to Gotham, he establishes the alternate identity of Batman, taking the name and black suit from the core of his childhood trauma – a bat. At the end of the film, Rachel, now a prosecutor in Gotham, welcomes Bruce home but not before admitting that he has changed. She hands him a box. Inside is the arrowhead and a small note, "Finders, Keepers". She leaves him with hope that he can find himself again.

## 36.3 Black Panther

When Ryan Coogler's *Black Panther* (Feige & Coogler, 2018) came to movie theaters, it was heralded as a triumph for black superheroes and black directors, breaking box office records and reaping critical acclaim. Black Panther (T'Challa) is a member of the Marvel Cinema Universe's Avengers, whose origin story was revealed in *Captain America: Civil War* (Feige, Russo, & Russo, 2016). Black Panther's father is the king of the advanced African nation of Wakanda. Before giving a speech in Nigeria, he is gunned down. T'Challa runs to his father's aid but is too late. His father dies in his arms. T'Challa is destined to rule Wakanda, vowing to become the righteous king he was meant to be.

T'Challa is challenged by a competitor, who has survived his own parental loss. Queen Ramonda encourages her son to take on his full power as king and says, "Show him who you are!" (Feige et al., 2018, 00:26: 22). His mother is a strong woman, more than capable of guiding her son. Wakanda's women are not only caregivers but also have powerful seats in the government and fight to influence Wakanda's politics and empower the nation (Allen, 2018).

## 36.4 Wonder Woman

Sometimes children discover new information about the deceased. Perhaps an accident is later revealed to be a suicide or circumstances of a death, long withheld, are exposed. Their bereavement story shifts dramatically, sowing confusion and doubt.

*Wonder Woman* (Roven, Snyder, Snyder, Suckle, & Jenkins, 2017) illustrates a shifting origin story. She is the third superhero to be introduced by DC comics. In 1941 William Marston conceived the character, who was based on his wife, a psychologist, and attorney. Unlike other superheroes, Wonder Woman did not kill her evil-doers, she reformed them. As the daughter of Hippolyta, she was sculpted out of clay and breathed into life by the gods. Also known as Diana, she lived without a father for years. However, in the 2011 comic book and the 2017 film, Wonder Woman's origin story dramatically changed. She learned her mother had a secret relationship with Zeus; she was a demi-God born of Zeus and Hippolyta, her superpowers explained by her paternal lineage (Roven et al., 2017).

Protective factors can mitigate negative consequences of loss and grief. A child's unique assets, interpersonal relationships, and social/physical environments can enhance coping and lessen stress (Gaffney et al., 2016). A positive self-image, supportive peer relationships, and nurturing families can minimize the severity of stressors. These protective factors are frequently noted in many superhero origin stories. How can adults channel their own inner superhero and give to their children what Alfred and Queen Ramonda have done so successfully with Batman and Black Panther?

## 36.5 Superheroes, Loss, and Grief: A Way of Healing

Recently there has been a surge of therapies, programs, and even bereavement camps that use superheroes thematically or as a therapeutic adjunct (Khazan, 2019). Some programs use superheroes symbolically: in a camp name, on capes and tee shirts, or the title of a funding campaign. One camp's superhero theme focused on skills to conquer their "villains" (Hospice of North Central Ohio, 2017), while another camp honored the adult superheroes in children's lives. Other approaches, Superhero or Geek therapies, are based on superhero narratives, inspiring reflection, and self-transformation (Khazan, 2019). Superheroes possess virtues of wisdom, courage, humanity, justice, temperance, and transcendence. Underlying these virtues are character strengths (e.g., kindness, self-regulation, curiosity, perseverance) essential to superhero work, promoting well-being, positive role modeling, and problem solving. Cohen-Manor (2019) describes character strengths as one's "true inner powers" and can be used as the foundation of strengths-based interventions (Scarlet, Innes, & Zahler, 2019).

Comics and film are valuable tools for the therapist. Children can explore superheroes and their origin stories as a way of coping with loss and recognizing their strengths – through bibliotherapy (Betzalel & Shechtman, 2017; Cohen-Manor, 2019), play therapy (Rubin, 2019), and for older children and teens cinema therapy (full films or clips of films) with groups and/or parents.

Film facilitates "therapeutic" experiences for viewers (Read & Goodenough, 2005). Specifically, it has the potential to "nurse maladies of the intellect and of experience" (p. x). The film director brings together images, sound, music, and story for the spectator's sensory and intellectual involvement (Bell, 2014). They guide their film-making with a specific philosophy or belief system. Christopher Nolan's Batman films dramatize the existential dimensions of grief (Bell, 2014). It would be difficult, if not impossible, to separate the story of the superhero from the power of the film experience itself. Film engages viewers using empathic engagement (Coplan, 2004), emotional contagion (Plantinga, 1999), identification (Oatley, 1999), and cinematic elevation (Algoe & Haidt, 2009), an uplifting emotion people feel when they observe a person helping another. These concepts illustrate how film inspires reflection and caring.

A number of themes emerge in superhero narratives. They can be organized into four major categories: the impact of trauma and loss (physical, behavioral, cognitive, and emotional reactions); coping/healing, self-care, and the care of others; relationships (how grief/trauma affects bonds); and meaning-making (Gaffney, 2002). These themes are a starting point. Using superheroes for personal exploration and growth is a creative process. Each individual will bring their own unique experiences, worldview, and talents to the material. It is also a fluid process, changing, and evolving over time. In addition to self-exploration, superhero stories offer opportunities for psychoeducation. The clinician can use film clips or comic book panels to illustrate how people react to loss and trauma and correct myths and misconceptions.

A number of settings are appropriate for using superhero stories. Teens can view films or read stories, individually or in groups. Parents of grade-schoolers can be guided to watch or read with their children. Clinicians must be well prepared when using superhero books and films in clinical or community settings for bereaved children.

Before initiating clinical superhero work, determine the purpose of using the superhero story by identifying goals. Professionals should read books and graphic novels and review films and film clips at least three times before using them in the clinical setting. The first read-through or screening is from a holistic perspective. Experience the film in much the same way as your client would, openly and without any preconceived ideas. During the second read or viewing, take brief notes at critical or instructive points. For the third time, consider what points you will want to address, and questions that arise after the book is read, or film viewed. Developing a manual or guide that highlights key points or "provocative passages" will be useful as you determine what films and books you may use in the future (Gaffney, 2017).

Identifying the above-mentioned themes, with prompts and questions for discussion or journal writing, can be included. Invite parents and teens to view films and film clips together (Work, 2017). Encourage them to share their impressions, reactions, coping skills, and how the superhero's experience is similar to their loss story. Children and adolescents can identify themes relevant to their own experiences and how they might differ from others. Perhaps the most useful strategy is to encourage children to identify their own "super" skills and strengths.

Superhero stories are extraordinary and meaningful tools when discussing loss and healing. Young people share their own origin stories and identify their inner strengths. These conversations unleash their "superpowers", allowing them to build meaningful lives, much like the heroes they so admire.

## References

Algoe, S.B., & Haidt, J. (2009). Witnessing excellence in action: The "other-praising" emotions of elevation, gratitude, and admiration. *The Journal of Positive Psychology*, 4(2), 105–127.

Allen, M.D. (2018). If you can see it, you can be it: Black Panther's black woman magic. *Journal of Pan African Studies*, 11(9), 20–23.

Bell, E. (2014). Grief time: Feeling philosophy in inception. *Film and Philosophy*, 18, 19–35.

Betzalel, N., & Shechtman, Z. (2017). The impact of bibliotherapy superheroes on youth who experience parental absence. *School Psychology International*, 38(5), 473–490.

Cohen-Manor, Y. (2019). The healing power of superhero stories: Bibliotherapy and comic books. In L.C. Rubin (Ed.), *Using superheroes and villains in counseling and play therapy: A guide for mental health professionals* (pp. 74–92). New York, NY: Routledge.

Coplan, A. (2004). Empathic engagement with narrative fictions. *The Journal of Aesthetics and Art Criticism*, 62(2), 141–152.

Feige, K. (Producer), & Coogler, R. (Director). Black Panther [Motion Picture]. (2018). United States: Marvel Studios.

Feige, K. (Producer), & Russo, A., & Russo, J. (Director). Captain America: Civil war [Motion Picture]. (2016). United States: Marvel Studios.

Gaffney, D. (2002) *911: The book of help: A guide for parents and professionals*. Chicago, IL: Cricket Publications.

Gaffney, D. (2017). Perilous journeys, the voices of Latina girls growing up in New York City. Unpublished manuscript, Columbia University.

Gaffney, D.A., Kaplow, J., Layne, C.A., & Primo, J. (2016). A selective literature review on childhood grief and bereavement: Current research findings and future directions. Unpublished manuscript.

Hospice of North Central Ohio has camp for grieving kids. (2017, July 24). Times-Gazette. Retrieved from https://www.times-gazette.com/article/20170724/NEWS/307249687

Kaplow, J.B., & Layne, C.M. (2014). Sudden loss and psychiatric disorders across the life course: Toward a developmental lifespan theory of bereavement-related risk and resilience. *American Journal of Psychiatry*, 171(8), 807–810.

Kaplow, J.B., Layne, C.M., Saltzman, W.R., Cozza, S.J., & Pynoos, R.S. (2013). Using multidimensional grief theory to explore the effects of deployment, reintegration, and death on military youth and families. *Clinical Child and Family Psychology Review*, 16(3), 322–340.

Khazan, O. (2019, October 22). The therapeutic potential of stanning. *The Atlantic*. Retrieved from https://www.theatlantic.com/health/archive/2019/10/superhero-therapy-im-batman/600475

Oatley, K. (1999). Why fiction may be twice as true as fact: Fiction as cognitive and emotional simulation. *Review of General Psychology*, 3(2), 101–117.

Plantinga, C. (1999). The scene of empathy and the human face on film. In C. Plantinga & G.M. Smith (Eds.), *Passionate views: Film, cognition, and emotion* (pp. 239–255). Baltimore, MD: Johns Hopkins University Press.

Read, R., & Goodenough, J. (2005). *Film as philosophy*. Palgrave.

Roven, C., Snyder, D., Snyder, Z., & Suckle, R. (Producers), & Jenkins, P. (Director). Wonder woman [Motion Picture]. (2017). United States: Warner Bros. Studios.

Roven, C., Thomas, E., & Franco, L. (Producers), & Nolan, C. (Director). Batman begins [Motion Picture]. (2005). United States: Warner Bros. Pictures.

Rubin, L. C. (Ed.). (2019). *Using superheroes and villains in counseling and play therapy: A guide for mental health professionals*. Routledge.

Scarlet, J., Innes, L., & Zahler, T. (2019). *Superhero kids change the world.* Pop Hero Coalition. http://www.superhero-therapy.com/wp-content/uploads/2019/04/SuperKids.pdf

Work, A. (2017). The value of parental co-viewing on children and families. *Cinesthesia*, 6(2). http://scholarworks.gvsu.edu/cine/vol6/iss1/3

# 37 Using Superheroes in Grief Counseling with Children and Adolescents

*Rachel A. Kentor and Julie B. Kaplow*

## 37.1 Superheroes in Socioemotional and Cognitive Development

In his volume outlining the utility of superheroes in child therapy and counseling, Rubin (2019) argued the fantasy of superhero lore promotes socio-emotional and cognitive development consistent with early theories of Piaget, Erikson, and Vygotsky, among others. Piaget (1962) posited that a central task of cognitive development is symbolic play, in which young children use abstract internal images and symbols to represent people, objects, or events that are not there. For example, a child may use a towel draped across their back to represent a superhero cape as they save their stuffed animals from an imagined villain. Erikson (1963) similarly purported, "... fantasy allows the child, free from the constraints of reality, to alter and experiment with otherwise unalterable constructs such as bodily limits, gravity, time, causality, and even identity" (Rubin, 2019, p. 4). By assuming the superhero role, children are empowered to tackle imagined challenges that parallel their own adversities (Rollins, 2018). For instance, a bereaved child may fantasize about having superpowers to turn back time and save a now-deceased loved one they were unable to "protect". Superheroes also allow children to operate in the "zone of proximal development" (Vygotsky, 1978), experimenting with concepts and capabilities beyond their own experiences. Whereas the majority of theories about superheroes' positive influence on children emphasize their superhuman powers and abilities, Fradkin et al. (2016) propose that teaching children about superheroes before their "moment of empowerment" (i.e., before they develop or become aware of their powers and emerge as a superhero) has the potential to instill hope in the future as a means of promoting resilience in the face of adversity.

## 37.2 From Theory to Research

Studies have demonstrated that self-distancing (i.e., cognitively distancing oneself from an egocentric perspective) is associated with less posttraumatic stress and more adaptive coping among children facing adversity (Kaplow et al., 2018). Drawing from self-distancing theory, several researchers have explored how emulating superheroes may help children perform and persevere on difficult tasks and foster prosocial behaviors. For example, White and Carlson (2016) found self-distancing improved child performance on an executive functioning task, particularly when children were instructed to take on the role of a fictional character (e.g., Batman). Similarly, children embodying an "exemplar other", such as a superhero, were found in another study to persevere longer on a difficult task than were children guided to use self-immersion or third-person thought (White et al., 2017). Other research has demonstrated the utility of superheroes in promoting prosocial behavior (Rosenberg, Baughman, & Bailenson, 2013) and decreasing disruptive and aggressive behaviors toward peers (O'Handley, Radley, & Cavell, 2016).

## 37.3 Superheroes and Childhood Grief

While the laboratory studies described above demonstrate initial promise for superhero-oriented interventions, extant literature is lacking with regard to the use of such interventions in assisting bereaved children. This is surprising, given that of the 20 most influential comic book superheroes (based on worldwide gross earnings), 49% had at least one parent murdered; in fact, being orphaned is the single most common superhero adversity (Fradkin et al., 2016). If the utility of incorporating superheroes into therapy lies in self-identification, it can be argued that superheroes are particularly well-suited to clinical intervention with bereaved children.

One study has examined the use of superheroes within an overlapping, while distinct, context. Betzalel and Shechtman (2017) examined effects of bibliotherapy on children experiencing parental absence, comparing superhero literature to affective bibliotherapy (i.e., stories not involving superheroes, focused on developing emotional insight). As compared to children in the affective treatment group, children in the superhero group demonstrated a significant decrease in anxiety, including a 50% reduction in the number of children falling within the clinical range. Similar positive effects were observed with respect to violent behavior and aggression, as well as future orientation in the superhero group. These outcomes were sustained three months postintervention. While this study focused predominantly on anxiety and aggression among children facing parental absence, further studies that examine the role of superheroes in assisting bereaved children with specific bereavement-related challenges are needed.

## 37.4 Multidimensional Grief Theory: A Framework for Identifying Bereavement-Related Challenges

Multidimensional grief theory (MGT) centers on a developmentally informed multidimensional conceptualization of grief, contextualized within a child's socioemotional environment (Kaplow et al., 2013; Layne et al., in press). The three theorized content domains of MGT include *separation distress, existential/identity-related distress,* and *circumstance-related distress.* MGT postulates that maladjustment and positive adjustment can co-occur within and across each content domain. Further, the different content domains may be differentially related to causal precursors (e.g., risk factors such as the circumstances of the death), causal consequences (e.g., functional impairment, developmental derailment), and moderators (e.g., culture, developmental stage). Contrary to traditional grief theories that view "maladaptive" grief as independent of developmental stage or one's social environment, MGT views childhood grief through the lens of rapidly unfolding developmental stages and the ways in which children's immediate caretaking environment can facilitate mourning. In other words, maladjustment in the context of childhood bereavement represents inadequate adaptation resulting from both intrinsic (e.g., cognitive coping skills) and extrinsic (e.g., parent–child communication) factors. The three content domains are explained below (Kaplow et al., 2013).

**Facing the Challenge of Separation Distress.** Normative or adaptive adjustment to *separation distress* involves missing the deceased person, longing to be reunited with them, and/or engaging in behaviors that help the child feel closer to the deceased person (e.g., looking at pictures of them). Maladaptive separation distress may include suicidal ideation motivated by reunification fantasies, developmental stagnation or regression (motivated by a desire to remain in the stage the child was at the time of death), or taking on unhealthy or dysfunctional elements of the deceased's life to feel connected to them (Kaplow et al., 2013).

**Facing the Challenge of Existential/Identity Distress.** Normative or adaptive adjustment to *existential/identity distress* involves finding meaning and fulfillment in one's life after the death, taking on new roles formerly provided by the deceased, and/or striving to live one's life in a way the deceased would have wanted. Maladaptive existential/identity distress is characterized by a severe and sustained personal identity crisis brought about by the loss. This may include perceived loss of one's identity, nihilism, survivor's guilt, and/or feeling resigned to a grim future blighted by their loss (Kaplow et al., 2013).

**Facing the Challenge of Circumstance-Related Distress.** Normative or adaptive adjustment to *circumstance-related distress* encompasses distress in reaction to a highly disturbing and/or traumatogenic death that recedes over time, replaced by increasing capacity to access more affectively neutral or positive memories of the deceased. Specifically, an adaptive response to circumstance-related distress may include engaging in prosocial activities that directly reflect the theme of vicarious wish fulfillment through repairing or preventing the cause of death (e.g., engaging in advocacy to prevent gun violence, aspiring to become a doctor to prevent cancer). Maladaptive circumstance-related distress occurs when preoccupation with *how* the person died leads to significant distress and functional impairment (e.g., behavioral avoidance, preoccupation with retaliation) (Kaplow et al., 2013; Layne et al., in press).

## 37.5 Applying MGT to the Superhero Narrative

Many components of MGT can be identified within superhero narratives. Take, for example, the story of Spider-Man (Lee, 1962). Peter Parker, a bright but socially outcast teenager, was bitten by a genetically altered spider and developed superhuman spider-like abilities. Shortly thereafter, his uncle was murdered by a burglar whom Peter had let escape only moments before. Following this event, Peter vowed to use his powers for a nobler purpose and donned the identity of Spider-Man. As a budding adolescent, Peter's actions were not motivated only by grief over his uncle, but also by the defining characteristics of adolescence. The death of Peter's uncle occurred when Peter was struggling to form his personal identity and make sense of his role in the world (Erikson, 1963). He assumed the identity of a masked vigilante superhero, while also navigating his roles as student, freelance photographer, best friend, and eager romantic. Rather than derailing his developmental progression, Peter was able to integrate these facets of his life into a cohesive evolution. Peter's adolescence was also what permitted him to fully capitalize on his superpowers. Among his other abilities, Spider-Man possesses a "spider-sense" that warns him of impending danger. With the ability to think abstractly and mentally manipulate the world, characteristic of the formal operational period (Piaget, 1962), Spider-Man was able to quickly plan and execute a response to the threat before it subdues him. Had Peter come into his superpowers and/or experienced the loss of his uncle in an earlier stage of development, his postbereavement adjustment may have manifested very differently. Peter's transformation into Spider-Man was also heavily influenced by his socioenvironmental context. In the wake of his uncle's death, Peter's aunt helped to foster a continuing bond between Peter and his uncle, imploring Peter to live his life in a way his uncle would have wanted for him, modeling adaptive coping in the face of loss.

Spider-Man's evolution can also be viewed through the lens of each of the MGT content domains. Peter pursues his uncle's killer to exact vigilante revenge (akin to maladaptive circumstance-related distress). However, as is the case with many other superheroes, Peter channeled his distress into an adaptive response, fighting for justice and protecting other innocent people from similar fates. Similarly, rather than dwelling on thoughts of a blighted future or losing his sense of himself (i.e., maladaptive existential/identity distress), Peter channeled his grief into living a life his uncle would have been proud of; demonstrating restraint and morality in a manner that honored his uncle's wisdom, "with great power comes great responsibility" (Ziskin, Bryce, & Raimi, 2002, 35:45). In responding to his uncle's death in such an adaptive manner across domains, Peter's grief became his "moment of empowerment", leading him to resiliency in the face of adversity (Fradkin et al., 2016).

## 37.6 Clinical Applications

Practitioners can utilize superheroes in their counseling with bereaved youth as a means of harnessing protective factors outlined in MGT. Below are several examples of clinical practice elements that can be used to promote adaptive coping within each of the grief domains. These elements can be incorporated into a general "loss narrative" (Kaplow, Layne, & Pynoos, 2019) or used independently, depending on which grief domains the child may be grappling with the most.

To assist a bereaved child facing the challenge of **separation distress**, a counselor might encourage that child/adolescent to imagine themselves as a superhero that reflects the best shared aspects of themselves and their deceased loved one (i.e., carrying the deceased person's best qualities as a means of remaining connected to them). Alternatively, the child might imagine the deceased as a sidekick to their own superhero, maintaining a sense of connection through shared imaginary adventures. For adolescents, a practitioner may help them to create a comic strip of their adventures as they continue to encounter important milestones (e.g., college), promoting their developmental progression beyond the stage they were at the time of loss.

To assist a bereaved child facing the challenge of **existential/identity distress**, a counselor may have them create a superhero that embodies the roles and values of their loved one and identify real-life ways in which they themselves can take on those qualities and/or live out the legacy of the person who died. This can also take the form of doing things that would make the deceased loved one proud (e.g., "I want to live my life like Batman, helping other people, so that my Dad would be proud of me").

To assist a bereaved child who may be grappling with **circumstance-related distress**, a clinician might ask them what superpower they wish they had that might protect others from dying the same way. For older children and adolescents, the practitioner could engage the client in identifying characters who instead became villains or antiheroes following a loved one's death (e.g., Harvey Dent or "Two-Face" from *The Dark Knight* [Thomas, Nolan, Roven, & Nolan 2008] or Killmonger from *Black Panther* [Feige & Coogler, 2018]), leading discussion about what causes some people to become heroes while others become villains in response to similar losses.

## 37.7 Conclusions

Superheroes have been theorized by many to represent core processes of child cognitive and socioemotional development. Initial research shows that encouraging children to assume the persona of a superhero fosters improved task performance, perseverance, and prosocial behavior. The application of superhero themes within the context of addressing childhood bereavement, however, is limited with regard to rigorous research. Multidimensional Grief Theory offers a framework that lends itself well to using superhero narratives to address bereavement-related challenges. Clinicians can use superheroes to guide a discussion of adaptive and maladaptive responses across MGT domains, promoting healthy functioning in the face of loss.

## References

Betzalel, N., & Shechtman, Z. (2017). The impact of bibliotherapy superheroes on youth who experience parental absence. *School Psychology International*, 38(5), 473–490.

Erikson, E. (1963). *Childhood and society*. New York, NY: Norton.

Feige, K. (Producer), & Coogler, R. (Director). *Black Panther* [Motion Picture]. (2018). United States: Marvel Studios.

Fradkin, C., Weschenfelder, G.V., & Yunes, M.A.M. (2016). Shared adversities of children and comic superheroes as resources for promoting resilience. *Child Abuse & Neglect*, 51, 407–415.

Kaplow, J.B., Layne, C.M., & Pynoos, R.S. (2019). Treatment of Persistent Complex Bereavement Disorder in children and adolescents. In M. Prinstein, E. Youngstrom, E. Mash, & R. Barkley (Eds.), *Treatment of disorders in childhood and adolescence* (4th ed., pp. 560–590) New York, NY: Guilford.

Kaplow, J.B., Layne, C.M., Saltzman, W.R., Cozza, S.J., & Pynoos, R.S. (2013). Using multidimensional grief theory to explore the effects of deployment, reintegration, and death on military youth and families. *Clinical Child and Family Psychology Review*, 16(3), 322–340.

Kaplow, J.B., Wardecker, B., Layne, C., Kross, E., Burnside, A., Edelstein, R., & Prossin, A. (2018). Out of the mouths of babes: Links between linguistic structure of loss narratives and psychosocial functioning in parentally bereaved children. *Journal of Traumatic Stress*, 31(3), 342–351.

Layne, C.M., Kaplow, J.B., Oosterhoff, B., Hill, R., & Pynoos, R. (in press). The interplay of trauma and bereavement in adolescence: Integrating pioneering work and recent advancements. *Adolescent Psychiatry (invited article for special issue on Adolescent Trauma).*

Lee, S. (1962). Spider-Man! *Amazing Fantasy*, 1(15).

O'Handley, R.D., Radley, K.C., & Cavell, H.J. (2016). Utilization of superheroes social skills to reduce disruptive and aggressive behavior. *Preventing School Failure: Alternative Education for Children and Youth*, 60(2), 124–132.

Piaget, J. (1962). *Play, dreams and imitation in childhood*. New York, NY: Norton.

Rollins, J.A. (2018). Superheroes to the rescue! *Pediatric Nursing*, 44(2), 59.

Rosenberg, R.S., Baughman, S.L., & Bailenson, J.N. (2013). Virtual superheroes: Using superpowers in virtual reality to encourage prosocial behavior. *PLoS ONE*, 8(1), e55003.

Rubin, L.C. (Ed.). (2019). *Using superheroes and villains in counseling and play therapy: A guide for mental health professionals*. New York, NY: Routledge.

Thomas, E., Nolan, C., & Roven, C. (Producers), & Nolan, C. (Director). (2008). *The dark knight* [Motion Picture]. United States: Warner Brother Pictures.

Vygotsky, L.S. (1978). *Mind in society*. Cambridge, MA: Harvard University Press.

White, R.E., & Carlson, S.M. (2016). What would Batman do? Self-distancing improves executive function in young children. *Developmental Science*, 19(3), 419–426.

White, R.E., Prager, E.O., Schaefer, C., Kross, E., Duckworth, A.L., & Carlson, S.M. (2017). The "Batman effect": Improving perseverance in young children. *Child Development*, 88(5), 1563–1571.

Ziskin, L., & Bryce, I. (Producers), & Raimi, S. (Director). (2002). *Spider-Man* [Motion Picture]. United States: Columbia Pictures.

# 38 The Superpower of the Expressive Arts

*Rebekah Near and Barbara E. Thompson*

Our human impulse to create and make art in response to grief and loss is evident across cultures and time. The power of the art making lies in its capacity to activate the creative imagination and a sense of agency through the shaping of materials, creation of images, and telling of stories related to grief and loss, a way of sense-making through the senses (Thompson & Berger, 2011). Art making grounds grievers in the present through somatic engagement and the images produced, in whatever expressive medium, make visible new perspectives on self and other that can be witnessed and shared. This process can prompt the creation of revised narratives or stories that integrate the loss differently, so that resources are revealed and perspectives widened (Thompson & Neimeyer, 2014). In this way, grieving is fundamentally viewed as a creative process and the expressive arts a means for the bereaved to find their way back into the world (Near, 2012; Thompson, 2019).

This chapter will explore the metaphor of grief as a journey and the emergence of the superhero with special powers as a response to loss, present a description of expressive arts therapy as an intermodal approach, and a case study that joins the two. Near (2013) states, "transformation cannot happen, personal or communal, unless we are in contact with 'what is'. Using the arts to dialogue with grief releases the vitality we need to carry on living and reconnect with the present" (p. 93). The expressive arts offer one more important tool to those working with the bereaved.

## 38.1 Expressive Arts Therapy: An Intermodal Approach

The expressive arts therapy field finds its origin in philosophy, psychology, and the use of multiple art forms working together (Knill, Levine, & Levine, 2005). It invites a person to move flexibly among media, following their creative instincts and interests, which distinguishes the expressive arts from its closely related disciplines of other creative arts therapies (Estrella, 2005). Working intermodally opens the auditory, visual and kinesthetic senses and accesses the emotions (Knill et al., 2005). Grounded in phenomenology, expressive art therapy explores the lived experience of grief, facilitating the inquiry by moving from one art modality to the next.

## 38.2 Superheroes and the Expressive Arts in Grief

The expressive arts can help to foster the emergence of the superhero within a grief story. The creation of the grief story is similar to any art-making process, in that the individual doesn't know what will unfold. The griever may discover many different characters inhabiting the internal landscape of grief, some helpful and some not, and on a journey that can seem perilous. The grief story may be layered with perceptions that are distorted or incomplete, and the griever may experience feelings of helplessness, hopelessness, or powerlessness with no way home. Being able to access internal resources, symbolized perhaps in the form of a superhero or a symbol representing a special power, can help the bereaved to embody enabling beliefs, mobilize capacities, and remind them of their strengths as they make their way in an unfamiliar landscape.

When people tell their grief story, they have some kernel that they start with, a memory, a perception, or an image that represents part of their lived experience of loss. As the story begins to be told and retold, there can be movement or stuckness. Intermodal expressive arts can help free people from repetitive loops in their grief story through physical activity, symbolic expression, metaphoric retellings, or reflections that reveal new trajectories, possibilities for action, and movement toward meaning.

## 38.3 Case Study

The following is a case example of how the expressive arts revealed an inner superpower figure that assisted a bereaved adolescent on her grief journey. It is written by the first author.

*I was introduced to the Swartz family in the last few weeks before Edmir, the father, died from cancer. He left behind a wife and four children ranging in ages from 14–18. At that time Shira was 15. The hospice rabbi made the referral and indicated that the family might not be receptive to expressive arts therapy. I knew that it was the arts (my own superpower) that would do the work of connecting me with these strangers.*

*Shira's superpower showed up when she needed it the most. The discovery of her power was made through an expressive arts session. During this session, we created a collaborative piece of art. Shira chose to create with paint. The palette was filled with a range of colors. As soft music played in the background, we closed our eyes and made the first mark. These marks inspired the rest of the image. With open eyes, we continued creating by rotating the paper, painting from many perspectives. A face began to emerge in the painting. Shira decided to make it more pronounced with highlighting. I followed Shira's lead, adding minimal marks to the painting. Shira guided the process until she reached a feeling of completion and appeared content (Figure 38.1). This image would act as a tangible reminder of the growth Shira achieved during our sessions together.*

*Figure 38.1* Good Grief Gary Representation by R. Near.

*Shira proudly named the face that emerged "Good Grief Gary". The intermodal shift from visual to dramatic form began at this point. We identified a place in the room for our stage, and I asked Shira to construct questions to use in interviewing "Good Grief Gary". Shira played the character of Good Grief Gary and held the painting over her face like a mask while I asked the questions she had already written. I added a few of my own. As she developed the character of Good Grief Gary, Shira spoke in a low-toned voice, unlike her own. I asked, "Where are you from?" Good Grief Gary responded, "I am from the land of grief. I have not always lived there, but I made it my home after my father died" (Near, 2013, p. 101) More questions followed, until finally I asked "Good Grief Gary" what advice he had for us on the grief journey. His response was, "Blow Away the Sadness: Even when you feel hopeless, know that YOU have the power to blow away the sadness" (p. 101).*

*The final phase of the expressive arts therapy session was to harvest the arts, helping Shira bridge her lived experience to her present-day reality. I guided Shira to make a connection from the arts to the actuality of her situation. Shira came to be aware that she possessed the tools to release her grief and transform it into renewed hope.*

The arts helped Shira to give shape and form to her grief as well as contain it, enabling her to transform her grief story. In narrating her grief journey through the arts, Shira discovered internal resources that renewed her sense of hopefulness and her capacity to re-create and narrate her journey back to life.

## 38.4 Integrating the Arts

The expressive arts meet the individual where they are and build on that foundation. Expressive arts clinicians do not interpret what is created from a detached stance; rather they help facilitate poesies – learning through making – and they partner in the creative process. Exploring the phenomenon of grief via the metaphor of grief as a journey and the superhero or person with superpowers as a resource on that journey, offers the bereaved an invitation to place one's own experience into a larger mythic narrative populated by figures that emerge from the personal and collective imagination. Inner resources can be discovered and amplified through the intermodal process as demonstrated in the case example above.

The arts can give expressive form and meaning to experiences that are often difficult to express in conventional language. While grief is universal, its expression is individual and influenced by multiple factors. In their model of grief language, Corless et al. (2014) noted the importance of recognizing and responding to the varied manifestations and dimensions of grief expression. They identify "a range of modalities for those who find themselves 'stuck' or who wish to express themselves in a variety of ways" (p. 142). While not specifically endorsing the expressive arts, the authors' model seems compatible as the expressive arts create the conditions for the bereaved to use narrative, symbolic, and metaphoric language through its intermodal approach.

While the arts are there for all to access, the work of the expressive arts therapist is a culmination of significant training, education, and practice. As with any therapy, practitioners should be trained. There are, however, many expressive arts techniques that can be used in conjunction with other therapies in an intuitive way. The following are examples in the context of superhero work:

- Collage (Create an image of your superpower or superhero.)
- Where does your grief superhero live? (Describe her or his home in poetic form. Where do you feel this in your body?)
- What is the superpower? (What is its color, sound, or shape, and how can it be used?)
- What advice does your superhero have for you? (What song does it sing? What would it say if your superhero wrote you a letter?)
- How does your superhero move? (What posture, movement, and gestures are made? Show me.)
- What symbol best represents the superhero's special abilities? (Create it for display or wear it as a reminder.)

Helping people to clarify and experience a felt-sense of their superpower or superhero capacities through multisensory approaches can help them to embody these qualities and enact them in their daily lives.

## 38.5 Conclusions

It is not the art product itself that is of primary importance, but rather the process of art making that is therapeutic along with a therapeutic relationship that encourages a process of discovery and transformation. Often, people think that the arts are a substitute for words, which is an incomplete view. Words can be a powerful catalyst for intermodal exploration and discovery. When we talk about grief, however, it is easy to intellectualize. The arts allow us to integrate our grief, building a bridge between our intellect and emotion, allowing us to play with possibilities and new ways of being in the world.

The shaping of experiences through the imagination that are translated into artistic form offer the client/artist new ways of seeing and widened perspectives. Thompson and Berger (2011) state,

> Images of grief and loss are allowed to take shape in whatever artistic medium is indigenous to the experience and consonant with the particular circumstances and needs of the individual or community. This freedom to move from one expressive mode to another prompts shifts in the articulation and elaboration of images as more of the senses are engaged.
>
> (p. 305)

As illustrated in the case example, Shira was able to engage in a full range of her expressive capability, and in doing so she was able to access her own personal superpower and blow away her sadness when she needed to rather than being blown away by it.

## References

Corless, I., Limbo, R., Bousso, R., Wrenn, R.L., Head, D., Lickiss, N., & Wass, H. (2014). Languages of grief: A model for understanding the expressions of the bereaved. *Health Psychology and Behavioral Medicine*, 2(1), 132–143.

Estrella, K. (2005). Expressive arts therapy an integrated art. In C.A. Malchiodi (Ed.), *Expressive therapies* (pp. 183–209). New York, NY: Guilford Press.

Knill, J., Levine, E.G., & Levine, S.K. (2005). *Principles and practice of expressive arts therapy*. Philadelphia, PA: Jessica Kingsley.

Near, R. (2012). Intermodal expressive arts. In R.A. Neimeyer (Ed.), *Techniques of grief therapy* (pp. 201–204). New York, NY: Routledge

Near, R. (2013). Expressive arts with grieving children. In C. Malchiodi (Ed.), *Art therapy in healthcare* (pp. 93–205). New York, NY: Guilford Publishing Company

Thompson, B.E. (2019). Therapies of the imagination. In N. Gershman & B.E. Thompson (Eds.), *Prescriptive memories in grief and loss: The art of dreamscaping* (pp. 9–23). New York, NY: Routledge.

Thompson, B.E., & Berger, J.S. (2011). Grief and expressive arts therapy. In R.A. Neimeyer, D.L. Harris, H.R. Winokuer, & G.F. Thornton (Eds.), *Grief and bereavement in contemporary society: Bridging research and practice* (pp. 303–314). New York, NY: Routledge

Thompson, B.E., & Neimeyer, R.A. (2014). *Grief and the expressive arts: Practices for creating meaning*. New York, NY: Routledge.

# 39 Grief and the Masks We Wear

## Secret Identities Are Not Only for Superheroes

*Sharon Strouse and Sarah Vollmann*

Masks are shaped to cover or guard the face. They are made from varied materials, including animal skins, leather, bones, feathers, wood, clay, plaster, plastic, cardboard, and metal. They are found worldwide. Rooted in prehistory, masks are used in folk traditions, ceremonies, and shamanic rituals of protection, initiation, and healing. "Masks symbolize our ability to change, to transform, to go to other worlds, to appease the spirits" (Nunley & McCarty, 1999, p. 15). In France, the Cave of the Trois Frères's paintings from 13,000 BC depict a prehistoric human masked and in animal costume exemplifying a "mystical participation" with the totem animal (Jung, 1964, p. 45). In that ritual, he or she becomes the animal, empowered with its spirit and attributes. From prehistoric to modern times, masks have served transformative and therapeutic purposes.

> *The mask I wear is heavy, yet it doesn't weigh an ounce. The mask I wear is stifling, yet it doesn't block my face. The mask I wear is tight, yet it doesn't cling at all. The mask I wear is a disguise, yet it looks like my regular face. The mask I wear is invisible, yet it hides my feelings. The mask I wear is suffocating, yet I breathe just fine. The mask I wear is removable, yet it never comes off. The mask I wear is "normalcy", yet I am grieving.*
>
> (Peaster, 2020, para 1)

The poem cited above shares the experiences of a bereaved mother who masks her grief from the world. This is often a common experience of the newly bereaved, as they negotiate and navigate a new social world while grieving. It illustrates the challenges of a meaningful world shattered by loss. Survivors of sudden deaths, accidents, homicides, suicides, disasters, and military combat are at higher risk for traumatic bereavement and complicated grief as they struggle with trauma and grief symptoms (Wortman & Pearlman, 2016, p. 25). They need safe opportunities to explore feelings of fear, guilt, anger, shame, and other unspeakable emotions. Survivors face "unique anguish, [casting them] outside the once 'normal' world of relationships shared with others" (Wortman & Pearlman, 2016, p. 6). It is understandable that they often develop a protective face to show the world, while a hidden face holds another story.

Attig (1996) describes the prevailing need to relearn the self and relearn the world after a significant loss, as one's identity and sense of the world is shaken. Art therapy mask making offers an ideal modality for the exploration and expression of shifting identities. Masks inherently allow us to try on new roles, to recreate ourselves, and to explore what is exposed and what is hidden. Masks may be especially beneficial for those facing traumatic loss, as their task of reconstructing a cohesive life narrative and sense of self can be particularly challenging (Neimeyer, Prigerson, & Davies, 2002).

Anna, whose name has been altered for confidentiality, lost her 25-year-old son to suicide. He was a soldier in Iraq. She created a mask in the Artful Grief: Open Art Studio (Strouse, 2013) at the Tragedy Assistance Program for Survivors (TAPS) National Suicide Survivors Conference. She worked with a partner. Wet plaster was molded over her face. After her mask hardened, she removed it, paused to reflect, and decorated it. Sharing her experience with the group, she said, "I was relieved removing my mask. It was constricting. It reminded me of its negative effect". This alluded to the heaviness of masking her feelings. She stated, "I enjoyed painting it. I see the two sides of myself, split down the middle by a broken heart and a red and yellow lightning bolt. I painted black question marks and crucifixes on the side that represents loss". The two sides symbolize her bereaved self and former self, pieces of identity that she is attempting to integrate. The split, a thunderbolt, depicts the trauma endured and a sense of before and after. The mouth is "stitched shut", an apt representation of the unspeakable aspects of her loss. She concluded, "I am surprised by my creation. Through making it, I feel lighter". Her willing exploration, with the guidance of experienced art therapists, allowed her to project her inner experience onto the created form of her own face. The process and product brought clarity to her inner and outer experiences of profound loss, fostering sharing, and transformation (Figure 39.1).

Numerous superheroes demonstrate the transformative qualities of masks, such as Batman, Spider-Man, and The Flash. Superheroes often don masks to hide their civilian self and to express their superhero identity. Their mask is a disguise, but it frequently reveals aspects of their truest sense of self.

Batman was created in 1939 by artist Bob Kane and writer Bill Finger. Unmasked, he is Bruce Wayne, a rich socialite born to parents who were shot and killed in front of him as a child. This trauma shaped his life. He pledges "to avenge their deaths by spending the rest of [his] life warring on all criminals" (Finger, 2016, p. 66). He has no superpowers, relying instead on an intimidating disguise to frighten criminals. He chooses the bat, the creature that he fears the most, as his emblem. As a child, he fell into a well and was terrified of the bats inside. His bat mask harnesses both his deepest fears and his story of trauma and loss, the source of his superhero persona. Batman takes on the qualities of the bat and becomes a creature of the night, able to see into the darkness and hunt down evil.

Bruce Wayne is his secondary identity. When asked his name, he replies, "It's not who I am underneath [the mask] but what I do that defines me"

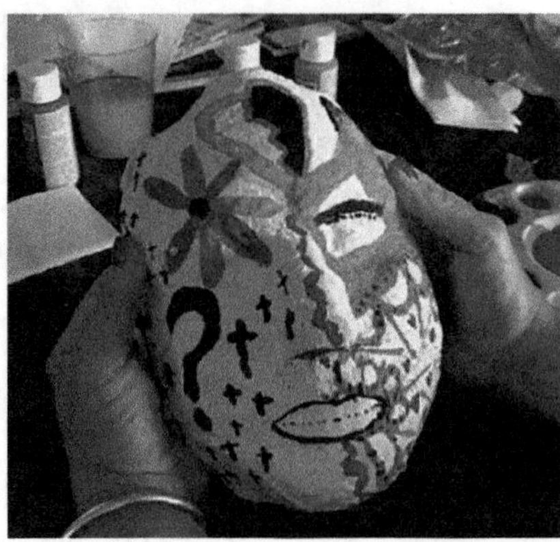

*Figure 39.1* Mask made be a bereaved military mother.

(Beatty, 2005, p. 62). He finds mastery and control in his crime-fighting. Batman believes in the sanctity of life, catching and sparing criminals. In the sparing, he realizes that his father's values exist in him. His innocent childhood self lives on in his superhero identity (Beatty, 2005, p. 133). His bat mask transforms him from victim into a powerful agent of change.

Spider-Man, also known as Peter Parker, was created in 1962 by writer–editor Stan Lee and writer–artist Steve Ditko. After Peter's parents die in a plane crash, he is raised by his aunt and uncle. A bright, socially awkward teenager, Peter is bitten by a radioactive spider. He gains superhero strength and the abilities of a spider to cling to surfaces, shoot spider-webs, and harness a "spider-sense" to detect danger. Initially, he dresses as Spider-Man simply to earn money as an entertainer. When a criminal runs by, Spider-Man refuses to help the police catch him. The same criminal murders his beloved uncle. Remorse ignites his resolve to help others. His true Spider-Man identity is born after this traumatic loss (Ditko & Lee, 2019).

Peter Parker wears a mask to disguise himself and to protect his loved ones from harm. His mask also serves as a shield, hiding expressions of fear from his enemies and allowing him to incorporate the spider's power as his own. Joking and acting brave, he takes on a more confident persona while in disguise. His Spider-Man identity empowers him. No longer in a victimized role, he can save others from crime and trauma.

The Flash was created in 1940 by writers Gardner Fox and Harry Lampert. Barry Allen, the fastest man alive, witnesses his mother's murder as a child (Berlanti & Nutter, 2014). His traumatic memories shape his life. He becomes The Flash, replete with superspeed powers after he is doused with chemicals and struck by lightning. His costume serves as a disguise and protects his loved ones. It also symbolizes his superhero powers and mastery over speed and time, powers that are used to save the world from meta-human villains. He runs toward danger, with lightning speed, rather than away from it. Like Batman and Spider-Man, The Flash harnesses his grief in service to the needs of humanity.

Today, we inherit a rich, universal tradition of mask making that utilizes the physical and psychological manifestations of "mask" for varied reasons. "Masks empower us to divulge our hidden, true selves or secret thoughts, exposing inhibitions or personality traits that we ordinarily contain or feel unable to express" (Nunley & McCarty, 1999, p. 17). Those facing traumatic loss may use masks to explore and author new life narratives. "Like the natural face, masks are expressions of the self, but the self we choose to be" (Baptiste, 1989, p. 47). Masks serve both fictional and real-life characters. Each wearer determines its functional or dysfunctional aspects and may choose to work with its properties for the greatest good and growth.

## References

Attig, T. (1996). *How we grieve: Relearning the world*. New York, NY: Oxford University Press.

Baptiste, D.A. (1989). Using masks as therapeutic aids in family therapy. *Journal of Family Therapy* 11 (1), 45–58.

Beatty, S. (2005). *Batman begins: The movie and other tales of the dark knight*. New York, NY: DC Comics

Berlanti, G. (Producer), & Nutter, D. (Director). (2014). *The Flash* [Television]. United States: Warner Bros. Entertainment.

Ditko, S., & Lee, S. (2019). *The amazing Spider-Man omnibus volume 1*. New York, NY: Marvel Comics.

Finger, B. (2016). *Batman, the golden age, volume 1*. Burbank, CA: DC Comics.

Jung, C.G. (1964). *Man and his symbols*. New York, NY: Doubleday.

Neimeyer, R.A., Prigerson, H.G., & Davies, B. (2002). Mourning and meaning. *American Behavioral Scientist*, 46(2), 235–251.

Nunley, J.W., & McCarty, C. (1999). *Masks: Faces of culture*. New York, NY: Harry N. Abrams.

Peaster, M.S. (2020, May 5). *Artwork – my mask*. The grief tool box. Retrieved from https://thegrieftoolbox.com/artwork/my-mask

Strouse, S. (2013). *Artful grief: A diary of healing*. Bloomington, IN: Balboa Press.

Wortman, C.B., & Pearlman, L.A. (2016). Traumatic bereavement. In R.A. Neimeyer (Ed.), *Techniques of grief therapy: Assessment and intervention*. New York, NY: Routledge.

# 40 Art Therapy Superhero Dolls

## Totems of Strength and Remembrance

*Sarah Vollmann*

Superheroes often emerge in the art therapy studio. Their narratives of courage and triumph over adversity resonate with people of all ages. Through their adventures we may gain confidence about facing our own issues, and our identification with them promotes a sense of mastery and control. Like myths, their stories "speak to us in the language of symbols.... Their appeal is simultaneously to our conscious and unconscious mind. In the tales' content, inner psychological phenomena are given body in symbolic form" (Bettelheim, 1976, p. 36).

Bereaved individuals in art therapy frequently create superhero dolls as symbols of self or a lost loved one. Dolls are imbued with the wishes and fears of their creators, and as self-shaped objects, they "access the creator's most urgent and prevalent issues. They provide a projective structure that facilitates the expression, organization, and symbolization of these issues, and they further the organization of an image of self" (Vollmann, 1997, p. 77).

The following case studies present superhero dolls as a transformative art therapy technique, effective in the treatment of loss. During the creative process, Restorative Retelling (Rynearson, 2001) takes place as bereaved individuals share, shape, and take control of their narratives of loss. The doll body is an outer landscape of an inner reality as survivors "attempt to reaffirm or reconstruct a world of meaning that has been challenged by loss" (Neimeyer, 2006, p. 102).

### 40.1 Wonder Woman

Ella, a soft-spoken woman in her twenties, lost her father to suicide when she was 13 years old. He was her sole parent, so she entered foster care after his death. In an art therapy session she decided to make a doll. She dressed it as Wonder Woman, creating a sparkling red cape, bullet-proof bracelets, and a starred headpiece. The doll looked like a self-portrait, with flowing brown locks that matched her own hair and a sweet smile that captured her kind approachability. She engaged carefully in binding, mending, and gluing to make her doll whole. This symbolic process mirrored her journey of rebuilding after her loss and promoted a sense of mastery as she successfully created a powerful self-symbol.

As her doll progressed, Ella explained that she identified with Wonder Woman because she was a survivor and not a victim. She shared about the trauma of losing her father to suicide, her intense grief, and her parentless teenage years. Foster care was a negative experience, and she essentially raised herself. We reflected on her extraordinary resilience. With pride and surprise she surmised that her Wonder Woman doll was a fitting symbol for her struggle, strength, and self-sufficiency. She had not initially realized that she was creating a self-symbol.

Much of Ella's identification with Wonder Woman was initially unconscious. The art therapy experience allowed her to give it shape. It is notable that Wonder Woman, like Ella, is fatherless and self-sufficient. She left her birthplace to assist in World War II and could never return (Marston & Peter, 2017). Created by Zeus and sculpted from clay by her mother, she is a powerful Amazonian princess. Many of her superhero gifts align with Ella's identity. She has superhuman strength, enhanced empathy, and healing capacities. Ella is employed in a helping field and assists the bereaved.

Ella's Wonder Woman doll gave form to a self-image altered by loss. As she created and shared her doll she organized and owned her life story, taking an active role as author and creator. She recognized her strength and heightened empathy as benefits gained from difficult beginnings. Her doll became a compelling symbol of her identity as an empowered survivor Figure 40.1).

*Figure 40.1* Wonder Woman doll created by a suicide loss survivor.

## 40.2 Superman

Alexis, a woman in her early thirties, was initially unsure about engaging in the art therapy studio. Her husband, a young soldier, had recently died of cancer. The doll-making materials inspired her to create a doll of her deceased husband.

She chose a tall doll to represent her tall husband. She paused in amazement upon discovering a piece of fabric with superhero logos, exclaiming, "You don't understand! My husband is Superman!" Working rapidly, she glued a Superman "S" on the doll's chest, added a cape, and selected dog tags to depict her husband's identity as a soldier. She then glued small bells on the doll's body. Their symbolism could be understood as funeral bells tolling, or as a celebration of her husband's life and service to his nation.

Like Superman, her husband has a hero's status. In the United States we often refer to our soldiers as heroes, and Alexis's husband served in Iraq. A theme of loss also connects both narratives. When Superman was an infant, his native planet was destroyed, and his parents perished. They saved him by sending him off in a spacecraft. He landed on earth and was adopted, but his adoptive parents died after he finished high school (Siegel & Shuster, 1939). Superman's Fortress of Solitude, where he keeps memorial statues of his birth parents, seems to represent his grief.

Despite his incredible strength, Superman is harmed if exposed to a material called kryptonite. Alexis's husband survived arduous tours in Iraq but died from cancer upon his return home. Like Superman, he had a vulnerability; even his strength and courage could not save him.

Alexis's husband is buried in Arlington National Cemetery, a symbolic and sacred place of burial for U.S. servicemembers – known often as fallen heroes. During graveside visits Alexis was astonished and moved to meet other families who also consider their lost loved one to be a superhero. Her husband is buried near Captain America and another Superman. His placement among other fallen heroes is comforting for her and regarded as an auspicious blessing.

With playfulness, Alexis shook the doll and giggled as the bells jingled. She joked about her artistic abilities. An art therapy object may simultaneously contain several meanings; I suspect that Alexis identifies with Superman and sometimes relies upon superhuman strength to cope as a widowed, single mother. The doll, while primarily a representation of her husband, could also serve as a symbol of self. She hugged the doll and spoke lovingly of her husband as "my Superman". The doll had become a transitional object that supported her continuing bond to her husband, and the title of Superman was a way to honor him. She showed me photographs. The art therapy process of doll making had opened up the transitional space between us, allowing for sharing and connection.

## 40.3 Clinical Considerations and Intervention Strategies

Art therapy doll making is aptly matched for Neimeyer's (2016) essential components of restorative retelling, known as bracing, pacing, and facing. Clients brace as materials help regulate strong emotions; for example, soft fabric or the rhythms of sewing may provide soothing. Clients pace themselves as they control and modulate their creative process. Finally, they face their story as mastery occurs; the doll becomes a significant symbol that fosters meaning making. There are limitless possibilities in therapeutic doll making. The bodies of Murdock's (1998) "spirit dolls" are made with canvas, fabric, gauze, rusted metal, bones, shells, gourds, or sticks. Personal mementos, objects from nature, photographs, poems, prayers, or journal entries may be sewn on the doll or hidden inside. An expansive repertoire of supplies and techniques opens up treatment possibilities.

Many art therapy approaches augment restorative retelling. Malchiodi (2013) uses drawing and journaling to allow patients to reauthor their life narratives, explore posttraumatic growth, and make meaning. Huss (2015) emphasizes the connection between art therapy and narrative theory, stating "art therapy uses images to generate new words, and expands words with images" (p. 75). She reminds us that art making is important for integration and reframing because "traumatic experiences are encoded nonverbally in the mind" (p. 76).

As seen in the case studies, superheroes may be powerful guides in Restorative Retelling. They offer rich opportunities to harness unconscious content, give voice to fears and hopes, and promote mastery and empowerment. Superheroes often come to life in the dolls, drawings, sculptures, and play of my bereaved clients. Their stories can help us to reframe our own.

## References

Bettelheim, B. (1976). *The uses of enchantment: The meaning and importance of fairy tales*. New York: Knopf.

Huss, E. f2015). *A theory based approach to art therapy: Implications for teaching, research and practice*. New York, NY: Routledge.

Malchiodi, C. (2013). *Art therapy and health care*. New York, NY: The Guilford Press.

Marston, W.M., & Peter, H.G. (2017). *Wonder Woman: The golden age, volume 1*. California: DC Comics.

Murdock, M. (1998). *The heroine's journey workbook*. Berkeley, CA: Shambhala Publishers.

Neimeyer, R.A. (2006). *Lessons of loss*. New York, NY: Routledge.

Neimeyer, R.A. (2016). Meaning reconstruction in the wake of loss: Evolution of a research program. *Behaviour Change*, 33 (2), 65–79.

Rynearson, E.K. (2001). *Retelling violent death*. Philadelphia, PA: Brunner-Routledge.

Siegel, J., & Shuster, J. (1939). *Superman, volume 1*. New York, NY: DC Comics.

Vollmann, S. (1997). Doll making and play: A therapeutic modality for an adolescent boy with gender identity disorder. *Pratt Institute Creative Arts Therapy Review*, 18, 76–86.

# 41 Mindfulness as Your Grief Superpower

*Heather Stang*

The intense suffering you feel after a major loss can be reduced by activating a superpower you already have at your disposal: mindfulness. Just as Spider-Man tunes into his spidey-sense to detect imminent danger, the superpower of mindfulness equips you to take back control when your body and mind are hijacked by grief. While it won't change the fact that loss occurred, mindfulness reduces physical and emotional suffering, boosts resilience to stress, and paves the way for meaning-making and posttraumatic growth (Stang, 2018).

At its core, mindfulness is self-guided mind control that results in neuroplasticity and physiological improvements, which may seem superhuman but are accessible to all of us. Unlike the toxic performance-enhancing chemicals that transform Norman Osborn into the ferocious Green Goblin (Ziskin, Bryce, & Raimi, 2002), mindfulness training shrinks the physical size of the amygdala, the part of the brain responsible for survival instincts that include fear and stress (Taren et al., 2015). It also rewires the brain, improving attentional control, emotional regulation, and interoception (Haase et al., 2014), an awareness of what is happening inside your body – your own personal spidey-sense.

Practiced regularly, mindfulness boosts immune functioning and cardiovascular health while reducing the genetic predisposition to other stress-related illnesses (Benson & Proctor, 2010). This is important during bereavement when the likelihood of heart attacks (Mostofsky et al., 2012) and other unpleasant physical and mental health symptoms increases (Stroebe, Schut, & Stroebe, 2007). Mindfulness can help you cope with side-effects of acute grief, including sleep disturbances, anxiety, nausea, muscle tension, headaches, emotional irritation, rumination, and more.

Imagine what would happen if, instead of focusing on his spidey-sense to defeat the Green Goblin, Spider-Man fantasizes about a conversation he hopes to have with Mary Jane, where he confesses his secret identity, and she professes eternal love (Ziskin et al., 2002). Or if, instead of protecting Earth, Superman hides in the Fortress of Solitude, or decides to hang up his cape and just be Clark Kent (Roven, Nolan, Thomas, Snyder, & Snyder, 2013). Neither Spider-Man's obsession nor Superman's avoidance will save the world, so if we are going to be our own superhero, we need to show up.

Mindfulness is the superpower of presence. It's an attitude that can be accessed any time by focusing your attention on *this* moment without clinging to or pushing away any one experience. When you are mindful, you witness the natural ebb and flow of your experience as it unfolds, through what you see, hear, feel, taste, and smell. Thoughts are a part of the experience, too, but rather than engaging with their content, you simply notice that you are thinking.

This present-moment awareness can elicit a peaceful mental state of equanimity – a calm and steady mind. Unusual on a good day, a calm mind may seem impossible when you are in the throes of grief. When you choose to simply observe your mind, you uncover habitual thought patterns and behaviors that contribute to your suffering. When what you did before to ease your pain no longer works, it's time to find a new approach, like Dr. Stephen Strange.

Dr. Strange loses control of his hands after a life-altering car crash (Feige & Derrickson, 2016). After the accident, his identity and purpose in life are shattered. Desperate, he turns to one thing he trusts unequivocally: medical interventions. When this fails, he seeks advice from a man named Pangborn, who can walk even though his spine was crushed. Pangborn sends Dr. Strange to a place called Kamar-Taj, offering a mysterious warning: "The cost there is high … and I am not talking about money" (Feige et al., 2016, 0:20:59).

Strange meets The Ancient One in Kamar-Taj, who reveals that it wasn't groundbreaking surgery that healed the paralyzed man, but a radical shift in Pangborn's consciousness and beliefs. Furious, Strange rages against The Ancient One, who responds by pushing the doctor's astral form out of his physical form. When asked why, The Ancient One replies, "To show you just how much you don't know" (Feige et al., 2016, 28:56).

Thus begins the transformation from the brilliant but callous surgeon he was to Marvel's Sorcerer Supreme, armed with mental flexibility, wisdom, and mystical powers to save Earth from Dormammu, ruler of the Dark Dimension. The high cost Pangborn referred to is the doctor's deeply ingrained beliefs. His whole identity and what he thought to be true had to be reexamined. Just as grief changes your identity and worldview, if approached mindfully, you may emerge on the other side armed with coping skills and beliefs never before imagined.

Unlike Dr. Strange's experience, you don't need to visit the astral plane. The physical body is the first foundation of mindfulness, housing sensations that connect us to presence (Gunaratana, 2012). Like Dr. Strange, mindfulness encourages us to observe our unchecked prejudices and preconditions, fostering mental flexibility, developing new coping skills, and helping us adapt to the changes we face after a major loss.

Grief can feel like a supervillain, an insurmountable nemesis who shattered your world, annihilated hope, and left you to feel powerless. But like all superheroes face their greatest challenge, the first step in preventing additional suffering is to remember that you have the power to control where you place your attention.

To master your attention in everyday life, it's helpful to train the mind through meditation. Just like exercise builds muscles, meditation helps build the mental fortitude you need to remain in the present. This is hard to do even on a good day, as the human brain is wired to scan for threats and opportunities. Grief feels like a personal attack, so go easy on yourself. Mindfulness is more than focus and presence – it requires compassion, too. Supervillains are focused and aware, but are they mindful? Not according to researcher and creator of mindfulness-based stress reduction (MBSR), Jon Kabat-Zin, who explains:

> In Asian languages, the word for *mind* and the word for *heart* are the same. So, if you're not hearing mindfulness in some deep way as heartfulness, you're not really understanding it.
>
> (Szalavitz, 2012)

## 41.1 I Am My Own Superhero

No one is more aware and in control of your internal thoughts and feelings than you or is more qualified to be your personal superhero. Even if you don't know how to make things better in your "thinking mind", meditation will rewire your brain and body to be trusty sidekicks as you cultivate self-compassion, focus, and open awareness. These five steps can be woven together in one meditation practice, or you can use them separately. Try it for 5 to 20 minutes each day. Only do what feels right for you. If any step in this practice exacerbates your suffering, take care of yourself and choose another step or skip it altogether.

**Step 1: Choose your posture:** Find a supportive but relaxed position that allows you to be as present as possible, either seated or lying down. Eyes may be open with a soft gaze or closed (Benefit: *A still body helps calm the mind*).

**Step 2: Set an intention for self-compassion:** What do you want to get out of your meditation practice? Find a reason that is rooted in self-kindness and will inspire you to stick with it. Examples include "May I be free from this suffering", or "To free myself from the grasp of anxiety". Single-word aspirations work, too, such as *peace, tranquility, space.* When you become distracted during your practice, use this intention as a reminder to begin again without being hard on yourself (Benefit: *Slows the cycle of self-imposed suffering that leads to feeling stuck and unworthy, helps you feel more connected to others who are suffering, inspires you to engage in self-care*).

**Step 3: Sharpen your focus:** Choose one of your senses to be your primary focus, placing 100% of your attention on what you hear, see, feel in your body, smell, or taste. Or, you could use a word or short phrase that you repeat silently to yourself each time you exhale. Refocus your attention as often as you need. (Benefit: *Gives the mind a place to go other than worry and fear, activates the body's relaxation response, the opposite of fight-flight-freeze*).

**Step 4: Open your awareness:** Once you feel your attention is steadied from focusing, allow yourself to notice your other senses *without seeking them out* – just notice them as they happen, and know you don't have to do anything with them other than be aware they are happening, and let go when they are complete. Reset your awareness to "open" as often as you need. (Benefit: *Expands attentional scope, cultivates mental flexibility, helps you see the big picture*.)

**Step 5: Rest and reflect:** Take a few minutes to rest and let go of all techniques. When you are ready, notice what stood out to you from this experience, and reflect on how you can apply your experience during meditation, so you can be your own superhero in your daily life.

## References

Benson, H., & Proctor, W. (2010). *Relaxation revolution: The science and genetics of mind body healing*. New York, NY: Simon and Schuster.

Feige, K. (Producer), & Derrickson, S. (Producer). (2016). *Dr. Strange* [Motion picture]. USA: Marvel.

Gunaratana, H. (2012). *The four foundations of mindfulness in plain English*. Somerville, MA: Wisdom Publications.

Haase, L., Thom, N.J., Shukla, A., Davenport, P.W., Simmons, A.N., Stanley, E. A., ... Johnson, D.C. (2014). Mindfulness-based training attenuates insula response to an aversive interoceptive challenge. *Social cognitive and affective neuroscience*, 11(1), 182–190.

Mostofsky, E., Maclure, M., Sherwood, J.B., Tofler, G.H., Muller, J.E., & Mittleman, M.A. (2012). Risk of acute myocardial infarction after the death of a significant person in one's life: The determinants of myocardial infarction onset study. *Circulation*, 125(3), 491–496.

Roven, C., Nolan, C., Thomas, E., & Snyder, D. (Producers), & Snyder, Z. (Director). (2013). *Man of steel* [Motion Picture]. United States: Warner Brothers Pictures.

Stang, H. (2018). *Mindfulness and grief: With guided meditations to calm the mind and restore the spirit*. London: Ryland Peters & Small.

Stroebe, M., Schut, H., & Stroebe, W. (2007). Health outcomes of bereavement. *The Lancet*, 370 (9603), 1960–1973.

Szalavitz, M. (2012, January 11). Q&A: Jon Kabat-Zinn talks about bringing mindfulness meditation to medicine. *Time*. Retrieved from http://healthland.time.com/2012/01/11/mind-reading-jon-kabat-zinn-talks-about-bringing-mindfulness-meditation-to-medicine/

Taren, A.A., Gianaros, P.J., Greco, C.M., Lindsay, E.K., Fairgrieve, A., Brown, K.W., ... Bursley, J.K. (2015). Mindfulness meditation training alters stress-related amygdala resting state functional connectivity: A randomized controlled trial. *Social Cognitive and Affective Neuroscience*, 10(12), 1758–1768.

Ziskin, L., & Bryce, I. (Producers), & Raimi, S. (Director). (2002). *Spider-Man* [Motion Picture]. United States: Columbia Pictures, Marvel Enterprises, Laura Ziskin Productions.

# Part X

# Conclusion

# 42 Finding Super Heroes All Around Us

*Jill A. Harrington*

From the beginning of time, myths, legends, folklore, and fairytales, across all cultures and religions, have helped provide an understanding of the mysteries of the world, such as supernatural events, traditions, and the struggles of humanity. They helped to provide meaning to the world people saw around them, serving to answer existential questions, as well as explain social systems and traditional customs ("Greek Mythology", 2020). These ancient oral stories through the ages progressively made their way into classical and modern literature. New stories are also being created as part of modern storytelling – via literature, films, comics, and music.

Throughout these stories, emerged heroes. Hero, comes from the Greek ἥρως (*hērōs*) – which means "protector" or "defender" ("hero (n. 1)", n.d.). And through these heroic tales, it illustrates both a historical and symbolic tale of humankind. They opened up an aperture to the very nature of humanity. These stories recount deeds of heroes, often complex and flawed – human, divine, or supernatural – fighting monsters of many kinds, allegories for human struggles, such as war, trauma, natural disaster, and death.

As we have evolved, so has our concept of a hero. In our modern society, we have heroes, and then we have superheroes. As if we gave the hero a jump in paygrade. With the advent of Superman, the popular comic book superhero and archetype was born into pop culture. Superheroes have become part of our modern mythology, providing us "teaching moments, archetypal moments, ideal moments" (Russell, n.d., p. 122) – lessons in the everyday struggles of life, death, and the human condition. Superheroes can be human, creature, or alien who are characterized as having some inherent abilities beyond that of normal humans, such as flight, telepathy, shape-shifting, and superstrength (Russell, n.d.).

In our modern times, the word *hero* has come to mean many things. A hero can be a real-life person or fictional character whose deeds display superheroic qualities. Social psychology has identified the great eight traits of heroes – wise, strong, resilient, reliable, charismatic, caring, selfless, and inspiring – as well as four domains of their primary functions – heroes provide wisdom, enhance us, provide moral modeling, and offer protection (Allison & Goethals,

2015). These heroic attributes make real-life heroes the most superpowerful, as they have no superpowers, only the ability to tap into their humanity.

In the human journeys of dying and death, there are many heroes to be found at the end-of-life and in the lives of the bereaved. They play an important and integral role for those suffering, and facing the humanly universal pain of grief, born of attachment and love. Heroes in the lives of the dying and bereaved can also play varying roles with differing acts – from large roles to small gestures.

Heroes can be the medical care team who tirelessly care for their patients and are compassionate with their families. As has been demonstrated with the COVID-19 pandemic, our medical heroes have provided frontline care, tireless hours, and worked in dangerous conditions to care for patients. They provided end-of-life care to dying COVID-19 patients, who were displaced from their families due to the contagion of the disease. Many medical professionals held the hands of the dying, clutched cell phones or tablets to their patients so their families could communicate with them in their final moments and corresponded with families through hospital windows to give them the sense of connection with their dying loved ones. Many of our medical heroes faced dangers to themselves by exposure and also potentially carrying the contagion home to their families. During these times of immense suffering, dying, and grief, under strenuous conditions and long hours, our medical heroes also had to return home to take care of their families. One of those heroes might come in the form of a nurse, who after long hours of caring for COVID-19 patients, changed shifts from nurse to mom, going home to care for a child with special needs.

Notwithstanding the COVID-19 pandemic, medical professionals provide daily heroic care to their ill and dying patients and their families, not only from their knowledge, experience, and superintellect but also through those that provide compassionate care, not focusing only on their patients as a medical disease but also as humans who are suffering. These medical professionals also include veterinarians and their staff who provide sensitive, kind and informed care while aiding us in often painful treatment and end-of-life decisions for our pet family members. And let's not forget our first responders, EMTs, paramedics, firefighters, and police who rise to the call of duty in assisting our dying, the deceased, and their bereaved families. One of those heroes might come in the form of your local EMT or paramedic who sits and holds the hand of your loved one while they may be dying or while they are being transported to their end-of-life care.

There are heroes who can also be found in the interdisciplinary teams of doctors, nurses, social workers, aides, and music and art therapists who deliver palliative and hospice care. These teams provide pain management and compassionate comfort care to relieve the symptoms of physical and mental stress associated with a terminal illness for the dying and their families. Sometimes the hero can come in the form of a hospice nurse who pursued hospice nursing after being widowed at a young age and understood the importance of end-of-life care. She wanted to make a difference to those who were dying and their families. Maybe she is the nurse that helped ease the suffering of your father as he was dying and showed up at his funeral service to express her support – conveying to you that your father was not just another patient, but a valued human being.

Let's not forget the heroes that come in the form of volunteers and contributors to hospice and other nonprofits supporting the bereaved. Grief services, camps, and retreats for children and adults could not happen without hero volunteers, peer mentors, workers, organizers, leaders, and financial supporters. Their tireless dedication, generosity, and selfless acts build those heroic safe harbors and healing communities for the bereaved. Let's also not forget the heroes who advocate for changes in the law to assist and care for the dying and bereaved.

Heroes can also be found in the mental health community – those providing emotional support to the dying and bereaved. This hero can come in the form of a therapist who takes a humanistic, compassionate, trauma, and grief-informed approach with their clients/patients. This can be the therapist that helps the dying work through unfinished business with loved ones before their death. Or someone who is sensitive to your pain and helps you embrace it and pace it in a way that is unique to you. This person could have also been your lifeline during periods of crisis in your grief.

Finally, let's not forget those that help us on our final journey. The heroes that can be found in mortuary, casualty, funerary, and cemetery services. Maybe that hero comes in the form of the morgue worker who respectfully carries and delivers the body/remains of your loved one or the funeral staff who provide steady guidance and the dignified care for your loved one as they journey to their eternal resting place. Let's also observe the cemetery worker who carefully tends the grounds.

Heroes for the dying and bereaved also come in many other forms using varying superpowers and abilities. Maybe they use the *power of kindness* to provide a meal to a newly grieving family. Maybe it is the teacher who uses the *power of intuitiveness* to recognize a grieving student and helps to support them. Maybe it is the *power of thoughtfulness* from a family member or friend who regularly picks up the phone to acknowledge your loss in the days, months, and years after your loved one has died. Maybe it is the bereaved parent/caregiver who uses the *power of strength and perseverance* in raising grieving children while they are grieving. Maybe it is the *power of understanding* of your loss and love for your deceased partner/spouse from a new partner/spouse who supports you as you both learn to integrate enduring love with starting anew. Maybe it is the *power of patience* that comes from the clerk as you are flustered with paperwork – trying to newly title a deceased family member's vehicle. Maybe it is the *power of dedication* a caregiver provides to their ill and dying loved one. Maybe it is the *power of faith* you find sparked within you from your spiritual or faith community. Maybe it is the *power of conviction* from demonstrators who peacefully gather in their shared communal grief and stand together in protest of discrimination, oppression, hate, violence, and injustice. Maybe it is the *power of courage* from another bereaved survivor who provides a glimmer of light that you can survive and somehow even grow through your loss. Lastly, one of the strongest of all these superpowers that human heroes can demonstrate, to help comfort and diminish the suffering of the dying and bereaved, is the *power of compassion*. It can come in the form of a police officer who recognizes the coat an acutely bereaved child is holding while sitting in his office at the station is his father's. With a simple act of compassion, he gently wraps the coat around the cold and traumatized child who had just witnessed the murder of both his parents on the streets of Gotham (Roven, Thomas, Franco, & Nolan, 2005).

We never know what influence heroic acts, both large and small, may have in the lives of the dying and the bereaved. But they can bring with them the *power of love*, and coupled with *compassion*, these most powerful human superabilities wielded together can provide *the power of hope*. For in grieving, it can feel amidst the heaviness of pain that there is only darkness and no light. It is hard to see that "darkness, the truest darkness, is not the absence of light. It is the conviction that light will never return" (Roven, Snyder, Berg, Johns, & Snyder, 2017, 1:46:46). It can be so hard to see through the veil of grief that "the light always returns to show us things familiar. Home, family, and things entirely new or long overlooked. It shows us new possibilities and challenges us to pursue them" (Roven et al., 2017, 1:47:24). Tapping into our heroic spirit within and opening ourselves up to others can allow the light to shine on heroes "coming out of the shadows to tell us we won't be alone again. Our darkness was deep and seemed to swallow all hope. But these heroes were here the whole time" all around us "to remind us that hope is real, that you can see it. All you have to do is look …" (Roven et al., 2017, 1:48:01–1:48:28).

## References


Allison, S.T., & Goethals, G.R., (2015). Hero worship: The elevation of the human spirit. *Journal for the Theory of Social Behaviour*, 46 (2), 187–210.

Greek mythology. (2020, May 8). Retrieved from https://www.history.com/topics/ancient-history/greek-mythology

hero (n.1). (n.d.). In *etymonline.com dictionary.* Retrieved from https://www.etymonline.com/search?q=hero

Roven, C., Snyder, D., Berg, J., & Johns, G. (Producers), & Snyder, Z. (Director). (2017). *Justice league* [Motion Picture]. United States: Warner Bros. Pictures.

Roven, C., Thomas, E., & Franco, L. (Producers), & Nolan, C. (Director) (2005). *Batman begins* [Motion Picture]. United States: Warner Bros. Pictures.

Russell, C. (n.d.). Heroic moments: A study of comic book superheroes in real-world society. *Explorations.* Retrieved from https://uncw.edu/csurf/explorations/documents/russell.pdf

# Suggested Resources

## African American Grief

Bordere, T. (2019). Suffocated grief, resilience, and survival among African American families. In M. H. Jacobsen & A. Petersen's (Eds.), *Exploring grief: Towards a sociology of sorrow*. New York, NY: Routledge.
Harris, D., & Bordere, T.C. (Eds.) (2016). *Handbook of social justice in loss and grief: Exploring diversity, equity, and inclusion.* Amityville, NY: Routledge.
Rosenblatt, P.C., & Wallace, B.R. (2005). *African American grief.* New York, NY: Routledge.

### Forward Promise

"Forward Promise is a national program that seeks to build and strengthen the villages that raise and empower boys and young men of color to heal, grow, and thrive". https://forwardpromise.org/

### Ambiguous Loss

Ambiguous Loss: www.ambiguousloss.com
Caregivers of Spouses with Dementia: https://www.nextavenue.org/caregivers-spouses-dementia-redefinition-marriage/

### Child/Adolescent Grief

The Dougy Center: https://www.dougy.org
Judi's House: https://www.judishouse.org
National Alliance for Grieving Children: https://childrengrieve.org

### Homicide

National Organization of Parents of Murdered Children, Inc.: https://www.pomc.com/survivors.html
Victim Connect – Resource Center: Homicide and Grief: https://victimconnect.org/learn/types-of-crime/homicide-and-grief/

Hotline: 1-855-4-VICTIM
Justice for Homicide Victims: https://justiceforhomicidevictims.org
Hotline: (310) 457-0030

**LGBTQI+**

Open to Hope: https://www.opentohope.com/grieving-loss-in-the-lgbt-community/
National Alliance for Grieving Children: https://childrengrieve.org/10-education/171-grief-and-bereavement-for-lgbtq-youth

**Military/Veterans**

Tragedy Assistance Program for Survivors (TAPS): www.taps.org

**Parent and Sibling Bereavement**

Bereaved Parents USA: https://www.bereavedparentsusa.org
Compassionate Friends – Supporting Families When a Child Dies (Parents/Siblings): https://www.compassionatefriends.org
Grieving for the Sibling You Lost: A Teen's Guide to Coping with Grief and Finding Meaning after Loss: https://www.newharbinger.com/grieving-sibling-you-lost
Open to Hope: https://www.opentohope.com/death-of-a-child/

**Pregnancy Loss**

Children's Hospital of Philadelphia: www.chop.edu/resources/loss-resources
Ending a Wanted Pregnancy: www.endingawantedpregnancy.com

**Restorative Retelling**

To download A Guide to Restorative Retelling and Support: https://www.virginiamason.org/workfiles/Manual_Accommodation_Violent_Dying.pdf

**Spousal Bereavement**

Liz Logelin Foundation: http://thelizlogelinfoundation.org/
National Widowers Organization: https://nationalwidowers.org/
Open to Hope: https://www.opentohope.com/death-of-a-spouse/
Soaring Spirits International: https://www.soaringspirits.org/

WAY Widowed & Young: https://www.widowedandyoung.org.uk/bereavement-support/
Widowed Young Support: https://www.careforthefamily.org.uk/family-life/bereavement-support/widowed-young-support

## Suicide Prevention and Postvention

### Prevention Training

Collaborative Assessment and Management of Suicidality: https://cams-care.com
ASIST: https://www.livingworks.net/asist
CBT for Suicide Prevention: https://beckinstitute.org/workshop/cbt-for-suicide-prevention/

### Postvention Training

Suicide Bereavement Clinician Training: https://afsp.org/suicide-bereavement-clinician-training

### Screening Tools

Question. Persuade. Refer: https://qprinstitute.com
Columbia-Suicide Severity Rating Scale: https://cssrs.columbia.edu

### Education and Support

American Association of Suicidology: https://suicidology.org
Alliance of Hope: https://allianceofhope.org
American Foundation for Suicide Prevention: https://afsp.org
*See TAPS for Military/Veteran

## Thanatology Education & Training

Association for Death Education & Counseling: https://www.adec.org
Portland Institute for Loss & Transition: https://www.portlandinstitute.org

# Index

Page numbers in **bold** indicate tables.

- Why This Book? Why now?
- How can The themes w/in it help Smokers?
- What is Thanatology & y is it important?
- Let's talk abt Batman.